The Writer's Guide to the Internet

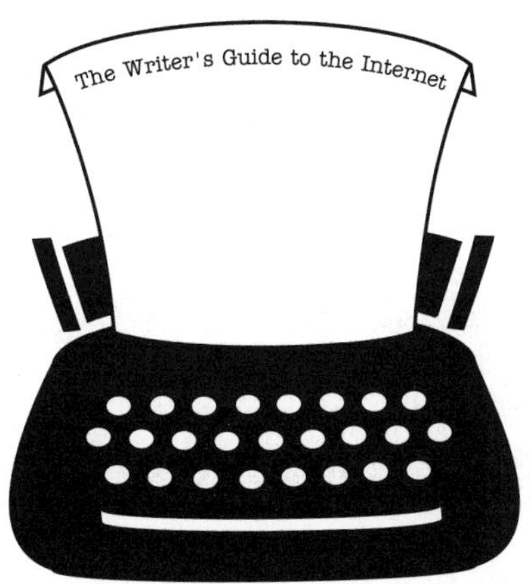

Dawn Groves

Bellingham Technical College
Whatcom Community College

FRANKLIN, BEEDLE & ASSOCIATES, INC.
8536 SW St. Helens Drive
Wilsonville, OR 97070
(503) 682-7668
http://www.fbeedle.com

President and Publisher	Jim Leisy (jimleisy@fbeedle.com)
Manuscript Editor	Eve Kushner
Interior Design and Production	Susan Skarzynski
	Karen Foley
	Tom Sumner
Cover Design	Steve Klinetobe
Marketing Group	Cary Crossland
	Victor Kaiser
	Eric Machado
	Sue Page
	Laura Rowe
Order Processing	Chris Alarid
	Ann Leisy

Dear Reader,

Because of ongoing software upgrades, this book does not come with the CD-ROM referred to on pages 2, 47, 69–70, 144, and 227. The software mentioned may be downloaded from the Internet. For links to these and other downloadable software packages, as well as a browser-ready, linkable index of all the URLs in this book, visit our Web site:

www.fbeedle.com

We look forward to your visit.

Jim Leisy
Publisher

Rights and Permissions
Franklin, Beedle & Associates Incorporated
8536 SW St. Helens Drive, Suite D
Wilsonville, Oregon 97070
www.fbeedle.com

Preface

This book is intended for writers who want to expand their use of the computer beyond the basics of word processing. As such, I assume that you know how to operate a computer. Further, since you'll need to link the Internet through a service provider and each hook-up will vary to some degree, I'm leaving those details in the able hands of the provider that you choose. My focus is on the tools and skills you'll need as a writer to take advantage of Internet resources and services.

Most writers agree that at this juncture in the Internet's development, its greatest strength is what it was originally designed for—research and communication. "For me, the best 'writer-oriented' feature of the Internet is the ability to network," journalist Richard Sherer writes. "I subscribe to a number of mailing lists aimed at increasing writers' knowledge of the resources available online, and participate in 'discussions' and trade e-mail with colleagues and other writers I wouldn't otherwise talk to once a year. In addition, the World Wide Web is the greatest library you can find if you know how to use it. As a reporter and writer with *very* eclectic interests, I am endlessly fascinated with the amount of information available. It reminds me of my freshman year at USC. I had been admitted as an honors student, which meant that I had stacks privileges in the library. I used to spend hours wandering around the lower levels, which were rarely visited by anyone else, looking at and reading 200-year-old treasures. The Web almost duplicates that experience at times, while being as useful as the reference rooms at the library, too."

Despite concerns about income and authors' rights, writers are finding that both opportunity and income are growing as a result of their online efforts. "As a small publisher, I firmly believe that the Internet and Web will only increase in importance as sales vehicles," says publisher and writing instructor Pat J. Bell of Cat's-paw Press. "I have two books listed on a book site and have made sales that I would not have otherwise. Likewise, I have promoted my books directly and indirectly using the Internet."

Columnist Jessie Shoop advises writers to "read and post on the writing newsgroups and the mailing lists. You wouldn't believe how many editors and publishers read them. The two column positions I now hold were, in part, because of my presence on the Web. I also know of a few writers whose work has been seen in an e-zine and then reprinted in a print mag. It is possible to create a number of contacts through the Internet. I think this area is just beginning for writers, and soon most writers will be on the Internet in one form or another."

Writer John Hewitt states: "I've made sales through Internet contacts, so I know it is possible. In addition, I have moved into the technical writing industry and my new, higher paying job, is at least partially due to my Web presence as well as directly due to an e-mailed resume."

In money actually earned there's progress but it's still a long road to the Emerald City. Executive Kate Jones of The NetShow Company, Inc., summed it up after she attended an Internet advertising convention. "One thing is obvious," she stated. "Nobody knows what they're doing." Fortunately, the Internet is maturing fast; the Emerald City could be just around the corner.

For writers this is good news. It means that the universe is still forming. There's room for all kinds of experiments and entrepreneurial efforts. A "who knows?" environment is fresh, exciting, and risky. You can carve a niche, to test new ideas, to fail miserably and try again. Qualities such as creativity, enthusiasm, talent, and persistence make all the difference. It's an electronic new world.

As you read this book, you'll learn many ways to make the Internet work for you. But if you look at writing only in terms of earning money this week, you're being shortsighted. Online material doesn't always have to translate into direct sales. Sometimes the indirect benefits of promotion and practice have even greater long-term value.

Of course, there's the other side of the coin. If you *don't* use the tools of the Internet, where does that leave you in the next five years? Online instructor Steve Moril graphically summed it up: "Writers who don't get on the information superhighway will end up as roadkill."

I can never adequately thank the many writers, publishers, critics, and friends who contributed their ideas, commentary, and energy as this book was being written. A partial list of these good folks follows:

Patricia J. Bell, Alon Bochman, Bob Brand, Bill Densmore, Bill DeRouchey, Wendy Chatley Green, John Groves, Paula Guran, John Hewitt, Don Johnson, Kate Jones, Whitmore Kelley, Robert Kendall, John Lancaster, Eric Leisy, Benedict O'Mahoney, Steve Moril, Stuart Moulthrop, Debbie Ridpath Ohi, Michele Picozzi, Richard A. Sherer, Jessie Shoop, Michael Shumate, Sol Stein, Alex Swain, Roger Williams, Brian Woodard, Ruth Zaslow, Lisa Cannon, Jack Miles, Sue Sumner-Moore, my students, and the Freelance writers mailing list.

My publishing company, Franklin, Beedle, and Associates, Inc. has been unfailingly patient during this rocky development cycle. Gratitude and appreciation is extended to the entire FBA team—Jim Leisy, Ann Leisy, Chris Alarid, Karen Foley, Victor Kaiser, Eric Machado, Sue Page, Laura Rowe, Susan Skarzynski, Daniel Stoops, and Tom Sumner. A special thanks also to my diligent manuscript editor, Eve Kushner.

I round out these acknowledgments with deep thanks to my husband, Dan, who bolstered my waning energy levels with bad movies, junk food, and continual encouragement, and to our soon-to-be-daughter, Holly, whose spirit kept both of us looking forward with anticipation and joy.

Contents

The Writer's Guide to the Internet
Chapter
1

Introduction to the Internet

The Internet is a global network of networks with a variety of characteristics and uses. Its academic and government database make it a tool for research. Its discussion forums turn it into a colossal electronic bulletin board. With its virtual cities it appears to be a community complete with homes, stores, meeting areas, game rooms, and infrastructure. With its e-mail and data transfer capabilities, the Internet is the ultimate communications convenience. And with its crazy, weird, and often fascinating Web sites, it appears to be a fantasy world where anything goes and everyone's got a bone to pick or a cause to promote.

Born in 1969 as a Department of Defense military network, the Internet quickly evolved into a university-based academic community with a distinctive culture and accepted rules of conduct. It has only recently gained widespread acceptance in the nonacademic community, due in large part to the birth of the World Wide Web (see Chapter 2).

In the past, Internet users fiercely defended the nonprofit sanctity of their electronic community. But with the commercialization of the Web and a tidal wave of new users who don't remember the good old days, senior "netizens" are being forced to accept advertising and for-profit ventures online as de rigueur.

Internet research resources are enough to make freelance writers and journalists drool. Beyond that, there's the addictive convenience of electronic mail, the accessibility of online workshops, classes, and support groups, the stimulation of a literal world of ideas, and the opportunity to participate in a no-holds-barred publishing arena that's as fresh, unsettled, and entrepreneurial as it gets. The Internet is a great place for writers to be.

Usenet

Born in 1980, Usenet is a worldwide network of computers that facilitates the most active, anarchistic region of the Internet. Think of Usenet as a worldwide bulletin board organized into topic-specific groups known as newsgroups. Participants mail (post) messages to newsgroups regarding topics of interest as well as other newsgroup messages. Several times each day, all Usenet computers send their latest posted messages to all other Usenet computers. Usenet has no central control, hence newsgroups participants from all over the globe can cover a wide array of subjects.

There are probably over 20,000 newsgroups currently available, though Internet service providers can choose which newsgroups they carry. Because most newsgroups are unmoderated, everybody's messages are posted without quality control or editing.

News reader programs (Figure 1.1) offer a variety of ways to participate in newsgroups, navigate through them, send mail to them, mark previously-read postings, customize newsgroup lists, and store downloaded data. Web browsers also let you read through newsgroups and send mail to them, but they lack the more sophisticated features available in a dedicated news reader program. A well-received news reader, Free Agent, is provided on the CD that comes with this book.

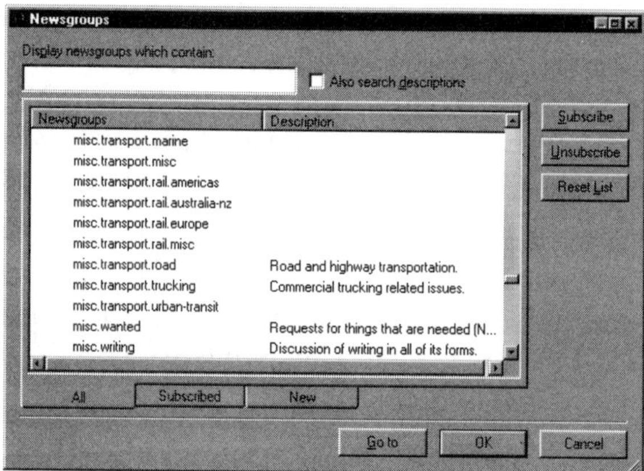

Figure 1.1 Usenet Newsgroups

The original Usenet topic hierarchy was divided into seven groups:

comp computers, operating systems, networking, etc.
Examples: **comp.graphics.apps.photoshop**, **comp.robotics.research**

misc miscellaneous topics that don't fall into a specific class.
Examples: **misc.writing.screenplays**, **misc.survivalism**

news news about Usenet and the Internet.
Examples: **news.answers**, **news.lists**

rec hobbies of all kinds, sports, music, reading.
Examples: **rec.travel.air**, **rec.arts.books.reviews**

sci hard sciences, such as chemistry, medicine, and astronomy.
Examples: **sci.agriculture.poultry**, **sci.med.diseases.cancer**

soc social issues, world culture topics.
Examples: **soc.geneology.methods**, **soc.religion.hindu**

talk opinions and general discussions, mostly political.
Examples: **talk.politics.china**, **talk.euthanasia**

Other group designators have evolved. Two of the better known are:

alt alternative, often nontraditional and controversial topics. The alt group contains many of the sexual topics we hear about from press stories.
Examples: **alt.animals.badgers**, **alt.e-zines**

clari ClariNet is a fee-based newsgroup service that distributes news feeds. It's excellent for research purposes because unlike other newsgroups, ClariNet reports from valid news sources. Because distributors must pay a subscription fee, not all news servers carry it.
Examples: **clari.news.terrorism**, **clari.sports.football**

A specialized group requiring a subscription is known as a mailing list. Mailing lists are frequently moderated and usually have a higher signal-to-noise ratio. That is, you don't see as many unnecessary or inappropriate postings because the group is confined to members only.

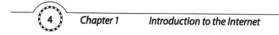

Newsgroups serve as support groups, soapboxes, research resources, or simply a way to keep track of the latest information about your favorite topics. As a writer, you'll definitely want to browse through them for ideas and research leads. But no matter what you learn, be sure to verify the sources. Usenet is a mixed bag of rumor and fact. You should also consider subscribing to mailing lists because they often contain more reliable, targeted information.

Chapter 5 talks about subscribing to newsgroups and mailing lists. It also contains the Usenet Rules of Order. Chapter 11 describes writing for Usenet audiences.

E-mail

Even though the publicity surrounding the Internet focuses on the Web, it is electronic mail (e-mail) that constitutes the bulk of Internet traffic.

E-mail (Figure 1.2) is special because, unlike snail mail (ground service), e-mail seldom contains junk. A piece of e-mail is like a real letter, not another unsolicited envelope of grocery coupons.

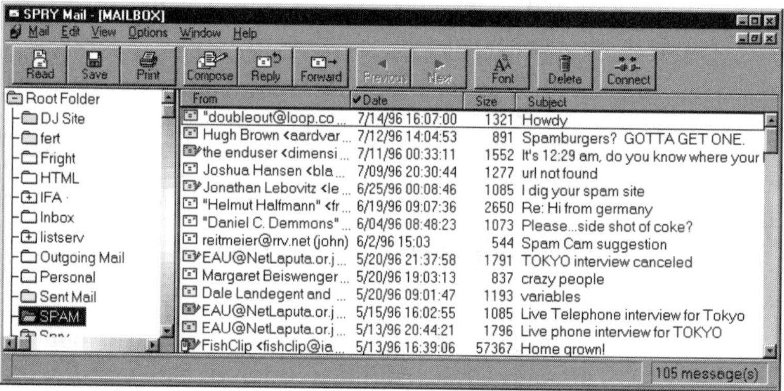

Figure 1.2 E-mail Screen

Writers have been using e-mail for years. What better way for a writer to communicate than to write? E-mail quickly and easily connects with any individual who has an e-mail address. (There are search engines that look for e-mail addresses exclusively. See Chapter 17.)

E-mail is used for basic correspondence and file transfer, and for posting messages to mailing lists. It is so popular and commonplace that it has evolved its own style guidelines and rules of composition. Because of the distraction e-mail provides, savvy Internet users confine themselves to checking their mailboxes once or twice a day at most.

E-mail can be especially useful for conducting interviews, querying markets, and transmitting manuscripts. Publishers, agents, and editors who specialize in technology topics or produce electronic publications are typically the most amenable to e-mail correspondence. Many traditional publishers still prefer hard copy letters.

Many rules of Usenet communication apply equally to e-mail (see Chapter 5 and the Usenet Rules of Order). Chapters 10 and 11 contain Usenet and e-zine composition hints that are also appropriate to e-mail correspondence. Chapter 18 explores the use of e-mail interviews as research tools.

Gopher

Gopher is a menu-driven program that searches for and displays information using a traditional menu structure and plain English titles, without the benefit of graphics (Figure 1.3).

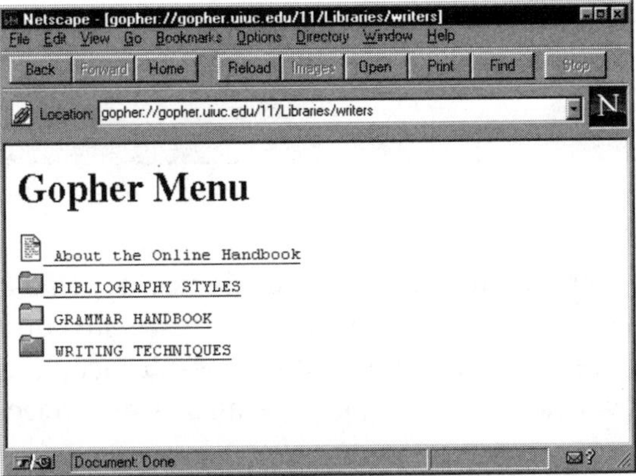

Figure 1.3 Gopher Menu

Most Web browsers (software used to view World Wide Web documents) can read Gopher sites such as the Gopher Jewels presentation (Figure 1.4), **http://galaxy.einet.net/GJ/**.

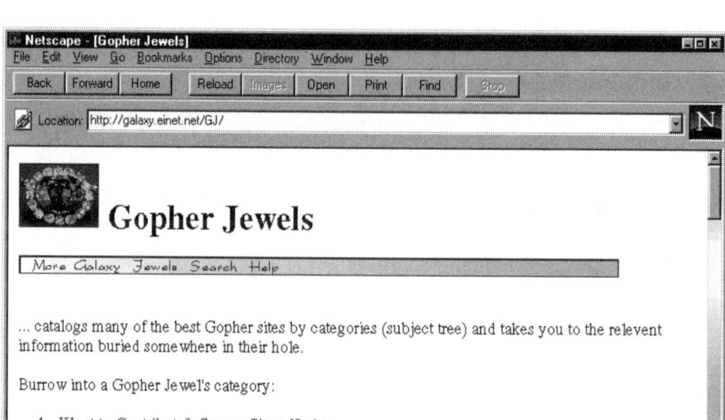

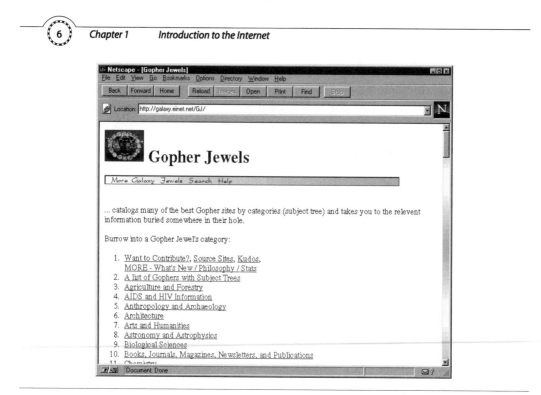

Figure 1.4 Gopher Jewels on the Web

There are upwards of 8000 Gopher sites around the world. Some are more popular than others, such as the original Gopher site at the University of Minnesota, **gopher://gopher.tc.umn.edu**. Gopher-formatted information doesn't include graphics, which makes Gopher a preferable download source for people with slower connections.

Gopher sites are replete with research material, much of it scholastic. This includes mountains of academic papers with excellent bibliographies. In researching this book, I actually found a great deal more information in Gopherspace than I found on the Web. Suites of Internet software usually include a Gopher program as part of the package; however if you're attached to the ease and familiarity of your Web browser, you'll find that most of Gopherspace (everything available to Gopher) can be accessed via the Web. Commercial online services such as America Online (AOL) also offer easy access to Gopher. To help you dig around Gopherspace, specialized search programs such as Veronica are available (see Chapter 15.)

File Transfer Protocol (FTP)

File Transfer Protocol is an older protocol that facilitates transferring files between computers. It was developed so that researchers could easily move their data and research reports from one institution to another. FTP is frequently used to transfer software and other forms of nontext data. Most people with Web sites upload their Web documents using an FTP program (Figure 1.5).

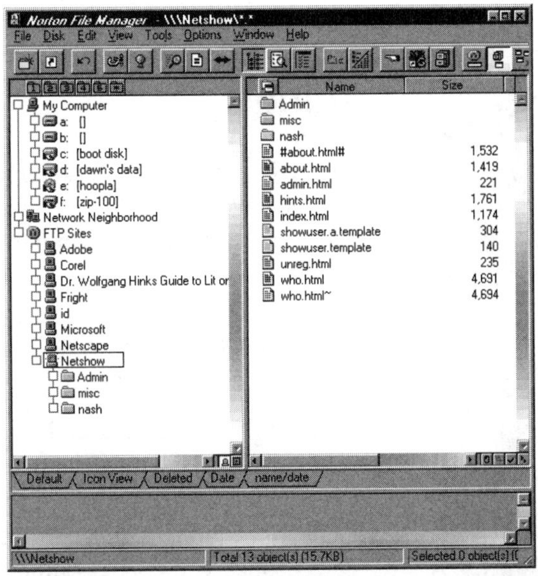

Figure 1.5 FTP

Web browsers have taken over much of the work of downloading files, but uploading still requires FTP. For example, if you visit a Web site to download a program, you simply click on a specified link in your browser window. But if you want to upload a new version of the file, you must use FTP.

FTP isn't necessary for research; most archives are accessible via the Web or Gopher. However, if you publish on the Net, you'll need an FTP program to upload your files to the Web server (the computer that makes your files accessible to the Web). This is the best way to transfer files from your local platform to the server platform. Of course, you might find a server administrator willing to accept diskettes from you, but more likely the administrator will take the time to teach you how to use FTP. Many FTP shareware applications are available via the Internet. Your computer probably came bundled with an FTP program as part of your Internet suite.

To use the program, you must know the name of the file to be downloaded and the directory where it resides (or the destination directory where you want to upload your local file). Log into the site using the word "anonymous" and enter your e-mail address as a password. Once logged in, you can then move through the directories until you find what you want. Not all FTP sites allow anonymous access; some require established accounts.

Eventually you will need to learn FTP because electronically sophisticated publishers will probably ask writers to send manuscripts via FTP, rather than e-mail. Chapter 7 discusses uploading a Web site using FTP and Chapter 15 covers searching FTP archives.

chat
An online conversation with multiple participants.

multiuser dungeon (MUD)
Originally a multiuser environment where ongoing games such as Dungeons and Dragons were played. Now MUDs also serve as communities where people can assign pictures (icons) to their screen persona and "walk" around the screen relating to other users.

Telnet

Telnet is used to log into remote computers on the Internet. When you "Telnet into" a site, your computer functions as a remote terminal. You are logged in as a user, just as if you were local. This is useful for accessing databases, running remote programs, engaging in online *chats*, and participating in *MUDs* (chat-based multiuser environments).

Although Telnet isn't complex, it can be confusing for someone who isn't technically inclined. You might want to explore Telnet if you maintain a Web site because it facilitates editing documents directly online. Unfortunately, once you change something online, your local page no longer matches it. Sooner or later you're going to have to download the corrected version. It's often less confusing to simply fix the typo locally and then upload the corrected document via FTP.

Telnet (Figure 1.6) usually requires the use of UNIX commands—a topic beyond the scope of this book. It you're interested in Telnet, talk to your service provider or enter the term "Telnet" into a search engine (Chapter 16) and research the topic online.

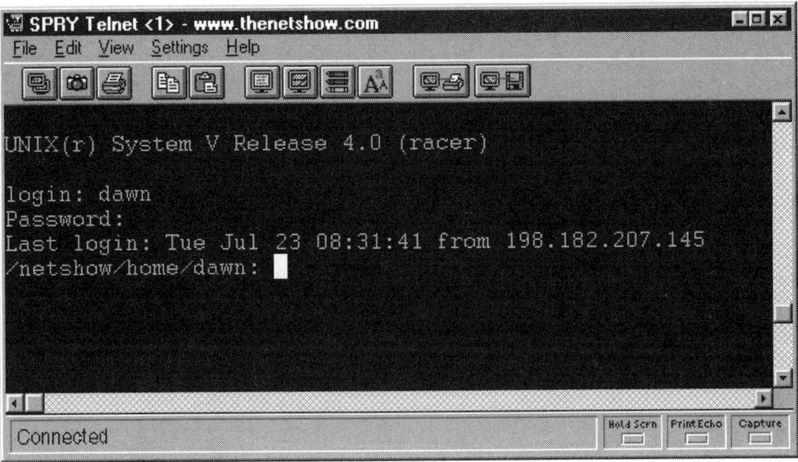

Figure 1.6 *Telnet*

Introduction to the World Wide Web

The best known aspect of the Internet is the World Wide Web (also known as the Web, WWW, or W3). The Web is a vast collection of Web-formatted documents, known as Web *pages* (the terms *document* and *page* are often interchangeable.) These pages include online magazines, newspapers, library and training resources, sound and video files, literature, shopping malls and museums, interactive newsgroups, software repositories, and much more.

Web documents exist on computers that run *HTTP* (*HyperText Transfer Protocol*) Web *servers*. Most Web servers are hosted on *UNIX* machines, but personal computers (PCs) and Macintosh computers can also be used. To access a Web server and display a Web page, you need *client* software known as a Web *browser*. Browsers are so named because they are easy-to-use programs that allow you to view Web pages for hours at a time. Netscape Navigator, Microsoft Internet Explorer, and Spyglass are examples of leading Web browsers.

The Web is one of the youngest regions on the Internet. It was originally developed in 1989 at the European Particle Physics Laboratory (CERN) in Geneva, Switzerland. Tim Berners-Lee created the Web to facilitate the transfer of information and research documents among

HTTP (Hypertext Transfer Protocol)
The Internet communications protocol used to transfer Web-formatted data between computers. Web page addresses are always preceded with "**http://**", indicating the communication scheme that the computers must translate.

server
A networked computer that runs server software. Servers "serve up" information to *client* programs. A Web server houses Web documents and controls data transfer to and from the Internet.

client
An end-user program that retrieves data from a server. Browsers "request" information from servers. A Web browser is a client program.

browser
The optimal tool for navigating the World Wide Web. Merely by pointing and clicking the mouse, you can view pictures, play sounds and music, read Web-formatted documents, transfer files, send e-mail, and access other forms of information.

UNIX
The computer operating system used on most Internet Web and non-Web servers.

HTML
(Hypertext Markup Language) The format for every Web-compliant document. HTML contains a set of tags that divide the contents of a Web document into structural elements such as headings, body text paragraphs, ordered lists, and so on. These elements can then be transmitted to any remote browser client located on a Web-compliant computer platform.

physicists. Web documents are formatted in *Hypertext Markup Language* (*HTML*). To publish a document on the Web, you must use HTML. (HTML is described in Chapters 7 and 8.)

Central features of Web documents are links, which are visually distinctive (often underlined and/or bordered) words, phrases, and graphics. A link contains the address of another Web document. When you click the link, the address is accessed and the referenced document is downloaded from the server to your screen. Each document contains a number of embedded links, creating an enormous web of topics to explore.

URL (Uniform Resource Locater)
A Web page address consisting of the method of transfer, the name of the computer where the page resides, the directory path, and the name of the document.

In the HTML world, a Web address is known as a *Uniform Resource Locator*, or *URL*. **The Cool Site of the Day** address, **http://www.infi.net/cool.html**, is a fairly typical-looking Web URL. As ugly as it may be, a URL is easy to interpret once you understand how it's constructed. Think of a URL as having three sections: how, where, and what (Figure 2.1):

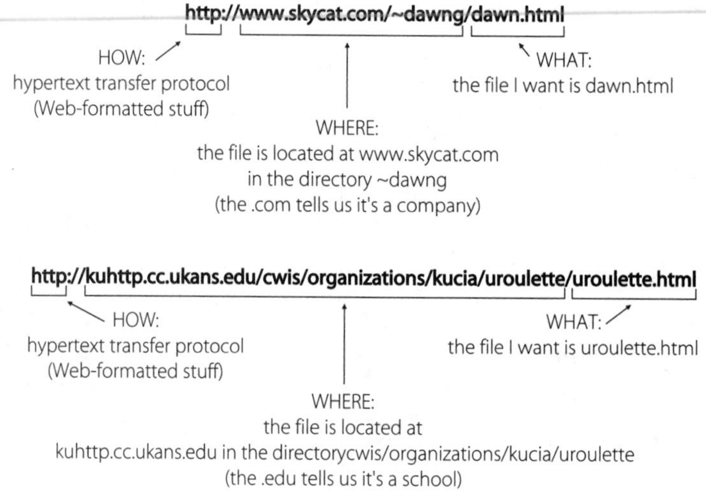
how you get it://where it is/what you want
http://www.skycat.com/~dawng/dawn.html
HOW:
hypertext transfer protocol
(Web-formatted stuff)
WHAT:
the file I want is dawn.html
WHERE:
the file is located at www.skycat.com
in the directory ~dawng
(the .com tells us it's a company)
http://kuhttp.cc.ukans.edu/cwis/organizations/kucia/uroulette/uroulette.html
HOW:
hypertext transfer protocol
(Web-formatted stuff)
WHAT:
the file I want is uroulette.html
WHERE:
the file is located at
kuhttp.cc.ukans.edu in the directorycwis/organizations/kucia/uroulette
(the .edu tells us it's a school)

Figure 2.1 The Organization of a URL

How you get it:

This is the method of access. On the Web, the common method of access is HyperText Transfer Protocol (HTTP). When you specify HTTP in a URL, you're accessing an HTTP (Web) server. Even though 90 percent of Web traffic travels via HTTP, URLs can contain other server protocols. Here are a few common protocols you might come across.

ftp:// Access File Transfer Protocol servers (**ftp://doman.edu/path/document.txt**). Browse through directories and transfer files to and from your computer.

gopher:// Cruise Gopherspace (**gopher://utirc.utoronto.ca/string**). Browse through Gopher menus and download files of interest.

news: Access Usenet newsgroups (**news:group.topic**).

telnet:// Log into a host computer (**telnet://server.big.edu**). Your computer functions as a remote terminal.

file:// Access local or networked files on your computer or local network, as opposed to accessing files on the Internet (**file://localserver/directory/file.html**).

Don't be concerned if the protocol list above confuses you. As you navigate the Web, most of the documents you access will have URLs starting with **http://**.

Where it is:

This is the location of the Web document you want to see. The location usually starts with the name of the HTTP server (the *domain*). Domain names often end with one of the following extensions:

.com (a commercial organization)
.edu (an educational institution, often a university)
.org (a nonprofit organization)
.gov (a governmental agency)
.net (a networking organization)

In Figure 2.1 above, the domain in the first URL is **www.skycat.com**. The domain in the second URL is **kuhttp.cc.ukans.edu**.

The domain name is separated from the directory path by a single slash. A directory path is like a street map leading to the location of the document you want to display. Directory paths can be simple or complex, depending on how many directories (streets) you have to navigate to reach your destination. If a directory path isn't specified after the domain name, the server defaults to a "root" Web directory identified by the system administrator. In the figure above, the directory path in the first URL is **/~dawng/** (only one street). The directory path in the second URL is **/cwis/organizations/kucia/uroulette/** (four streets).

domain
A name used to identify computers on the Internet. It usually reflects the company, organization, or Web topic it will host. Domain names are submitted to the Internet Network Information Center (INTERNIC) for approval before they can be used. For example, **hwg.org**, **fright.com**, and **ucsd.edu** are all domain names. In a URL, the domain name is usually preceded by the name of the computer housing the Web server. This is commonly (though not always) **www.**

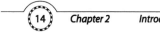

What you want:

In general, the last part of a URL is the filename for the Web document you want to download. The filename is typically the last item in the URL. Web documents usually include an **.htm** extension if they're on PCs and an **.html** (or similar) extension if they're on Windows 95 PCs, Macintosh computers, or UNIX machines. If a filename isn't specified in the URL, the server defaults to a document known as an index page. The index page functions as the home page for the Web site and is usually named **index.html**. Web site developers often name their home pages **index.html** so that when someone opens the directory without specifying a document, the system will default to the proper home page.

> *Important:* Whenever you type a URL, make sure you copy it exactly as it is referenced. URLs are case-sensitive and inflexible. For example, the URL **http://www.whozits.com/whoopah.html** is not the same as **http://www.whozits.com/Whoopah.html**. Also note that Web addresses used in sentences sometimes include periods, commas, or other punctuation marks at the end of URLs. Do *not* type the final punctuation mark (unless it is a slash) when you copy the URL into the browser window. If you do, the URL will be wrong.

Some Web pages are classified as home pages. A home page often resembles a snazzy table of contents with links representing Web servers around the world. This could be a site such as Yahoo, **http://www.yahoo.com**, that catalogues and categorizes all other sites, or a highly rated list of hot Web sites such as Netscape's What's New page (Figure 2.2), **http://home.netscape.com/escapes/whats_new.html**. Most Web travelers select a home page that they use as a starting point for their Web journeys.

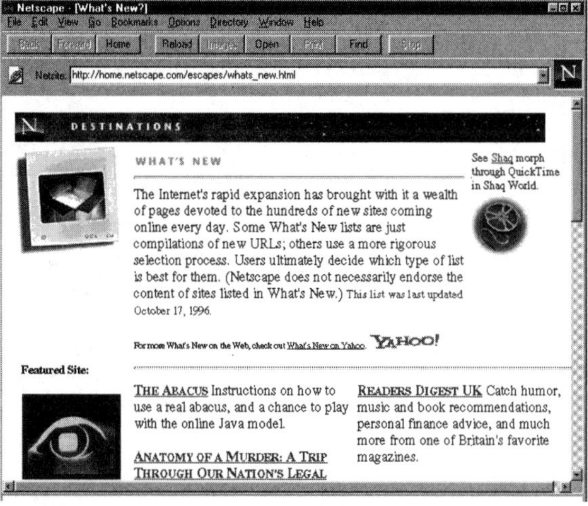

Figure 2.2 Sample Home Page: Netscape's What's New

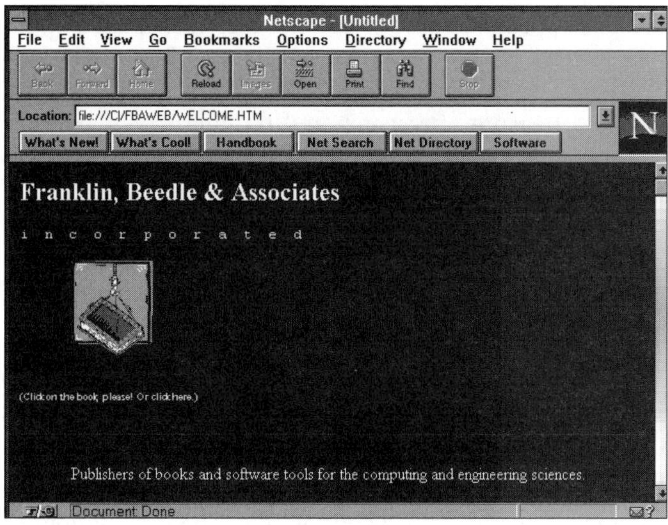

Figure 2.3 *Business Home Page: Franklin, Beedle, & Associates, Inc.*

The opening page to an individual Web presentation is also known as a home page. A personal home page is usually written by and about a single person or family. It can include everything from scanned photos to business projects, resumes to writing clips, political preferences to favorite jokes. A business home page functions as a front door, briefly introducing the company and offering links to the interior of the site (Figure 2.3). It can include product information, employee e-mail addresses, registration forms, anything that customers would find useful.

> *Note:* Busy writers may not always have time to develop creative, lively home sites. For months my home page was simply a statement that I didn't have a home page yet. I didn't have time to develop a personal Web page, so I had an introductory statement, a short link list of sites I had developed, and my e-mail address to answer any individual questions. I even toyed with calling it my anti-home page and making the whole thing black, text included. (That was in response to a long day slogging through Web documents containing blinking text, huge graphics, and god-awful slow connections. It wasn't pretty.) By the time this book is published, I'll probably have a more elegant setup. But I'll keep the old one for reference. It does the job.

Because of its universal appeal and ease of use, the Web has opened up new possibilities to writers:

- The Web is a treasure of research and training resources. Search engines have created catalogues of sites and topics that are easy to index and access. Online classes and support information are readily available, and often free of charge (though copyright protected). And most high-end browser software can also connect you to newsgroups, perform file transfers, and even send e-mail.
- The Web is an outlet for promotion. Writer registries and job banks almost always expect you to have a personal home page containing your credentials, writing clips, and pertinent personal information. Book jackets are starting to include e-mail addresses and home page URLs. Writers attest to receiving job offers based on the material they've produced and published on the Web.
- The Web is an outlet for publishing. Web pages can be accessed by any of the up to thirty million people with Web browsers. The distribution network is staggering. This is also the area that is least predictable because it's still so new. Problems with electronic publishing include getting people to visit your site, making money for your efforts, and preparing the material for online presentation. Additional concerns revolve around quality control and copyright. These matters are discussed in the body of this book.

Each chapter in this book contains Web sites of special interest to writers. Chapters 20 and 21 include comprehensive lists of Web sites that you may find particularly useful and motivating. Keep in mind that with the ever changing nature of the Web, the listed addresses were as current as possible at the time of publication but may need to be relocated.

Getting Started Online

If you're not already wired (online), this chapter will help you get up to speed. If you're overwhelmed by the many directions to travel, then "Taking it Step by Step" later in this chapter will help simplify your options once you're online.

Requirements

Getting wired demands a basic suite of hardware and software as described below. If you have questions about what you read, talk to your *Internet Service Provider* (*ISP*). This book isn't meant to serve as an encompassing technical tutorial.

You will need the following items:

1. A fast computer. To be Internet tolerant, a PC must have at least 4 MB RAM (Random Access Memory—the active area of the computer's brain—measured in megabytes). If you only have 4 MB, upgrade to at least 8 MB. It makes your programs run more efficiently. You'll also need storage space in case you download video titles—at least 250 to 500 MB. For greatest PC efficiency, purchase the Windows 95 operat-

Internet service provider (ISP)
A business that connects you to the Internet. ISPs can be local providers, or national companies such as Netcom, Earthlink, Pipeline, and so on. Commercial online services such as America Online (AOL), CompuServe, Prodigy, and the Microsoft Network (MSN) offer friendly electronic communities in addition to Internet access, though you may pay extra for the amenities.

modem (modulator/demodulator)
Device that transforms a computer's binary data (ones and zeros) into analog data (sounds) that can travel over phone lines.

Internal modems slide into a slot inside the body of your computer, requiring neither additional cabling nor a separate power supply. External modems are little boxes that sit on your desk, plugging into your computer and your phone. Modems can be purchased at any computer store.

ing system with 16 MB RAM and a 1 GB hard drive.

2. A fast *modem*. If you plan to spend time on the Internet, it behooves you to invest in the fastest modem you can afford. Currently, this is 28,800 bits per second (bps). If you're purchasing a new computer, you can specify this speed. If you already own a computer, it may have come with an internal 2400 bps, 9600 bps, or 14,400 bps modem already installed. 14,400 is acceptable but not great, 9600 is pretty slow, and 2400 is a waste of space. One thing's for sure—no matter how fast you receive and transmit data, you'll want it to be faster.

   Faster forms of access are available but cost hundreds of dollars more. There's also a lot of chatter about the eventual use of cable as a means of transport, but this is still in the early talking stages. Unless you're a technically well-fixed writer or you work for a computer company or university, you're probably stuck with a modem. For now, that's 28,800 bps at best.

3. Communications software. This software hooks you up to the Internet and displays the resulting information on your computer screen. The most recognizable program is the Web browser. Other programs include File Transfer Protocol (FTP), news readers, e-mail, and so on.

   Most software can be supplied by your service provider. Commercial online services such as America Online (AOL), CompuServe, or Microsoft Network (MSN) usually provide everything on a single diskette. If you're hooking up using a university system, you'll receive guidance from the network administrator. One piece of advice: If you plan to spend time on the Web, use a high-end browser (such as Netscape Navigator, Internet Explorer, or Spyglass) that displays the latest Web enhancements.

4. Internet service provider. Look in the phone book or local newspaper for ISP references. Local computer store representatives may offer good recommendations. Check the prices of your local providers and compare them against regional or national ISPs. You might also talk to your local phone company, which is also getting into the ISP act. Don't rule out joining a commercial service; they're now providing good Internet access and some are offering competitive pricing arrangements. I use a local ISP because I have fast access lines and the rates are competitive, but I also joined a few commercial services because I liked their research databases and writer communities.

Writers (and other non-technical folks) often wonder what to look for in an ISP. Here are a few suggestions:

1. Full Internet access, enabling you to send and receive e-mail, subscribe to newsgroups, and transfer files to and from your computer.

2. Disk space on the Web server for your home page (when you develop it). Some ISPs automatically provide 2 to 4 MB of server space when you subscribe; others charge for it. Find out if they structure their Web site fees by traffic limits, disk storage, or both.

3. A local access phone number so you don't have to pay long-distance charges. If you live in Podunk, North Dakota, your town may not have a local ISP. In that case, a commercial online service such as AOL or CompuServe might be your best bet. They provide 800 numbers for a surcharge, but also have local access.

4. Easy access when you travel. If you spend a lot of time on the road, you're better off with a service provider who maintains many local access numbers around the country and has an 800 number option. Using an 800 number usually applies a surcharge to your account.

5. Competitive monthly rates ranging from $20 and up, depending on a variety of factors including the pricing structure, how much help you require, and how much server space you reserve. The ISP might charge a flat rate for unlimited hours, or it could be calculated based on usage.

6. A dial-in modem speed at least as fast as your modem. Hopefully, that's 28,800 bps.

7. An understanding of beginner's problems and concerns. This includes helping you configure your system properly and supplying software (such as FTP, Telnet, or browser if necessary).

8. Enough modems to service their subscriber base comfortably. There's nothing worse than trying to go online and hearing a busy signal.

By turning each of the above ISP requirements into a question, you'll know what to ask your prospective providers when you call them.

If you can't find an ISP in your area, ask one of your wired friends to visit TAG Online (Figure 3.1), **http://www.tagsys.com/Providers/index.html**. When you enter an area code into the search engine, you'll receive a list of service providers based in that locale.

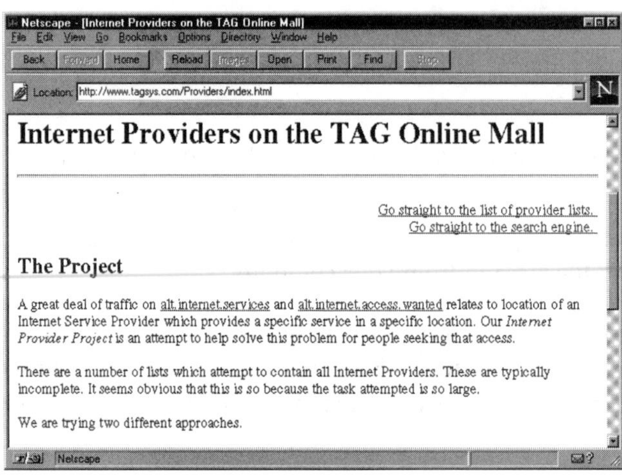

Figure 3.1 TAG Online ISP Search Index

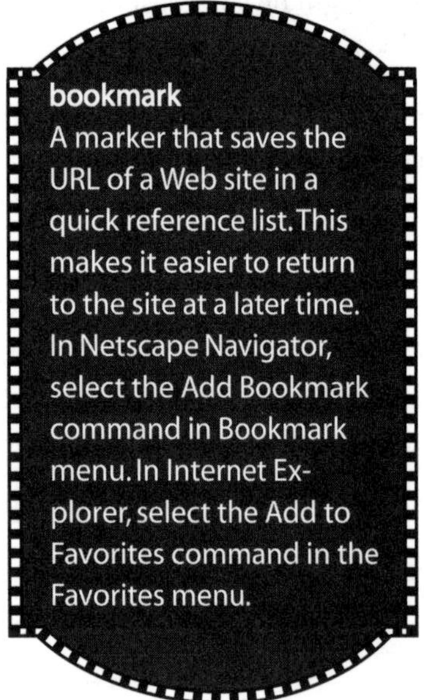

bookmark
A marker that saves the URL of a Web site in a quick reference list. This makes it easier to return to the site at a later time. In Netscape Navigator, select the Add Bookmark command in Bookmark menu. In Internet Explorer, select the Add to Favorites command in the Favorites menu.

Taking it Step by Step

Even when you're wired and ready, it's easy to become overwhelmed by the Internet. What should you do first? Which sites should you visit? And how often should you visit them? The following guidelines will help you narrow your focus. It's a good way to get the most information with the least amount of confusion.

1. ***Bookmark* an index site on the Web that caters to authors. Use it as your starting point for guidance, news, and updates.**

There are hundreds of Web sites containing links for writers. It's easy to get lost in the mass of information. If you concentrate on only one site, eventually you'll add other others once you know the lay of the land. Suggestion: The Inkspot, **http://www.inkspot.com/~ohi/inkspot/** (Figure 3.2). This is an excellent site with comprehensive links to most writer-related pages on the Web.

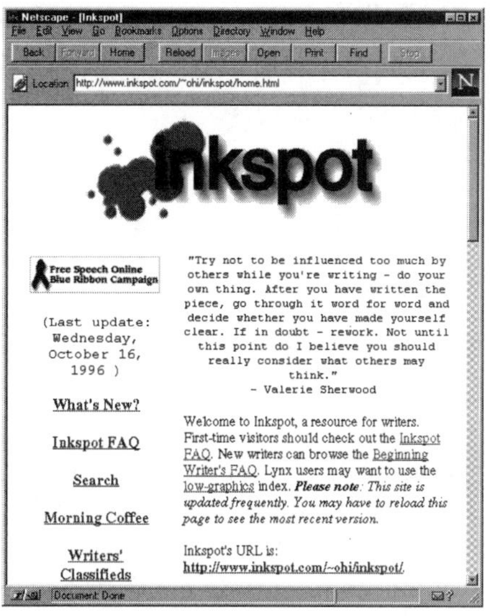

Figure 3.2 The Inkspot

2. **Participate in one or two newsgroups that target your genre.**

   Usenet may have a reputation for buffoonery, but there are also countless newsgroups that share useful information and positive insights. Find a newsgroup that appeals to you and *lurk* for a while. Not only will you learn about newsgroups, but you'll probably also gather some research leads. You may even find a specialized mailing list that appeals to you. Suggestion: **misc.writing** (Figure 3.3). This is a popular, active newsgroup suitable for amateur and professional writers.

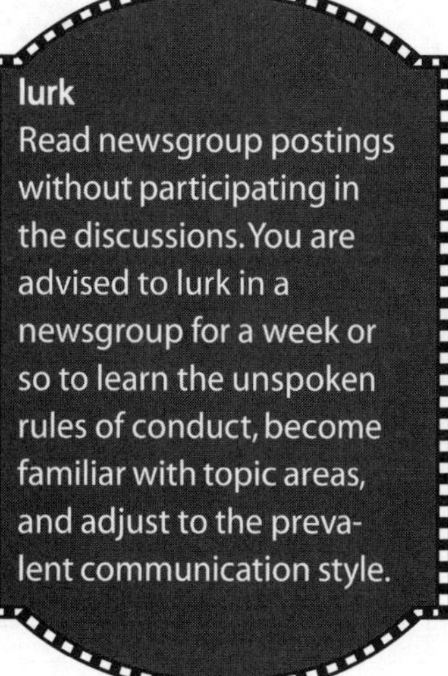

lurk
Read newsgroup postings without participating in the discussions. You are advised to lurk in a newsgroup for a week or so to learn the unspoken rules of conduct, become familiar with topic areas, and adjust to the prevalent communication style.

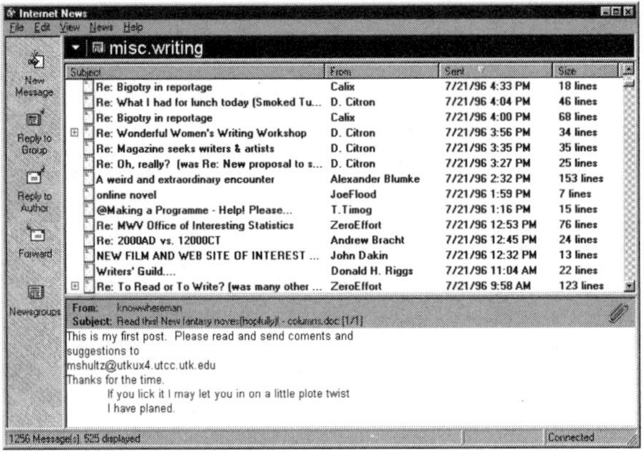

Figure 3.3 The misc.writing Newsgroup

3. **Select one search site to serve as your training ground.**

   Search sites provide the option of browsing through pages of interesting links organized hierarchically by topic, or simply searching on a specific keyword. Pick a search site and get used to it (see Chapter 16). Learn how to employ advanced search techniques. Once you're comfortable, you can then transfer those skills to the countless other search sites available. Suggestion: Yahoo, **http://www.yahoo.com** or HotBot, **http://www.hotbot.com/** (Figure 3.4). Yahoo has an excellent hierarchy of topic categories and HotBot is a fast, thorough search site.

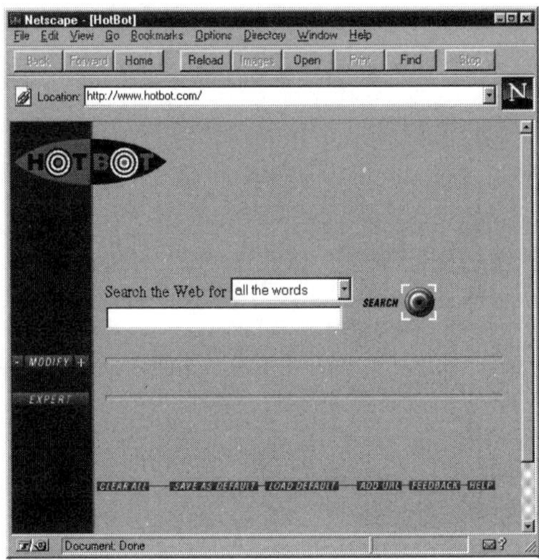

Figure 3.4 HotBot Search Site

4. **Subscribe to a writer's newsletter or electronic magazine.**

   Newsletters often contain targeted market updates, lists of new links, and other information you'll find useful. In most cases, they can be delivered via e-mail, making it very easy to keep up with new online developments. Suggestion: Inklings, **http://www.inkspot.com/~ohi/ink/inklings.html** (Figure 3.5). Inklings is a respected newsletter containing specialized reviews, market information, and much more.

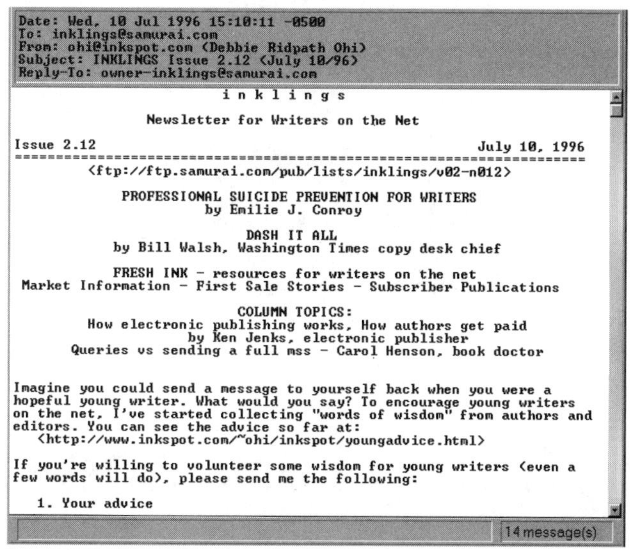

```
Date: Wed, 10 Jul 1996 15:10:11 -0500
To: inklings@samurai.com
From: ohi@inkspot.com (Debbie Ridpath Ohi)
Subject: INKLINGS Issue 2.12 (July 10/96)
Reply-To: owner-inklings@samurai.com
                         i n k l i n g s

                  Newsletter for Writers on the Net

Issue 2.12                                             July 10, 1996
=====================================================================
       <ftp://ftp.samurai.com/pub/lists/inklings/v02-n012>

          PROFESSIONAL SUICIDE PREVENTION FOR WRITERS
                     by Emilie J. Conroy

                         DASH IT ALL
         by Bill Walsh, Washington Times copy desk chief

          FRESH INK - resources for writers on the net
 Market Information - First Sale Stories - Subscriber Publications

                       COLUMN TOPICS:
       How electronic publishing works, How authors get paid
                by Ken Jenks, electronic publisher
     Queries vs sending a full mss - Carol Henson, book doctor


Imagine you could send a message to yourself back when you were a
hopeful young writer. What would you say? To encourage young writers
on the net, I've started collecting "words of wisdom" from authors and
editors. You can see the advice so far at:
   <http://www.inkspot.com/~ohi/inkspot/youngadvice.html>

If you're willing to volunteer some wisdom for young writers (even a
few words will do), please send me the following:

   1. Your advice

14 message(s)
```

Figure 3.5 Inklings Newsletter

5. **Subscribe to a commercial online provider (optional).**

   AOL, CompuServe, MSN, or Prodigy include proprietary research resources, classes, and writer's clubs. If you're Internet shy, you might try subscribing to the commercial provider first, then going out into the Web from there. But don't cheat yourself by sticking to the service alone; commercial providers are simply one of many of fascinating cultures to explore online.

The five steps above will provide you with a good feel for the resources available on the Internet. They'll help you to decide where you want to go with your online publications and will allow you to connect to other writers with similar interests.

The Writer's Guide to the Internet
Chapter
4

Online Writing Labs and Classes

Take advantage of the many opportunities to expand you writing skills online. Try joining in classes, participating in critique groups, developing professional e-mail relationships, and reading Net-published works. Internet education and training resources are so valuable that it almost doesn't matter if the Internet becomes a moneymaking bonanza. (*Almost* is the key term here. I haven't lost my mind completely.)

Online Writing Labs

Many universities are creating Internet versions of the writing labs they offer to their students. At the time of this writing, over fifty online writing labs can be accessed from the Web alone. This number could easily double over the next couple of years.

Online writing labs (sometimes called OWLs) provide tutorial documents and resource links for writers on and off campus.

Most OWLs maintain comprehensive link lists of reference sites, online writers' haunts, professional organizations and electronic discussion groups, and Usenet newsgroups. They also provide a variety of style guides (Figure 4.1) and support materials covering specific writing genres. Some OWLs offer online classes and workshops. One of the best known and longest running OWLs is maintained by Purdue University, **http://owl.english.purdue.edu** (Figure 4.2).

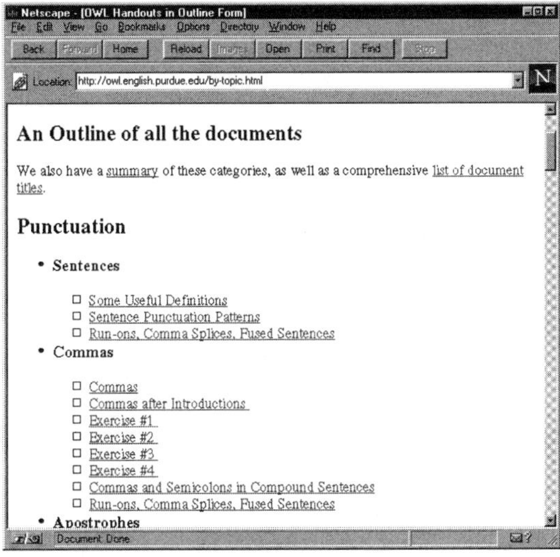

Figure 4.1 Style Guides at Purdue University OWL

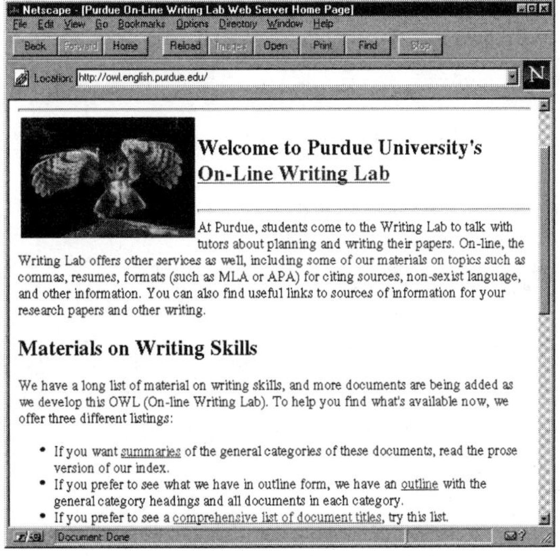

Figure 4.2 Purdue University's OWL

The Purdue OWL is a well-organized Web site. Their considerable library of writing handouts contains documents covering punctuation, sentence structure, active/passive voice issues, parts of speech, research paper composition, spelling, English as a second language, resumes, business/professional writing, proofreading strategies, and much more. These handouts serve as succinct, quick-reference resources that many writers will find useful.

Some OWLs are targeted at university students, while others provide classes and learning environments for a wide array of individuals outside the university popularion. The easiest way to become acquainted with the OWLs is to visit a lab site, access the OWL resource list, and start clicking through the options (Figure 4.3).

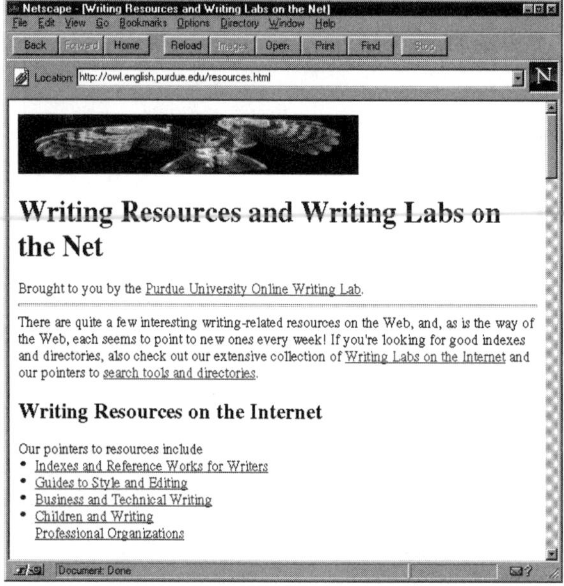

Figure 4.3 *Purdue OWL Resource List*

How Online Classes Work

Online classes are a great way to receive instruction and critique without leaving the comfort of your computer. If you subscribe to a commercial online service such as AOL, CompuServe, MSN (Figure 4.4), or Prodigy, you can register for a variety of excellent writing courses available throughout the year.

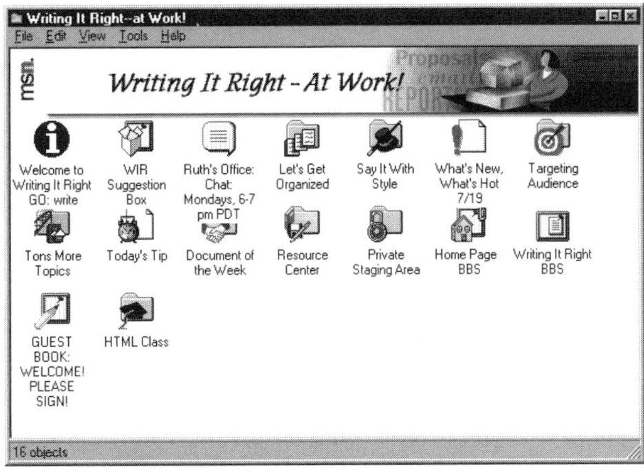

Figure 4.4 MSN HTML Class

Online classes cover basics, such as how to find an agent, all the way through advanced dialogue techniques. Other courses are offered through university OWLs, some of which are accredited. Online degree programs are still in their infancy, but their numbers are growing each month.

Online classes operate in much the same way as real-world classes. Class meetings are conducted in an assigned *chat room* once or twice a week where students type in questions for the instructor. To avoid confusion, most instructors employ a communication protocol which they explain during the first class meeting. Instructors usually have a bulletin board area where they can post a class syllabus, discussion questions, supplementary materials, and a log of the previous class lecture.

chat room
A window where two or more users can converse via typed submissions. In the context of a class, chat rooms are scheduled and monitored by instructors for meetings, lectures, and interviews. Other groups use them to arrange for periodic gatherings with other folks of like mind. The more infamous chat rooms are the private one-on-one conversations between consenting adults of dubious gender.

Here's an excerpt from an online chat for an HTML class taught by MSN instructor Ruth Zaslow:

DawnGroves:
  In the FAQ you can easily address potential concerns without boring the more savvy visitors with unnecessary detail.

DawnGroves:
  Another way of handling this issue is to provide a Hints page, especially if optimal viewing is obtained by setting certain defaults or sizing your browser window appropriately.

DawnGroves:
  Just don't expect people to actually follow your suggestions!

Host:
  Dawn, could we hold here for questions?

Host 2 (student):
  I do have one question. I want to have some text on the bottom of a page for search purposes and I do not want the page to scroll that far. How do I do this?

DawnGroves:
  You mean like adding a bunch of words for keyword search engines?

Some classes provide forum areas where students can leave messages for each other, engage in friendly chats, and just virtually hang out together. It's not the same as the student union or the coffee shop, but when you live 500 miles away from the university and you work full-time, the virtual classroom is an excellent way to receive good instruction that would otherwise be out of the question.

Students can download the graphics, text files, or logs, and then post responses to the discussion questions. Tests can be e-mailed to students who are timed from the moment they download the file. In a university setting, teachers usually make themselves available for optional phone consultations. Final written pieces can be posted online and instructors can even edit them on screen.

Online classes have the following advantages:

- No missed classes or notes. Lectures and all discussion can be logged and stored, then posted on the class bulletin board for downloading.
- Proactive participation. The students must participate; there's no way to fade into the woodwork. They have to send e-mail, comment on assignments, and respond to discussion questions. Surprisingly, some instructors feel that they can get to know students better online than in a physical classroom.

 Efficient, customized scheduling. This is especially important to busy adults with other commitments. Class lectures and material can be downloaded and read during the wee hours of the morning. Compositions and response papers can be uploaded late at night. No time is wasted driving to class, searching for a parking place, or waiting for other students to show up.

Of course, online instruction can't duplicate the vitality of classroom dialogue; it isn't meant to. Instead, it broadens educational options for adults and children alike. It suddenly makes accessible and user-friendly what was previously unavailable. To explore other online classes, visit the following:

Alliance for Computers and Writing

http://english.ttu.edu/acw/operations/news.html

Provides a page of internet class listings as well as a variety of other writer-related links.

University of Missouri Online Writery

http://www.missouri.edu/~wleric/writery.html

Touted as "a place where communities of writers can flourish," this is a well-organized OWL with many interesting resource pages.

Writers on the Net

http://www.writers.com/

A group of published writers who are also teachers. This site includes resources and assistance for every writing genre.

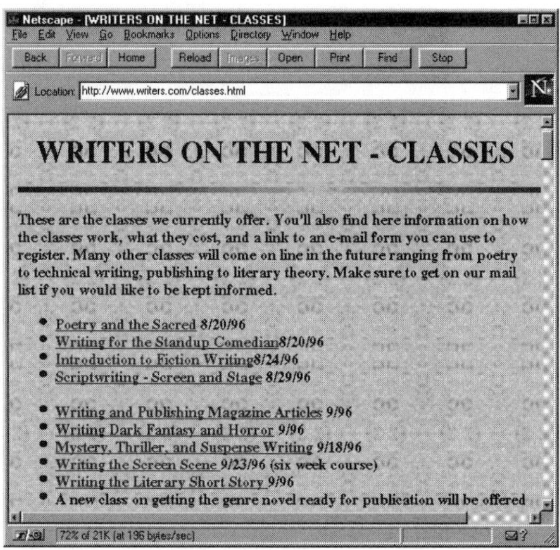

g Courses and Workshops

p://www.inkspot.com/~ohi/inkspot/courses.html

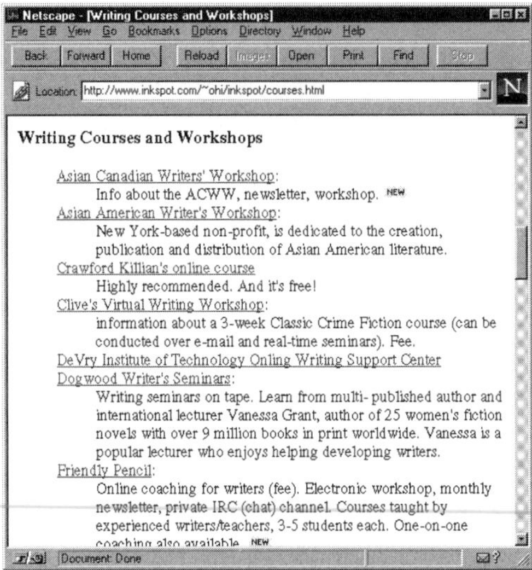

Lists of graduate writing programs, writing courses, and workshops, as well as links to sites for writing teachers, university writing centers, and critique groups. If you're looking for a lab or a class, start with this list first.

The Writer's Guide to the Internet
Chapter
5

Newsgroups and Mailing Lists

As a writer, you'll find great support in writer-specific Usenet *newsgroups* and *mailing lists*. They can also be a rich source of research and inspiration. You'll need to verify facts taken from newsgroup and list postings, but oftentimes you can glean directions and ideas from the material you read. (Before participating in Usenet or mailing list discussion, be sure to read the Usenet Rules of Order below.)

To find a newsgroup that interests you, either look through the groups in your news reader program, or check the Web site directory, *WWW view of Directory of Scholarly and Professional E-Conferences*, **http://n2h2.com/KOVACS/** (Figure 5.1). This directory contains descriptions of discussion lists, Internet interest groups, Usenet newsgroups, and forums on topics of interest to scholars and professionals for use in their scholarly, pedagogical, and professional activities.

newsgroup
Topic-specific bulletin board. *Posting* a message or article to a newsgroup is like tacking a note on a community wall. When someone else tacks up a response to your message, a *thread* is created.

thread
A series of messages on a particular theme or subject, similar to an ongoing conversation.

mailing lists
Groups of people who exchange e-mail about specific topics. Membership is generally by subscription. Some mailing lists are handled by automated programs such as listserv or majordomo.

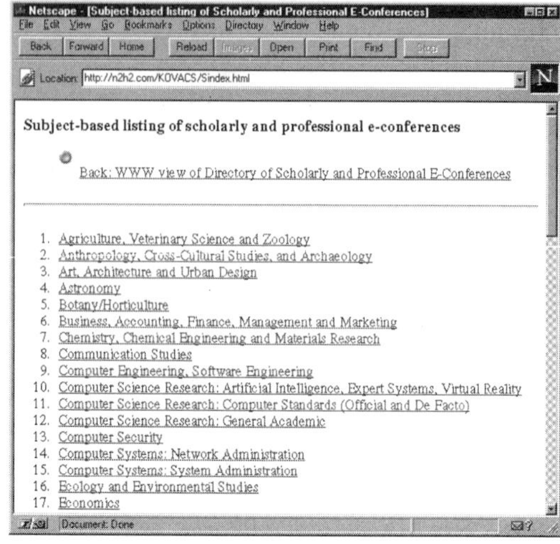

Figure 5.1 *The Directory of Scholarly and Professional E-Conferences*

Newsgroups

Some newsgroups are obnoxious and infantile in content and purpose. But there are many more that provide valuable support and guidance (such as **rec.arts.books** in Figure 5.2).

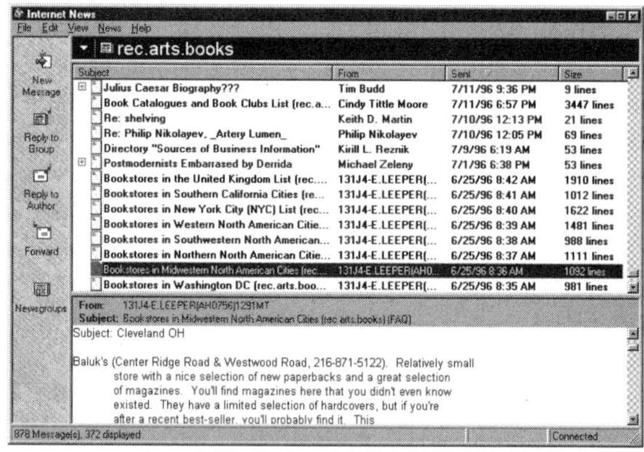

Figure 5.2 *The rec.arts.books Newsgroup*

For writers, newsgroups offer a wealth of input. But before we get into the details, you must familiarize yourself with Usenet "netiquette." Conduct is a big issue in bulletin boards and forums.

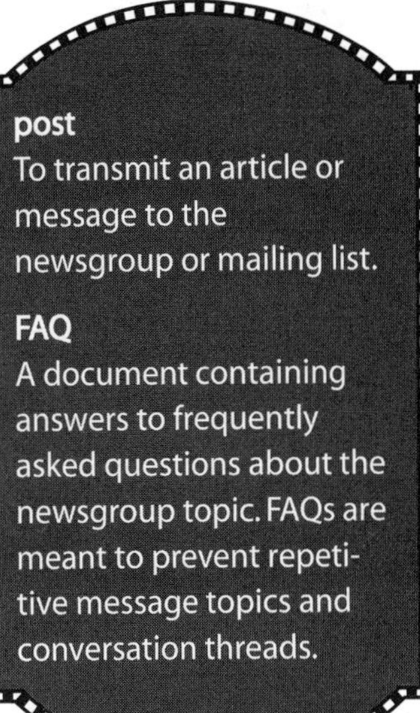

post
To transmit an article or message to the newsgroup or mailing list.
FAQ
A document containing answers to frequently asked questions about the newsgroup topic. FAQs are meant to prevent repetitive message topics and conversation threads.

The Usenet Rules of Order

The Internet is a global community. As with any community, commonly accepted rules of behavior have evolved. Nowhere is this more apparent than in Usenet newsgroups. If you break the rules, Usenet participants may become offended, even hostile and retaliatory. For your sake and the sake of the newsgroup, review the rules of order before posting any messages.

1. Don't *post* before reading the *FAQs* (Frequently Asked Questions).

   To avoid asking the same tired questions that the newsgroup has already answered a thousand times, read the FAQs. Most newsgroups maintain FAQs that are posted periodically to the various lists. If you don't see the FAQ in the newsgroup messages, you can politely ask where it is or look it up in one of the FAQ index sites such as Oxford University, **http://www.lib.ox.ac.uk/search/search_faqs.html**.

2. Lurk before leaping.

   When you browse without posting a message, you're *lurking*. It's a good practice to lurk around a newsgroup for at least a week or two before leaping into the conversation. Lurking helps you determine the forum's range of subject matter as well as the accepted level of discussion (scientific, sassy, soporific).

3. Don't post mail or news (especially advertising) that has nothing to do with the newsgroup.

   Newsgroup participants become angry if you take up their valuable space with unrelated text or self-serving advertisements. If you follow rule 2 above, you won't make this mistake.

4. Don't reply to a newsgroup posting or letter with the entire original embedded in your reply.

   If you must include the original message in the letter you're answering, only use the pertinent lines. This keeps your responses (and you) from seeming bloated and repetitious. Also avoid sending "me too" messages unless you have new information to add.

flame
A particularly offensive e-mail or newsgroup message. Flaming is usually inappropriate and often inane.

spam
A term describing the much-hated act of posting inappropriate messages to several unrelated newsgroups. Also a canned meat food product.

emoticon
Also known as smileys; little faces that indicate humor or irony in messages. The most common smileys are versions of :-) smiling, ;-) winking, and :- (frowning. Refer to the table of Commonly Used Smileys in Appendix B.

5. Don't blindly reply to a news post containing multiple crossposting addresses. Make sure you send it only to the appropriate list recipient.

   Blind replies will not only send your message to the targeted newsgroup, but it will also post it to all the other addresses in the To: line. Your message could clutter up a dozen other newsgroups or mailboxes that have nothing to do with your subject. This is poor form and you're likely to receive a mailbox full of flames.

   Send personal replies to the individual, not the newsgroup. If your message is only of interest to the individual, don't burden the list with it.

6. Don't send a *flame* or respond to one.

   There are plenty of ways to communicate your disagreement without becoming offensive. If you receive an offensive piece of e-mail, remember that its purpose may be to provoke reaction. The best way to respond is to ignore it.

7. Never spam.

   Spamming is a term that describes posting a message to everybody and their mothers. It isn't difficult to send something to every newsgroup in the country, but it's very bad form and will surely get you flamed.

8. Communicate clearly and minimize the jargon.

   Communicating by typed word alone can sometimes create messages that seem too harsh. Watch how you word your postings. Here are some tips:

   - Punctuate your messages with *emoticons* to indicate humor or irony. (A list of common emoticons can be found in Appendix B.) But be conservative about including them. Many of these symbols are silly or unclear. Overuse could make you seem—for lack of a better word—*uncool*.

- Don't overuse acronyms. They make the reader work harder to understand your message. If possible, write them out.
- Don't SHOUT except when appropriate. USING ALL CAPS MEANS THAT YOU'RE SHOUTING. Use this form of emphasis when you want to make a point, not as a standard format for typing.

General Newsgroups for Writers

The following newsgroups provide general support for writers. Also, check the genre references at the end of this chapter for newsgroups and mailing lists dedicated to topics such as romance, children's writing, technical writing, and so on.

alt.journalism

The main newsgroup for journalists. Keeps you up to date on trends in journalism, research resources, and other topics of interest to journalists.

alt.usage.english

Questions and answers about anything to do with the grammar, punctuation, and meanings of words.

bit.listserv.literary

An academic mailing list distributed over Usenet as a newsgroup. Characterized by a more academic thrust than rec.arts.books. Not available on all news servers.

misc.writing

A supportive group for writers of all kinds. Participants gladly offer advice and direction on most writer-related issues and concerns.

news.newusers.questions

A safe place to ask newbie questions about Usenet in general.

rec.arts.books

The primary newsgroup for writers and book lovers. Includes discussions about various books, questions and answers about book genres and locations, and announcements of new electronic bookstores or other book-oriented news on the Internet.

soc.libraries.talk

Questions and answers about where to find what resources, what libraries are out there; basic library chatter.

listserv and majordomo Programs that automate the management of mailing lists. They add and delete subscribers, distribute messages and files, and take care of the tedium of mailing list administration. Subscribing to a listserv or majordomo requires specific commands typed in the body of an e-mail message.

Mailing Lists

Some informal mailing lists are simply lists of addresses pasted into the To: line of the e-mail message. One person collects all the addresses of interested parties, and mails a message to the group with all the addresses typed out. Participants then post messages to each member of the group.

Other more established lists are administered by a program (robot) and not a person. The most common mailing list programs are called *listserv* (Mailing List Server) and *majordomo*.

Mailing lists are especially useful because of their subscription-oriented nature. In many cases, mailing list subscribers are more serious about the topic than those who visit newsgroups. Off-topic chatter and spams are minimized. Mailing list topics can become more specific than newsgroup topics. Some mailing lists offer digest versions in the form of a single periodically mailed file of messages instead of countless daily individual postings.

As good as they are, mailing lists do have the following drawbacks:

1. Busy mailboxes. If the mailing list is busy, you could conceivably receive a hundred or more e-mail messages a day. If this is a problem for you (some people like lots of e-mail), write to the administrator of the service and see if they offer a digest version.

2. Cliquish behavior. Mailings lists often develop close communities. Some people participate off and on for years. Before you jump in with hoopla and ballyhoo, lurk for a little while. Then respectfully introduce yourself.

3. Unchecked mail. If you travel for days or weeks on end, your mailbox could overflow with unchecked mail, causing problems for your service provider. Consider unsubscribing for a period of time or ask the list administrator if there's a way to temporarily suspend delivery until you return.

Subscribing to a Mailing List

Most of the time, you'll find subscription information described in the list announcement, probably located via a search site or posted in a newsgroup. Keep in mind that you're usually sending a message to a computer program, not a person, so you don't need to write a bunch of nonsense about how happy you are to find the list. To submit to a listserv, simply address your subscription request to the program address, leave the subject line blank, and type the following in the body of the message: **subscribe *name-of-list your-name***

Example: **subscribe FREELANCE holly barrett** (Figure 5.3)

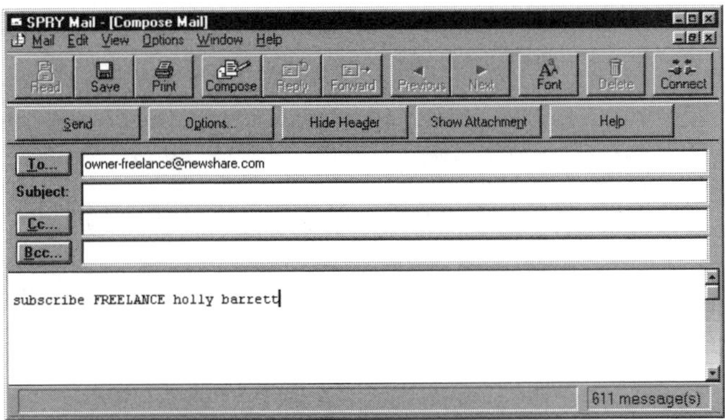

Figure 5.3 Listserv Subscription E-mail

If the mailing list is administered by majordomo and not listserv, don't include your name in the above message. To receive information about the mailing list without subscribing, type **info** instead of **subscribe**. You don't have to include your e-mail address because the program takes it directly from the message header. Remove *sig lines* from the message, as they can confuse the mailing list program.

Once successfully subscribed, you'll receive an automated confirmation message as well as information about how to unsubscribe. Be sure to save this message. To read more about mailing lists, visit The Reporter's Guide to Internet Mailing Lists at **http://www.daily.umn.edu/~broeker/guide.html**.

sig
Signature lines at the bottom of e-mail messages. Sigs are often saved in sig.txt or signature.txt files. Most mail and news programs automatically append your customized sig to your messages. Often, sigs contain your name, e-mail address, and perhaps your business or home page URL.

Locating a Mailing List

There are many ways to stay informed about new mailing lists or to search for a mailing list that covers a specific topic. Here are a few suggestions:

1. Check the following Web pages:
   - Liszt Directory of E-mail Discussion Groups at **http://www.liszt.com/**. One of the biggest indexes of mailing lists and newsgroups.
   - *Online Magazine*'s List Servers of the Internet at **http://www.online-magazine.com/listsvr.htm**. This searches 7530 mailing lists by e-mail address, title, or descriptions.
   - Publicly Accessible Mailing Lists (PAML) at **http://www.NeoSoft.com/internet/paml** or **http://www.cis.ohio-state.edu/text/faq/usenet/mail/mailing-lists/top.html** (Figure 5.4). This is another master list of mailing lists.

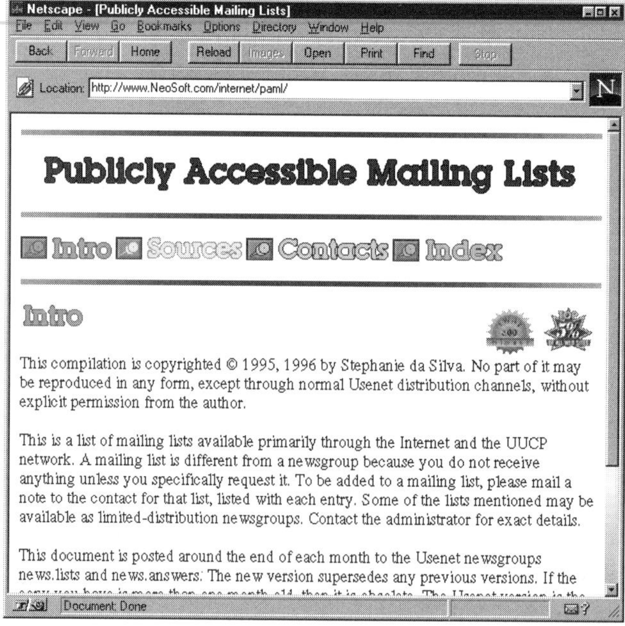

Figure 5.4 Publicly Accessible Mailing Lists Web Site

2. Post a message in a related newsgroup. For example, if you're a big Raymond Chandler fan, you could ask if there are any mailing lists that focus on Raymond Chandler's writing.

3. Check **news.lists** and **comp.internet.net-happenings** newsgroups. Mailing list announcements are posted in these two groups.

4. Subscribe to the Net Happenings newsletter by sending e-mail to **majordomo@dsmail.internic.Net**. In the message area, type **subscribe Net-happenings**. This is a daily newsletter containing a synopsis of everything that's new on the Net. (This could be more information than you actually need.)

5. Check the WWW view of *Directory of Scholarly and Professional E-Conferences*, **http://n2h2.com/KOVACS/**.

General Mailing Lists for Writers

The following mailing lists provide helpful support for writers:

AuthorsNet

Writers discuss marketing and other writing-related topics. To subscribe, send e-mail to **listserv@authors.woodybbs.com**. In the subject line, type: **subscribe authorsnet-ml**.

In the body of the message, type: **subscribe authorsnet-ml** ***your_first_name your_last_name@your_e-mail_address***. For more information, contact **sandra.greenwood@authors.woodybbs.com**.

Correspondent's Exchange Network

An international discussion forum where foreign correspondents, writers, editors, and publishers can meet to exchange thoughts, information, and material with other professionals and publications.

To subscribe, send e-mail to **majordomo@true.net**.

In the body of the message, type: **subscribe correx-l**.

Freelance Writers

An unmoderated listserve for independent journalists and nonfiction writers who want to exchange information markets and professional expertise. To subscribe, send mail to **owner-freelance@newshare.com**.

In the body of the message, type: **subscribe FREELANCE** ***your_first_name your_last_name***.

Include your name and address and a few words about your interests. For more information, send e-mail to **SYNDICATE@newshare.com**.

List of Mailing Lists for Writers

http://vanbc.wimsey.com/~sdkwok/mwmlist.html

A master list of mailing lists specifically for writers. Includes subscription information. Fiction, nonfiction, technical, romance, novel, and children's genres.

Small Press Mailing List

Authors and editors involved with small and independent presses. Printers and services; announcements; calls for submissions; readings; advice for writers, editors, and self-publishers. To subscribe, send e-mail to **small-press-request@world.std.com**. This message is read by a person and not a program, so you can write a note in the body of the message. For more information, contact **ctan@world.std.com**.

Writers' Online Workshop

Excellent online critique group with five categories available: fiction, novels, nonfiction, young adults, and poetry. Minimum participation required to retain membership. To subscribe, send e-mail to **listserv@psuvm.psu.edu**.

In the body of the message, type: **subscribe listname** ***your_first_name your_last_name*** replacing **listname** with **fiction**, **novels-l**, **nfiction**, **yawrite**, or **poetry-w**. For more information, contact **lkraus@voyager.net**.

Writers' Workshop

Unmoderated workshop where writers discuss the craft of writing and share works in progress. To subscribe, send e-mail to:

listserv@mitvma.mit.edu
or
listserv@mitvma.mit.bitnet

In the body of the message, type: **subscribe writers** ***your_first_name your_last_name***.

Publishing Online

> We have read your manuscript with boundless delight. If we were to publish your paper, it would be impossible for us to publish any work of lower standard. And as it is unthinkable that in the next thousand years we shall see its equal, we are, to our regret, compelled to return your divine composition, and to beg you a thousand times to overlook our short sight and timidity.
>
> —Found on the the Internet, translated from a Chinese journal

Most published writers tell you that getting published doesn't make you a writer. But of course, they're all published.

Trying to get published the traditional way has until recently been a mysterious, lengthy process often culminating in repeated rejections. If you couldn't find a publisher, your only option was the self-publishing route. Even though this route commands more respect than it did ten years ago, it still requires a considerable outlay of money and energy on the part of the writer/publisher, not to mention the burden of marketing and distribution.

Electronic publishing is similar to traditional publishing in that you either find a publisher for your work or you publish it yourself:

1. Find a publisher. There are a few electronic/multimedia publishers, such as Eastgate Systems, **http://www.eastgate.com** (Figure 6.1), who work strictly with Internet and CD-based works. Most freelance material, however, is published on personal Web sites, in Usenet newsgroups, and in electronic magazines (e-zines).

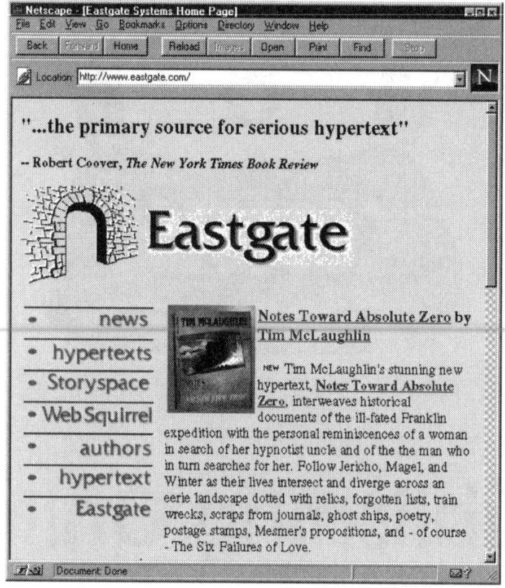

Figure 6.1 Eastgate Systems Publishing

Most publishing-related links lean heavily toward discussing the book world, not the on-screen world. Online newsletters and e-zines struggle to keep up with industry news, gossip, and trends. There are also many online booksellers with big, active Web sites such as The Amazon Bookstore, **http://www.amazon.com** and BookWire, **http://www.bookwire.com** (Figure 6.2). Most hard copy book publishers also have their own sites.

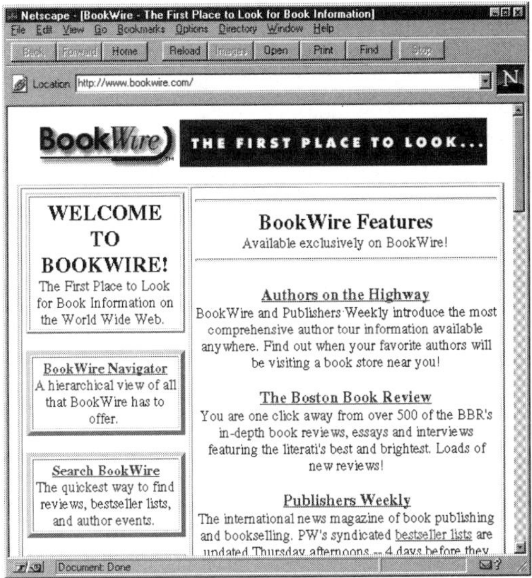

Figure 6.2 BookWire Web Site

E-zines can be corporate giants with major hard copy counterparts such as *Time* magazine and *USA Today*, or they can be strictly cyberspace publications such as the Web's HotWired, **http://www.hotwired.com/** (Figure 6.3) and Slate, **http://www.slate.com**. There are also thousands of independently published e-zines that showcase new writing.

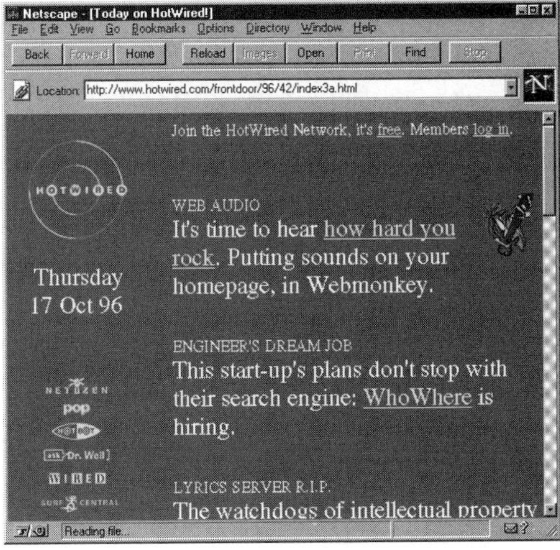

Figure 6.3 HotWired E-zine

2. Self-publish. It takes comparatively little money and effort to publish your own material online. If you create a Web site, you may have to pay a monthly fee for server space. If you publish on Usenet or in mailing lists, there's no fee beyond that required to keep your e-mail address active.

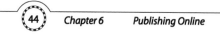

   On the Web you can publish anything from a hypertext version of your thousand-page historical romance (please don't) to a series of short articles you've written about foreign adoption programs. On Usenet you can publish material in any of the writing newsgroups. If you subscribe to a commercial online service, you can publish articles, advice columns, messages, and whatever you can successfully pitch to the company.

Drawbacks

Unfortunately, electronically published materials often suffer from second-class status. This has to do with the following drawbacks:

- Quality control. Good and bad things happen when everyone becomes a writer. Creative, talented people finally get the recognition that they richly deserve, and that's good. But most of us have to wade through piles of garbage to find those talented people, and that's bad. (Chapters 9 and 13 discuss quality issues.)
- Promotion. Your site is a piece of straw in the global haystack. You need lots of arrows pointing to it (see Chapter 14).
- Money. Unless you create your own Web site and have big-bucks sponsors, or you publish a fine piece of journalism with one of the heavy-hitter e-zines, you're not likely to earn much money—yet. Fortunately, this is changing rapidly as online transaction and royalty distribution systems come of age (see Chapter 19).

Some writers are unsure about the future of Internet publishing, especially as it relates to the entertainment industry. "Online entertainment is still in its infancy," writes television and interactive fiction writer John Groves. "Reading text on-screen is difficult, so it is less likely to be pursued for entertainment as opposed to getting information. I suspect all current online text fiction will be superseded by interactive programs and live action video within a few years. It may well be that the Internet market is a passing thing, like radio fiction or live TV drama."

Hypertext fiction author and teacher Robert Kendall predicts changes once the technology is upgraded. He says, "The biggest obstacle to the widespread acceptance of electronic books and magazines is currently the primitive state of the technology for reading them. Staring at today's computer screen just doesn't have the same attraction as curling up with a good book. However, industry experts expect the eventual arrival of an inexpensive paperback-sized computer with a screen that matches the readability of the printed page. Then the electronic publishing boom will begin in earnest."

Writers and editors bitterly complain about the quality of workmanship available on the Internet. Most publications brim with poorly edited, narcissistic homilies that make you want to hang yourself. The bottom line is that electronic credits don't pull much weight unless they're established productions with a track record and a lot of good press.

Why Bother?

Despite these disadvantages, there are still compelling reasons to explore and publish on the Internet:

If you look at this strictly from a profit-making standpoint, you'll see that the opportunities to earn income from online publications are looking up. The National Writers Union took an unequivocably enthusiastic stance in a position paper on online publishing, **http://www.igc.apc.org/nwu/docs/e-money.htm**. They noted," income-producing self-publishing on the Net could be a great boon not only for freelance writers, but for readers as well. The ability to earn a living from online distribution of one's work will encourage a wider range of writers to produce a wider range of materials for a wider range of audiences. While many Net publishers will continue to make their material available at no cost, new techniques of digital commerce are emerging that make it possible for those who live off their writing to receive payment—even tiny amounts per user—directly from their online readers."

If you look at this from a broader perspective, you'll see that the Internet is a wellspring of fresh energy. It provides writers with inspiration and new opportunities in a cost-effective, convenient, and timely manner. Research resources, communities, classes, tools, professional and personal communications, publishing outlets—they're all out there. We're nuts not to take advantage of them.

Where to Publish Online

There are a variety of online structures into which you can fit your writing. Each of the following is discussed at length later in this book:

- **Web Presentation.** Easily the most common and recognizable form of online publishing, Web presentations can be as simple as a resume with clips or as elaborate as a fully illustrated novel. Hypertext fiction—text with links embedded in it—is rapidly gaining respect as a new genre (see Chapter 12). Web pages can include sounds, video clips, and animation enhancements and can only be viewed with a Web browser.
- **E-zines and Newsletters.** An e-zine is an electronically distributed magazine. Some are e-mailed to a subscriber list; others reside as Web sites. E-zines can be idiosyncratic and quirky, or impressive, professional online journals. Newsletters are similar to e-zines, except that they're more likely to contain market information and "how to" articles. It's not difficult to generate your own e-zine or newsletter, and the resulting publicity can garner a new audience for your work.
- **Usenet and Mailing Lists.** Usenet newsgroups and mailing lists offer three publishing options: 1) you can post your work in specific newsgroups for critique, 2) you can start your own newsgroup, or 3) you can e-mail articles to the newsgroup. Usenet articles are read by potentially thousands of newsgroup participants. Many writers attest to receiving work queries based on articles they've posted in Usenet.
- **FAQs (Frequently Asked Questions).** FAQs are important to Usenet and the Web because they provide useful information about Web sites and newsgroups in a simple question/answer format. Originally developed to prevent newsgroups from going over the same information repeatedly, FAQs have become a staple on the Internet.
- **Commercial Service Provider articles**. If you subscribe to commercial providers such as America Online (AOL), CompuServe, the Microsoft Network (MSN), or Prodigy, you have an enormous outlet for publishing written works. Commercial online communities electronically publish articles and support materials provided by instructors and experts. These materials are listed in forums and on bulletin boards, and some are used as online class curriculum. The writing is practical, basic, and motivating.

The Writer's Guide to the Internet
Chapter
7

How to Create a Web Page

This book isn't meant to be a complete Hypertext Markup Language (HTML) guide; however, the following information can help you understand what it takes to publish a simple Web document. You'll find short explanations of the most common features of HTML as well as a tutorial using the simple template contained on the CD that comes with this book. As you go through this chapter, you might also want to download one of the quick reference HTML guides available on the Web such as *The Bare Bones Guide to HTML*, **http://werbach.com/barebones/** (Figure 7.1).

tags
HTML labels enclosed in angle brackets, **<HR>**, **<HTML>**. Tags identify structural elements such as links, headings, subheadings, body text paragraphs, numbered and indented lists, line breaks, and so on (Figure 7.3). Tags also indicate where to insert graphics, how to emphasize characters, where to include fill-in forms, and where to insert horizontal lines. Most tags come in pairs (also known as containers because they mark the beginning and ending of elements). For example, the text contained in the tag pair **<H1>...</H1>** is a level 1 heading element. Some tags are single, such as **<HR>**, which inserts a horizontal rule into a document.

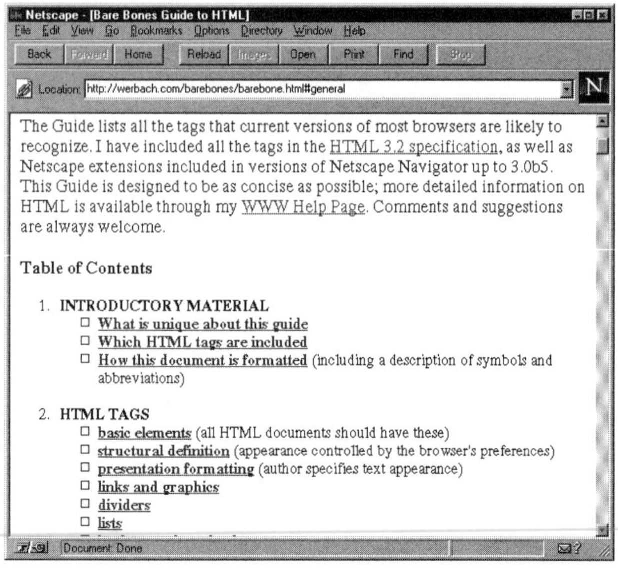

Figure 7.1 The Bare Bones Guide to HTML

If you plan to publish material on the Web, you'll probably also need to purchase a good hard copy HTML tutorial eventually to help you with the details. (See the end of this chapter for book references.) You'll also want to check out HTML index sites such as WWW Help, **http://werbach.com/web/wwwhelp.html#guides** and the HTML Writers Guild, **http://guild.infovav.se/** (Figure 7.2).

Web pages (also known as Web documents) are ASCII text files punctuated with HTML *tags*. Web documents can be created in any word processor, but many people use specialized HTML editor programs to simplify the task. One of the easiest to acquire and use is HotDog, available from Sausage Software at **http://www.sausage.com**. Another useful tool is the Word for Windows HTML Assistant add-on program which can translate Word documents directly into HTML. WordPerfect has a similar program. But you can always type the text into a simple text editor such as Notepad.

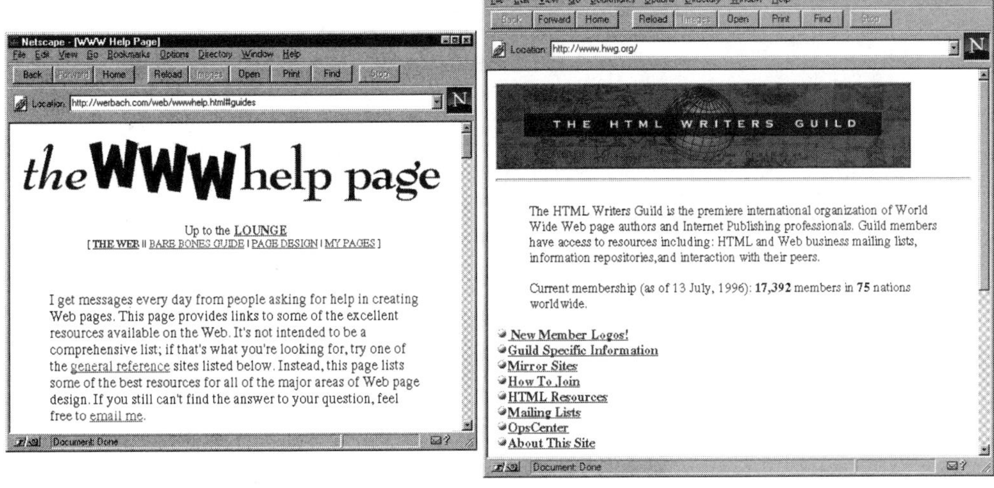

Figure 7.2 Online HTML Resource Sites

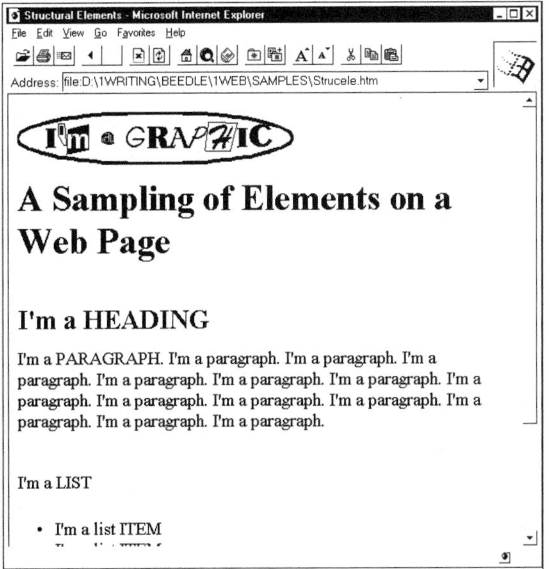

Figure 7.3 Structural Elements Tagged in HTML

Ideally, you should compose HTML documents based on how you want the information organized and *not* on how you want it to appear visually on the screen. This is difficult to understand because most of us think about how something looks, not how it's built. Even though HTML lets you identify document elements as paragraphs, numbered lists, headings, and so on, each browser applies its own internal set of formats to the tagged elements. For instance, a bulleted list displayed in Netscape Navigator can be interpreted differently by Internet Explorer, which may use another font size, indent value, and bullet character.

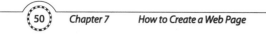

Each platform displays the structural elements in a locally consistent, logical manner. The integrity of your document's structure is always maintained, even if the font sizes and styles differ from computer to computer, browser to browser. A level 1 heading will always be a dominant element, clearly emphasized over lower-level headings and body text.

Unless you have a natural affinity for and interest in Web page design, resist the temptation to employ too many HTML bells and whistles (such as multimedia enhancements). Human nature being what it is, people tend to tire easily of sexy features. You're better off spending time on content. The pages that wear the longest are multibrowser-compatible, contemporary-looking, easy to use, and filled with good solid content.

Tag Fundamentals

source
The HTML text file with all the tags revealed. (WordPerfect users might recognize this as the Reveal Codes display.) In the following examples you'll see browser views and source views. With most browsers, you can view the HTML source by selecting a View Source command in the File or View menus. It's useful to view source documents because you can study how other Web pages are constructed.

Here are a few things you need to know about tags:

- Tags are enclosed in left and right angle-bracket symbols: **<TAG>**. This is how browsers distinguish between the document text "HTML" and the tag **<HTML>**.
- Tags are case-insensitive. It doesn't matter whether you type **<HTML>**, **<html>**, or **<HtmL>**. However, for ease of use and consistency, choose a case preference and stick with it. Tags are all capitalized in this book.
- When the browser doesn't understand tags, it ignores them. Typographical errors usually render tags invisible to the browser.
- Many tags come in pairs. For example, the **<H1>** *start tag* indicates the beginning of a level 1 heading element, and the **</H1>** *end tag* indicates the end of the same element. The text sandwiched between the two tags is the heading text displayed in the browser window. (Note the slash symbol / identifying the end tag.)

- Some tags are single entities such as **
, which indicates a line break, or **<HR>, which indicates a horizontal line. They don't have end tags.
- Some tags contain *attributes* that modify the start tag in a special way. For example, the **<P>** (paragraph) tag can include the **ALIGN=CENTER** attribute, indicating that a paragraph should be centered in the window. The tag would then be **<P ALIGN=CENTER>**. Without an **ALIGN** attribute, paragraph text defaults to left alignment. Some attributes are mandatory; most are optional.
- Tags and the text they modify must be correctly positioned relative to other tags. For example, a paragraph **<P>** element isn't legal unless it's nested inside of **<BODY> </BODY>** tags. A title **<TITLE></TITLE>** element isn't legal unless it's nested inside of **<HEAD></HEAD>** tags.

start and end tags
In a pair of HTML tags (a container), the start tag begins the HTML element and the end tag completes the element. The text of the element falls in between the start and end tags. The end tag contains a slash to identify it clearly. For example, **<H1>** *text* **</H1>**.

attributes
A characteristic that modifies a start tag. For example, the **<HR>** tag that inserts a horizontal rule (line) into the document can be modified with the **WIDTH=50%** attribute. **<HR WIDTH=50%>** means that the rule will display at 50 percent of the size of the window. Without a width attribute, the rule defaults to the full width of the window. Some attributes are mandatory; others, such as **WIDTH**, are optional.

Creating Your First Web Page

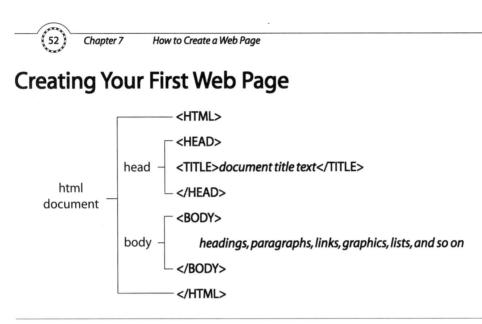

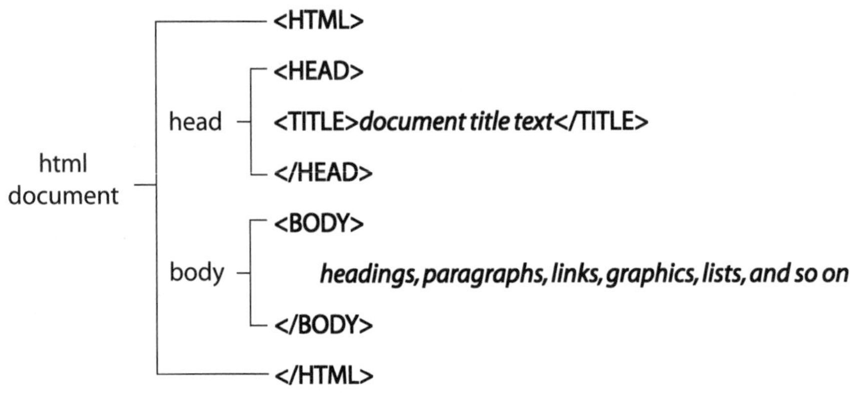

Figure 7.4 The Outline of a Web Page

The Minimum Tags Necessary

The following tags represent the bare minimum necessary to generate a Web page.

Tag Name	Function
<HTML>...</HTML>	Starts and ends the entire document. Everything falls in between this tag pair.
<HEAD>...</HEAD>	Contains header information, especially the document title.
<TITLE>...</TITLE>	The title of document, usually displayed in a special text box or in the title bar of the Web browser. Often, the title matches the first heading in the **<BODY>** of the page.
<BODY>...</BODY>	All of the document excluding the head. The majority of basic tags such as headings, paragraphs, lists, and so on fall in between this tag pair.
<P>	Identifies text as a paragraph. Insert a **<P>** tag in front of each new paragraph.
<H1>...</H1> <H2>...</H2> <H3>...</H3> <H4>...</H4> <H5>...</H5> <H6>...</H6>	There are six levels of headings. Each level has a distinctive font style and size dictated by the browser displaying the Web page. Use headings just as you would use them in a typical word processor. The level 1 headings **<H1>** are at the top of the structural hierarchy. The level 6 headings **<H6>** are at the bottom.

You can publish any document by placing these main tags properly. If you use only these tags, you'll have a big dull page, but this at least gives you an idea of how easy it is to format Web documents (Figure 7.5). All other tags are optional, helping to structure the document and provide links to other related information.

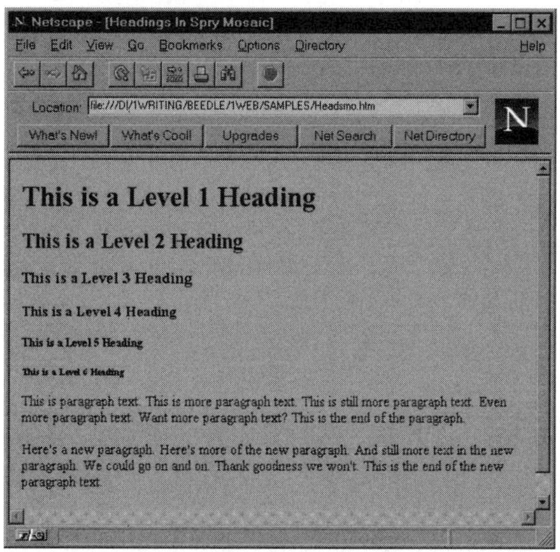

Figure 7.5 Headings and Paragraph Text on a Web Page

In the following figure, note the proper placement of the five main tags in the document. You can see the HTML source and how it appears in a browser window (Figure 7.6).

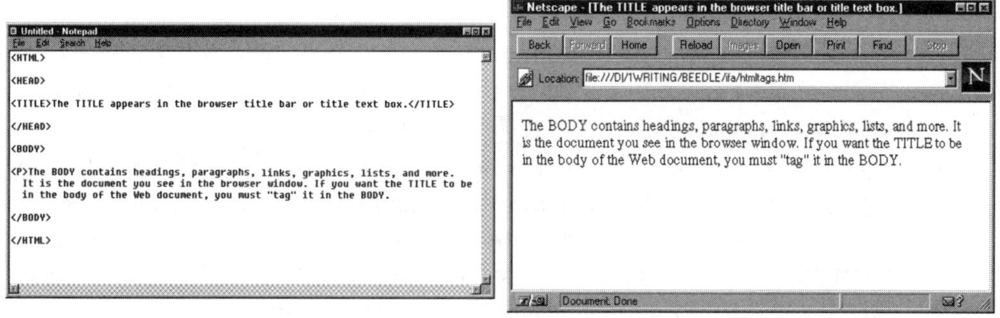

Figure 7.6 The Minimum Necessary HTML: Source and Browser Views

Adding a heading provides more structure. In Figure 7.7, note the addition of the level 1 heading tags **<H1>...</H1>**.

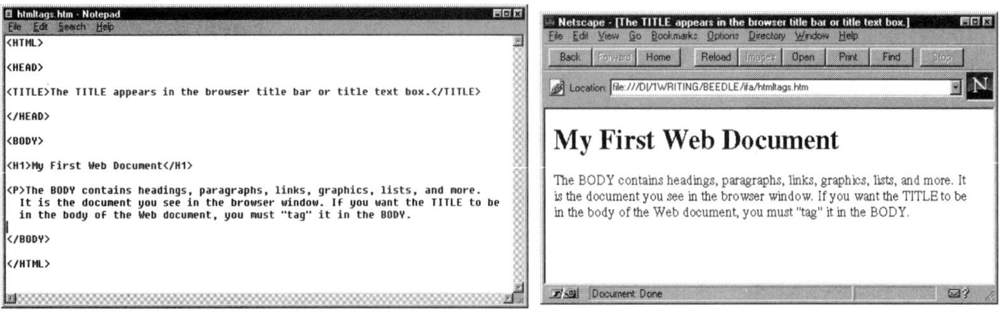

Figure 7.7 Additional Tags with the Minimum Necessary HTML: Source and Browser Views

> *Important:* The browser you use determines the amount of white space above and below paragraphs, headings, and so on. When you create a Web page, you should try to view it using different browsers.

In most cases, you must save an HTML document before you view it in the browser. The save function is standardized, usually in the File menu of the editor you're using. There are a few simple conventions to follow when naming and saving an HTML document:

- Save everything in one directory. This includes your art, your Web pages, everything that you use for the Web site. For example, you might create a directory called **website** on your hard drive and then save the Web page **index.htm** and all other Web pages in the **website** directory. This is the least complicated way of transporting data from your local computer to the server because it minimizes any editing of paths (you don't want me to get into that subject). As your Web site becomes more complex and you learn more about addresses and links, you may want to reorganize your directory. But for now, keep it very simple.
- Stick to the filenaming conventions for your home computer since you'll be testing your files locally. For Windows 3.1 computers, this means naming files with an **.htm** extension (**mypage.htm, index.htm**). When the documents are uploaded to the server, their extensions will likely need to change to **.html**. (Check with your server administrator about renaming and uploading the files.)
- To minimize confusion, type filenames in lowercase letters. Some servers are case-sensitive, meaning that **Iguana.htm** and **iguana.htm** are two different files.

When you create the Web page on your local hard drive, save it frequently and view the saved versions in the browser. This helps to catch formatting errors during the development cycle.

To view the saved Web document, select the Open File command in the browser window. (In Netscape, Open File is in the File Menu; in Internet Explorer go to the File menu and choose the Open command.) Select the HTML document you just created in the editor. As you view the document in the browser, switch back to the editor to make corrections and add new material. Each time you make a substantial change or correction in the editor, save the document again and click the Reload button in the browser window to reload the same document with the new edits.

Note: These instructions are generic; browsers and editors may vary in the location of commands and the manner in which they display corrected Web pages. For example, Internet Explorer automatically updates the browser to show the latest saved document.

Once you've completed local construction of your Web page, it's a good idea to run it through a validation program such as Weblint, **http://www.khoral.com/staff/neilb/weblint.html**. Validation programs detect formatting errors and highlight questionable tags. This helps to insure that most browsers will read your tags. If you don't have a validation program installed on your computer, try using Webtech's Validation Service, **http://www.webtechs.com/html-val-svc/**, to check the document once it's uploaded. You can find validation programs for all computer platforms on the webreference.com Web page, **http://webreference.com/html/validation.html**.

The Lowdown on Links

Links give the Web its dynamic character and appeal. They are visually distinctive elements that are colored and/or underlined. When you click any part of a link, you download the file from the location dictated by the link's address (its URL). Links are also known as hypertext and hotspots.

Links are typically found in menu-style lists (Figure 7.8); however, they can also be embedded in paragraph text.

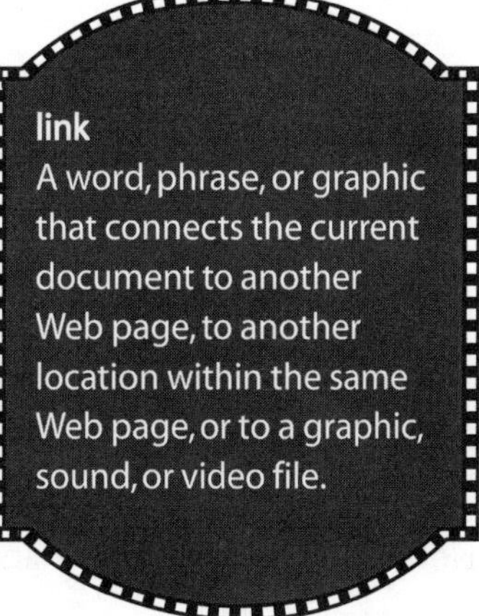

link
A word, phrase, or graphic that connects the current document to another Web page, to another location within the same Web page, or to a graphic, sound, or video file.

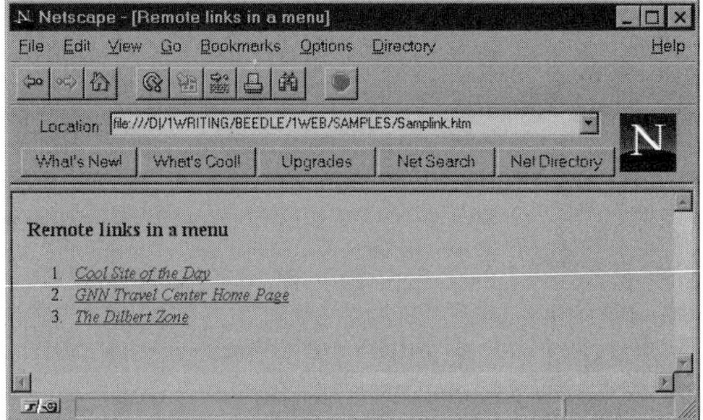

Figure 7.8 Sample Links in a List

The Anatomy of a Link

In HTML, a link tag is designated by the tag pair **<A HREF=>...</A>**. Because links contain URLs and other associated information, they can often look complex and intimidating. However, when you understand the layout of a link, you'll find that it's a fairly simple construct with a few basic components. Figure 7.9 dissects the Cool Site of the Day link.

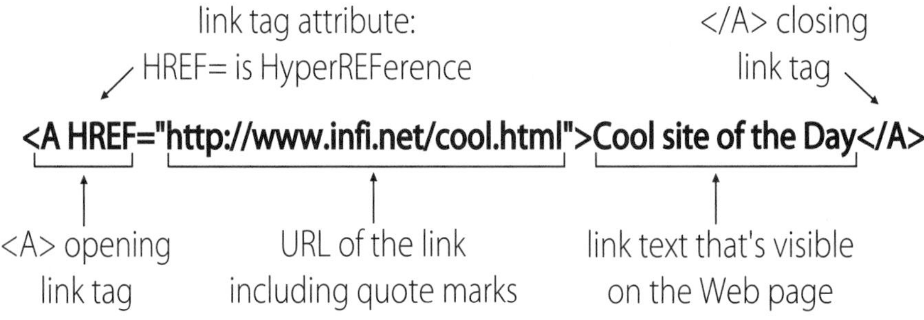

Figure 7.9 The Anatomy of a Link

Note the following features in this figure:

- The **<A>** start tag contains a commonly used attribute, **HREF=**. Attributes modify tags. Unlike filenames, attributes are not case-sensitive. The **HREF=** attribute stands for Hypertext REFerence, indicating that the text after the "=" is a URL. (Reminder: URLs are addresses for Web-formatted documents.)
- The **<A HREF="*filename*">** start tag contains the URL of the file you want to see. The URL is enclosed in quotations with the closing angle bracket > immediately following the closing quotation mark.

- The **</A>** end tag closes the link.
- Between **<A HREF="*filename*">** start tag and **</A>** end tag is the text that will serve as the virtual link, sometimes called the hotspot. This is what you'll see and click on the Web page.
- Links adopt the format of the element surrounding them (Figure 7.10). In other words, if the link is inside a **<P>** paragraph, it'll look like paragraph text. If it's inside a level 2 heading, it'll look like heading 2 text.

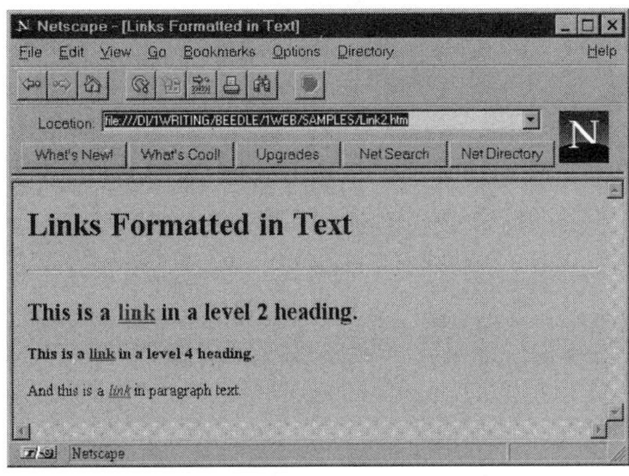

Figure 7.10 Links Formatted in Text

There are four commonly used links in Web documents. These links can be:

- from one *internal Web page* to another
- to a Web page on a remote server
- to an image
- to a specific location on a Web page

Because this book covers HTML in a nutshell, we'll explore only the simplest forms of links including links from one *internal Web page* to another and links to a Web page on another server. To learn about other kinds of links, visit one of the many excellent HTML tutorial sites described by the HTML Writer's Guild, **http://www.hwg.org**, or drop by Ian Graham's HTML Documentation tutorial at **http://www.utoronto.ca/webdocs/HTMLdocs/NewHTML/intro.html**.

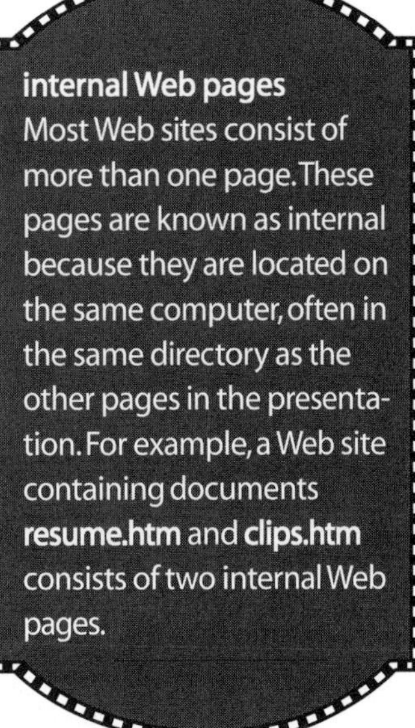

internal Web pages
Most Web sites consist of more than one page. These pages are known as internal because they are located on the same computer, often in the same directory as the other pages in the presentation. For example, a Web site containing documents **resume.htm** and **clips.htm** consists of two internal Web pages.

Links between Internal Web Pages

To make linking between pages as simple as possible, save all your internal Web pages and related art in one directory. Many personal Web sites include one or more internally linked documents such as a resume, a publicity photo, and an assortment of additional pages describing hobbies and haunts (Figure 7.11).

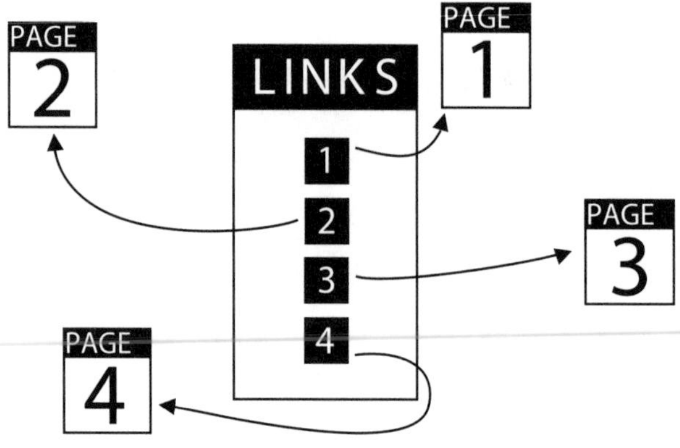

Figure 7.11 Links to an Internal Web Page

Internal files located in the same directory are very easy to format into links. The format is as follows:

<A HREF="*filename*">*the text of the hotspot*</A>

<A HREF="resume.htm">RESUME</a>

In the following example, The Dog Page contains a link to a page about terriers. The page **terriers.htm** is located in the same directory as The Dog Page. Thus the link on The Dog Page looks like this:

<A HREF="terriers.htm">Terriers</A>

Notice that in Figure 7.12, the Terriers link is embedded in a bulleted list. (In HTML this is known as an unordered list.)

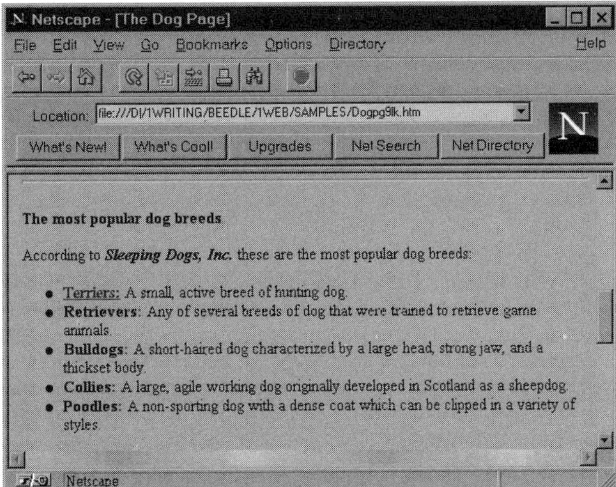

Figure 7.12 Links to an Internal Web Page

Note for folks who understand directory paths: if **terriers.htm** is located in a directory subordinate to The Dog Page directory, you can reference it by including the subdirectories:

<A HREF="/others/terriers.htm">Terriers</A>

Links between Remote Web Pages

Aside from internal links, the most common links you'll see are those to a Web page on another computer. When a site contains a list of favorite Web sites, the locations of these sites are almost always outside of the Web site's home server. Regardless of whether the remote server is in the next city or across the globe, the link format is constant.

<A HREF="*URL of remote document*">*the text of the hotspot*</A>

<A HREF="*http://iguana.images.com/dupecam.html*">Iguana Cam</a>

Let's consider The Dog Page example above. If **terriers.htm** were located on a different server, the full URL would be cited instead of just the filename. (Reread Chapter 2 if you have forgotten the structure of a URL.) The link might look like this:

<A HREF="http://www.server.com/AKC/terriers.html">Terriers</A>

Link Etiquette

Links should be clearly listed, easy to find, and descriptive without being verbose. Here are some tips:

1. Unless it's part of the style of your presentation, don't bury links in a lot of text. They should be easy to find, easy to understand, uncomplicated, and probably in a list if there are more than a couple of them.

2. Make your link names descriptive. If your link doesn't clearly reference its subject matter, it's less likely to be found in a search. Descriptive link names are also easier for the user to understand.

   Not as good:

   To **learn more** about potted meat, visit The Spam Cam.

   Good:

   To learn more about potted meat, visit **The Spam Cam**.

   Not as good:

   Check out these potted meat sites:
   http://www.fright.com/spamcam
   http://www.domain.edu/ewwww/uglymeat.html

   Good:

   Check out these potted meat sites:
   The Spam Cam
   Potted Meat Artistry

3. Resist the "click here" temptation. The word "here" doesn't describe anything.

   Not as good:

   Click **here** to learn more about potted meat.

   Good:

   Visit **The Spam Cam** to learn more about potted meat.

The Lowdown on Images

Images add color, energy, and excitement to a Web page. They also slow down transmission time. Before adding an image to your Web page, ask yourself if it is truly necessary. When in doubt, don't include it.

Images (graphics) come in two flavors: *inline* and *external*. Generally speaking, *inline* images download to your screen automatically, whereas external images require you to click an associated link (Figure 7.13).

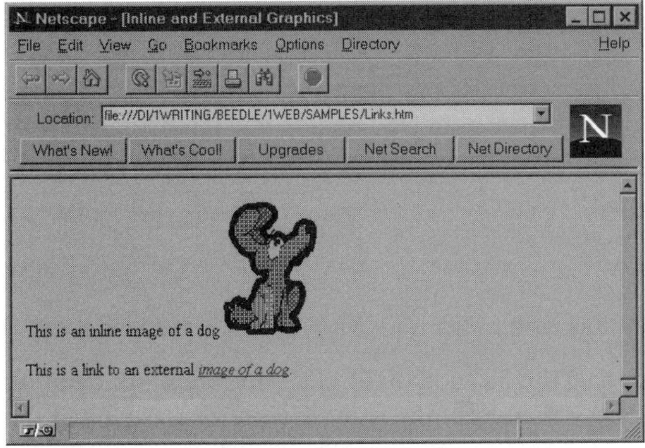

Figure 7.13 An Inline Image and a Link to an External Image

Common graphic file formats used on the Web are:

GIF	.gif	Currently, the most common inline image file format. Best used for line art and images with fewer colors.
JPEG	.jpeg, .jpg	Most but not all browsers can display inline JPEGs. JPEG format is best used for photos and complex colored images. A photo saved as a JPEG is a smaller file size than the same photo saved as a GIF.

inline image
A graphic that downloads to your screen when the document is displayed. Some browsers let you disable the automatic download to speed up data transmission. (Netscape:View menu, Options command, Appearance tab, Show Pictures check box.)

external image
A graphic linked to the site. You must click the link to initiate a download sequence and launch the necessary external *viewer program.*

viewer program
A program that interprets and displays an external file, often an image. Viewer programs, sometimes called "plug-ins," are also used to play video and sound files.

To convert a graphic into a GIF or JPEG, use an editing program such as Adobe Photoshop or View Pro, a shareware program at **http://world.std.com/~mmedia/lviewp.html**.

Two important points to consider:

- If you plan to use images that you haven't created yourself, then make sure you get permission from the originator.

- Use repeat images for logos, return icons, and bullets, because they lend consistency to your Web pages. Repeat images also save time because no matter how often they're referenced, they only need to be downloaded once by the visitor.

Inserting Inline Images

Like links, images can be embedded in most any HTML element or they can be placed in their own line of text. The simplest way to insert an inline image into your document is to save the graphic in the same directory as the Web page itself and insert the following HTML:

<IMG SRC="*filename*">

<IMG SRC="iguana.gif">

The **<IMG>** tag is not a container, i.e. it has no end tag. The **SRC=** attribute is mandatory.

The above tag inserts a left-aligned image at the location of the tag. If the tag is inserted into a line of text, most browsers will align the bottom of the graphic with the baseline of the sentence. To center an image (or any element) horizontally in the browser window, enclose it in **<CENTER>...</CENTER>** tags.

alternative text
Descriptive text inserted into an **<IMG>** tag using the **ALT=** attribute. Appears in place of an image when graphics are disabled. In Internet Explorer "Alt" text pops up when the mouse cursor rests over the image.

To make the image tag useful to visitors who disable their graphics (to speed file transmission), include *alternative text* by adding the **ALT=** attribute. Alternative text appears in place of the image and helps visitors know what is supposed to be there, even if they choose not to view it. The format is as follows:

<IMG SRC="*filename*" ALT="*alternative text*">

<IMG SRC="iguana.gif" ALT="Picture of a smiling iguana, 10k.jpg">

The following figure shows you how alternative text helps to define graphic areas that don't download.

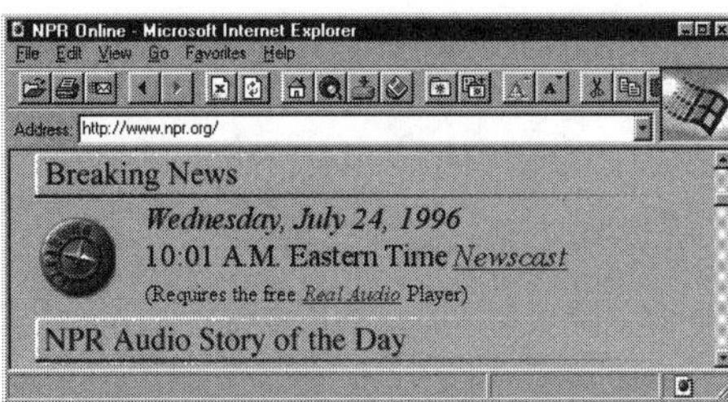

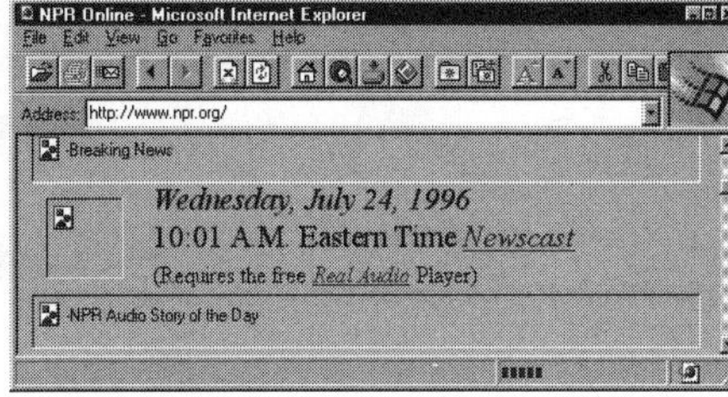

Figure 7.14 Alternative Text

Including External Images

An external image is linked to a Web page. In a manner similar to external Web page links, you download the image by clicking the link. Unlike external Web page links, the images are usually part of the local Web presentation and don't require the full URL for access. The format for an external image link uses the standard **<A HREF=>** tag, but instead of linking to an HTML document, you link to an image file.

```
<A HREF="image filename">visual hotspot</A>

<A HREF="iguana.gif">A smiling iguana</A>
```

If possible, external links should be followed by text that explains the format and size of the file. This helps visitors decide if they want to click the link. For example:

```
<P><A HREF="iguana.gif">A smiling iguana</A> (5k .jpg)
```

The link hotspot can be text or a *thumbnail* (smaller) version of the graphic. Web pages such as museum sites and shopping malls contain galleries of thumbnails. To use a thumbnail, simply insert the **<IMG>** tag into a link pointing to the full-scale graphic file. For example:

```
<A HREF="bigpic.gif"><IMG SRC="thumbnail.gif"></A>
```

Figure 7.15 shows a simple external link and an image link using a thumbnail graphic. Note that in both cases, the size and format of the file are included in the paragraph text.

thumbnail
A thumbnail is simply a scaled-down version (or small section) of a much larger image. To create a thumbnail, open an image-editing program, resize your graphic or crop a small sample of it, and save it under a different filename.

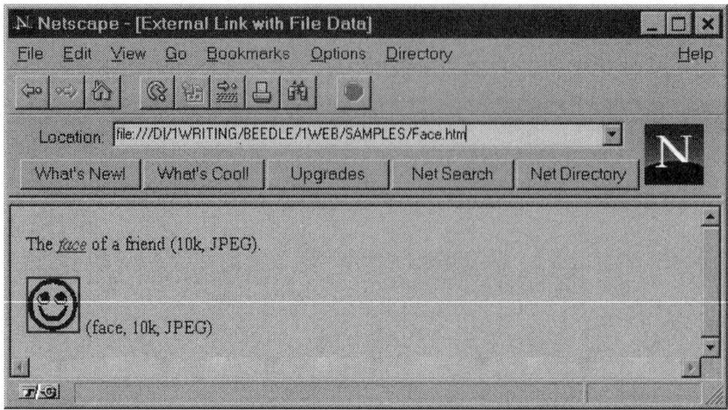

Figure 7.15 External Image Links with Descriptive Text

Here is the HTML for the above figure:

```
<BODY>
<P>The <A HREF="face.jpg">face</A> of a friend (10k, JPEG).
<P><A HREF="face.jpg"><IMG SRC="face.gif"></A> (face, 10k, JPEG)
</BODY>
```

More Style and Structure Tags

In addition to the basic tags outlined above, HTML includes other style and structure tags that are easy to use. The following table briefly describes some of the most common. This is by no means a comprehensive list. It's merely offered as a way to get you started. To practice using these tags, go through the tutorial in the next chapter.

HTML Lists

Tag Name	Function
<OL>...</OL>	Ordered (numbered) list. Each item in the list is tagged **<LI>**.
<UL>...</UL>	Unordered (bulleted) list. Each item in the list is tagged **<LI>**.
<LI>	List item. Used to describe each item in ordered and unordered lists.
<DL>...</DL>	Definition list. Contains terms and definitions similar to a glossary or dictionary. Each term is tagged **<DT>**. Each definition is tagged **<DD>**.

<DT>	Definition term. The term being defined in a definition list, as in a dictionary or glossary.
<DD>	Data definition. The definition of a term in a definition list, as in a dictionary or glossary. Always follows the term itself, which is tagged **<DT>**.

HTML Font Style Tags

Tag Name	Function
<B>...</B>	Bold
<I>...</I>	Italic
<U>...</U>	Underline
<STRONG>...</STRONG>	Strong (usually bold)
<EMPHASIS>...</EMPHASIS>	Emphasized (usually italicized)
<TT>...</TT>	Teletype (monospaced) font

HTML Dividers

Tag Name	Function
 	Line break (without creating a new paragraph)
<HR>	Horizontal rule (line). Include the **WIDTH=x%** attribute to specify a width relative to the width of the window. For example, **<HR WIDTH=50%>**.

Other Tags

Tag Name	Function
<CENTER>...</CENTER>	Center the text relative to the window width.
<ADDRESS>...</ADDRESS>	A signature block (sig). Typically includes name, e-mail address, and copyright statement.
<!— ... —>	Comment tags. Text contained inside the tags doesn't display onscreen.
<PRE>...</PRE>	Preformatted text, rendered in monospaced font. Useful for preserving the spacing and line breaks of code listings, tables, and text.

Upload Your Web Site

When you upload a site, you're literally moving the entire local Web site directory to the server. Once on the server, the site becomes open to the Web. Uploading isn't an intuitively obvious task, but it isn't rocket science either. Once you do it a few times, you'll find that it's a simple, rote procedure. Typically, uploading is accomplished via FTP (see Chapter 1). You'll need to talk to your service provider about how best to do it. Don't be shy about seeking assistance.

The cost of renting Web space on a server varies greatly from provider to provider. If your site is mostly text, you may be able to get away with using very little disk space—2 MB to 10 MB. If your site is a catalog filled with images, you may need more server space. Your provider will calculate the fee based on how much disk space you require and the number of hits per day you're likely to receive. Customized features such as forms (fill-in pages for gathering information) can add to the monthly fee. If you can't find a local provider to rent you Web space, send an e-mail message to **listproc@einet.net** with **get inet-marketing www-svc-providers** in the body of the message.

Most important, find out what kind of server you're using. If it is a UNIX machine, two minor conversions are needed to render your Web documents compliant to the new platform:

- Rename the Web documents with **.html** extensions *after they're uploaded* (unless you run Windows 95, in which case you can use the four-character extension locally). Remember that whenever you rename a file, you also have to update the associated HTML link that calls it.
- If you use a PC locally, convert all backslashes (\) used in document paths to UNIX forward slashes (/). Check with your service provider, as these changes may not always be necessary.

> *Note:* UNIX is case-sensitive, which means that you must use the same upper- and lowercase lettering in your Web document link references as is used in the associated filenames; **Chinadoc.htm** is not the same file as **chinadoc.htm**. There's never a problem if you confine all filenames to lowercase letters.

Once the site is uploaded, you'll periodically upload corrected and new documents to the server. This is standard Web maintenance and shouldn't take more than a few hours a week if your site is simple.

Obviously, there's a great deal more to links and HTML than this brief introduction covers. If you plan to publish on the Web, you'll need to invest in an HTML book. You'll also want to explore the many online and offline resources that can help you expand your HTML skills. The following Web sites and books will get you started:

Web Resources for HTML

The Bare Bones Guide to HTML

http://werbach.com/barebones/

An easy-to-use quick reference list of HTML tags along with a variety of other HTML resource links.

Dave Siegel's Home Page

http://www.best.com:80/~dsiegel/home.html

An extravaganza of blasphemous Web page design advice coupled with gorgeous examples and down-to-earth work-arounds. Well worth studying but you need a browser that can display HTML tables.

The HTML Writers Guild Home Page

http://guild.infovav.se/

From this source you can find most any HTML-related information you're seeking. This includes online tutorials, supportive articles, Web page development software (browsers, editors, translators, converters, etc.), HTML newsgroups for sharing ideas and asking questions, HTML software and book reviews, and much more.

webreference.com

http://webreference.com/html/validation.html

"From Net beginners to webmasters, webreference.com is the fastest way to learn about the Web and the art of Web site creation." Includes Web Wizard awards and pays for articles about Web design. Go to the site map and sample the wide array of excellent links. You can get everything you need from this one site.

Word

http://www.word.com/index.html

When you want to see just how wild Web pages can be (and you have a fast connection), take your table-friendly browser to this e-zine.

Reference Books for HTML

HTML for Dummies, by Ed Tittel & Steve James

A fairly detailed description of HTML in an easily accessible language and style.

HTML for Fun and Profit, by Mary E. S. Morris

A no-nonsense, detailed, clearly-written description of HTML. An excellent resource book for serious HTML developers.

HTML: The Definitive Guide, by Chuck Musciano & Bill Kennedy

An excellent, detailed book that is easy to use. Published by O'Reilly & Associates, Inc., a company with an admirable track record of Web-related books.

Teach Yourself Web Publishing with HTML 3.0 in a Week, by Laura Lemay

An easy tutorial and reference organized on a day-by-day basis. Simple, humorous, and thorough. Good for beginners.

The Web Page Workbook, by Dawn Groves

Distills sound Web development, design, and promotional advice into simple practices and quick-reference lists. Includes a tutorial and sample Web site, Earthlink's Total Access (with Netscape) and HotDog Web Editor.

A Quick HTML Tutorial

The following tutorial quickly helps you generate a simple Web site using the template included with the *Author's Guide to the Internet* CD. Remember, this is a nutshell tour of a few basic HTML tags. At some point you should purchase a book containing a comprehensive tutorial and a complete HTML index.

In this step-by-step tutorial, you'll edit a Web site called Dan's Fish Fry. Although the tutorial is divided into subject areas, it is meant to be executed in a linear fashion. Each set of steps builds upon the previous set. *You must already know how to use a text editor and a browser.*

Getting Ready

As you edit the HTML source document in your word processor or text editor, don't be concerned about the extra blank lines between the sentences. Remember that HTML doesn't concern itself with extra character or line spaces. In most cases, the browser will display no more than a single blank character space between words, no matter how many times you press the spacebar. In the same manner, the browser will also ignore extra blank lines (unless you're using the **<PRE>** tag).

1. Copy the **template** directory from the CD to your hard drive. Keep the directory intact when you copy it. You'll edit the files from the hard drive.

2. Launch your browser and keep it open. You'll use this to view your work as you make changes to the source. The figures in this book show Netscape Navigator, but any browser will do.

   Note: Each browser displays screen elements in a unique manner. Don't be surprised if your browser elements look somewhat different from those pictured in this tutorial.

3. In the browser, open the **template/index.htm** file. (In Netscape, type CTRL + O to open a local file; in Internet Explorer, type CTRL + O and click the Open File button.) Your screen should resemble the following:

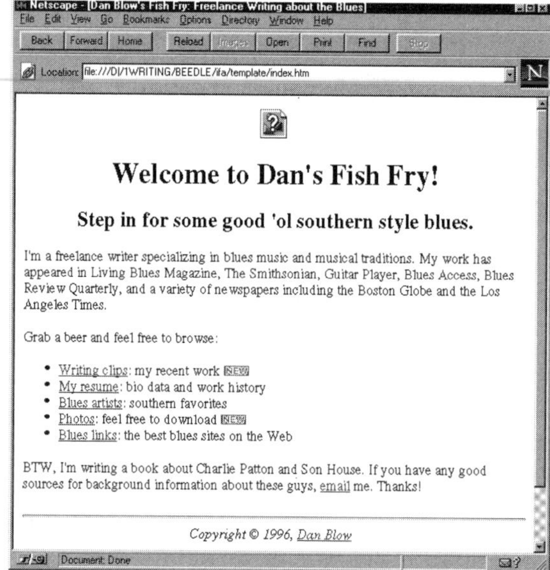

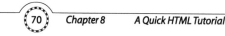

   Note: The placeholder ( ) above the title indicates that an HTML image tag **<IMG>** is present in the source; the image file name is either incorrect or the image file can't be located. We'll insert a correct file name into this placeholder later in the tutorial.

4. Launch a text editor or word processor. The screen captures in this book show Windows 95 Notepad, but you can edit a text file using almost any word processor on any platform.

5. In the text editor, open the **template/index.htm** file. This is the source document. Your source should resemble the following:

```
index.htm - Notepad
File Edit Search Help
<html>

<head>

<!--Insert the title of the site.-->

<title> Dan Blow's Fish Fry: Freelance Writing about the Blues</title>

</head>

<!--Background color is white. -->
<!--ffffff is hexidecimal for white. -->

<body bgcolor=#ffffff>

<!--CENTER tag is a container.-->

<center>

<img src="filename" alt="text describing your graphic">

<!--Insert welcome graphic if you have one.-->

<h1>Welcome to Dan's Fish Fry!</h1>

<!--Insert the title of the page -->

<h2>Step in for some good 'ol southern style blues.</h2>

<!--Insert a level 2 heading, or perhaps -->
<!--change it to a paragraph -->
```

The files are heavily commented (using the **<!--...-->** tag container) to help you understand what you're reading.

Note: All Fish Fry files are located in the template directory. As such, it won't be necessary to include directory paths in the links and image tags that you type.

Editing Text

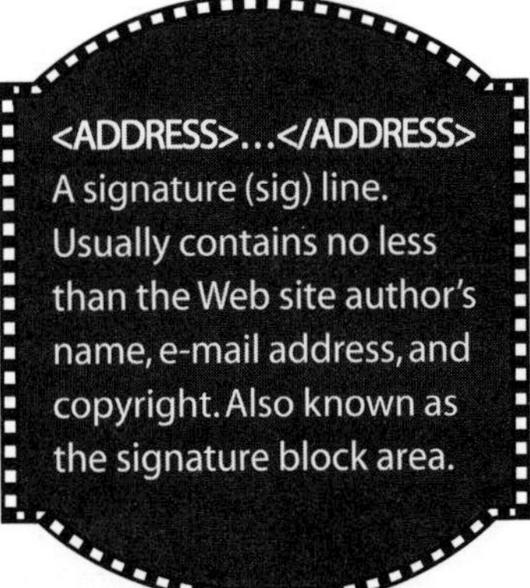
<ADDRESS>...</ADDRESS>
A signature (sig) line. Usually contains no less than the Web site author's name, e-mail address, and copyright. Also known as the signature block area.

Editing text in HTML is identical to editing text in any other document. Simply make the changes in the word processor or text editor and then save the file. Check your edits frequently in the browser window so that you can fix errors as they occur. If you use a PC, try pressing the **Alt** + **Tab** key combination to switch efficiently between the browser and editor windows.

1. In the text editor, change all name references from Dan Blow to your name. This includes references inside the **<TITLE>**, **<H1>**, and ***<ADDRESS>*** elements. The source should resemble the following:

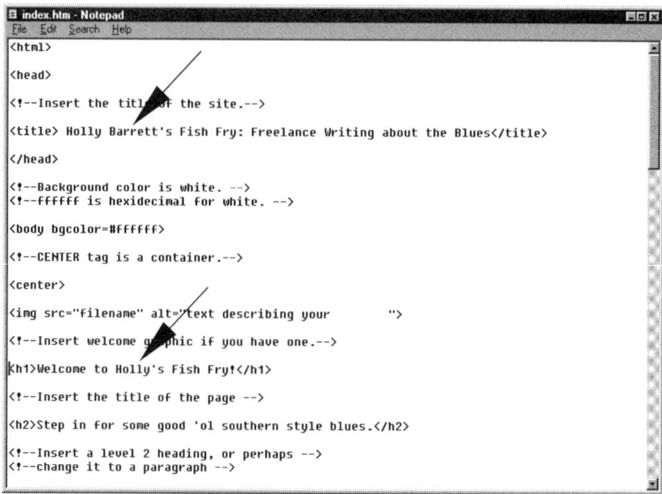

2. Save the document as text (not a Word or WordPerfect format) and keep the **.htm** file extension when you save it.
3. Switch to the browser window.
4. If necessary, click the browser's Reload button (or similar function button) to display the updated version of your source. Your screen should resemble the following:

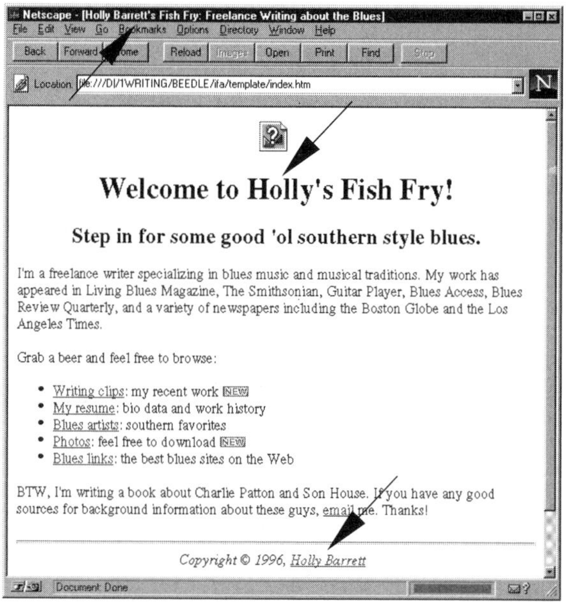

Note: In general, you should name the opening page of your Web site **index.htm**. When a browser accesses your directory (on the server) without specifying a page to download, the **index.htm** file is automatically displayed.

Editing Tags

When you add, edit, or remove tags, make sure your typing is accurate. Browsers are unforgiving when it comes to displaying Web documents. Typographical errors often render tags invisible. This means your text will either display as an incorrect element, or it won't display at all.

1. Switch back to the text editor window. Remove the **<CENTER>...</CENTER>** tags enclosing the two headings and the **<ADDRESS>** signature block.

2. Save the document in the text editor, switch to the browser window, and view the updated document. (Remember to click the Reload button if you don't see the results of your HTML updates.) Your screen should resemble the following:

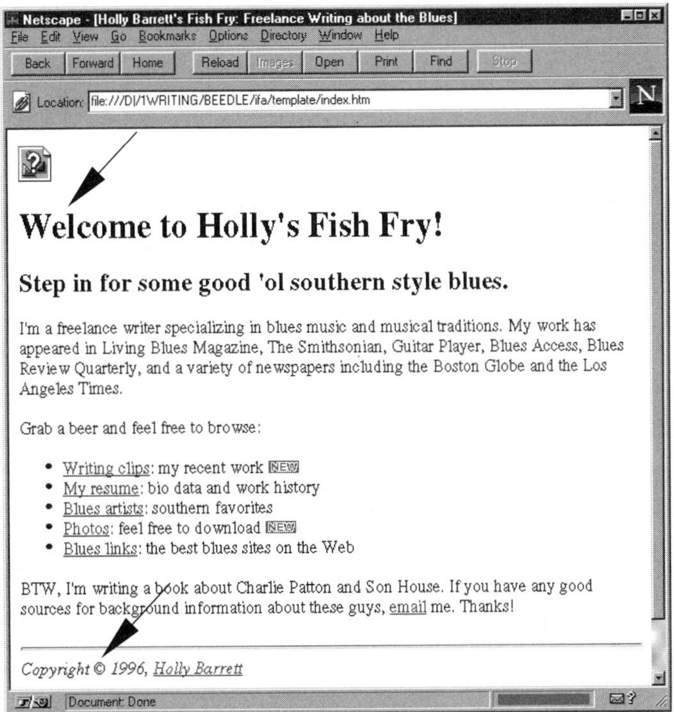

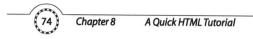

3. Switch back to the text editor window. Change the unordered (bulleted) list to an ordered (numbered) list. Do this by replacing **<UL>...</UL>** with **<OL>...</OL>**.

4. Still in the text editor, change the paragraph following the ordered list into a level 4 heading. Do this by replacing **<P>** with **<H4>**. Don't forget to insert the end tag **</H4>** at the end of the paragraph! Your source should resemble the following:

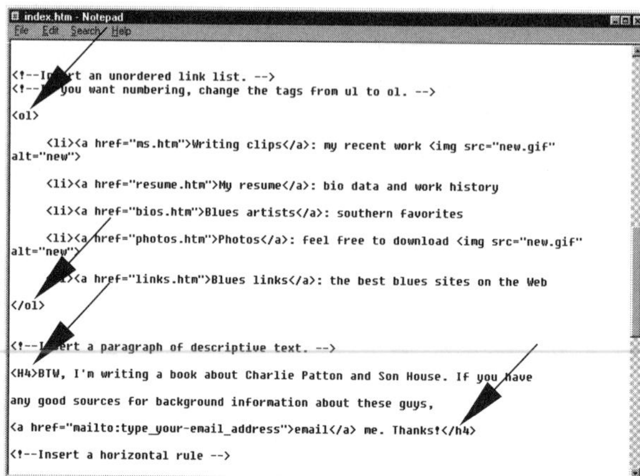

5. Save the document in the text editor, switch to the browser window, and view the updated document. Your screen should resemble the following:

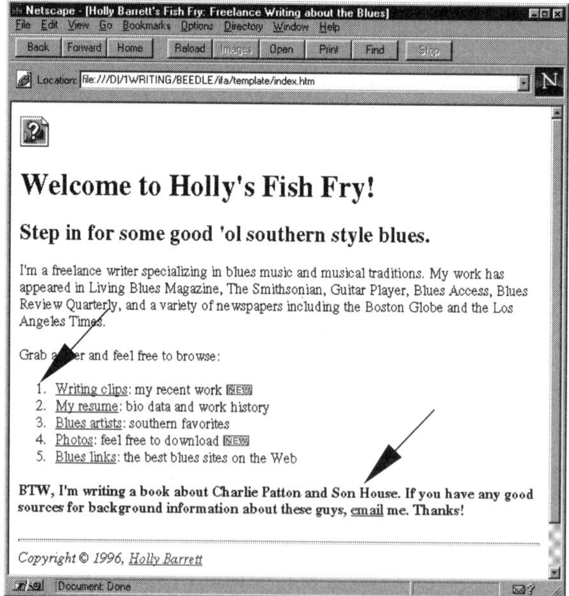

Inserting Graphics

Graphics are easy to insert provided they're saved in the same directory as the rest of the documents. If they're saved in a subordinate directory, include the directory path in the **<IMG>** tag.

1. Switch back to the text editor window. Rewrite the placeholder image tag at the top of the page **<img src="file name" alt="text describing your graphic">** to display the **welcome.jpg** graphic. Change the **ALT** text to **Unknown guitarist live at a blues festival.** The **<IMG>** tag should now read as follows:

   <img src="welcome.jpg" alt="Unknown guitarist live at a blues festival.">

2. Save the document, switch to the browser window, and view the updated document. Notice how the graphic pushes text down the screen. Your screen should resemble the following:

3. Switch to the text editor and add an attribute, **ALIGN=LEFT**, to the **<IMG>** tag as follows:

   <img src="welcome.jpg" alt="Unknown guitarist live at a blues festival." align=left>

Note: The **ALIGN=LEFT** attribute wraps text along the right side of a left-aligned graphic. **ALIGN=RIGHT** wraps text along the left side of a right-aligned graphic. (The **ALIGN** attribute doesn't work in all browsers.)

4. Save the document, switch to the browser window and view the updated document. You may need to widen the browser window to accommodate the new page layout attractively. Your screen should resemble the following:

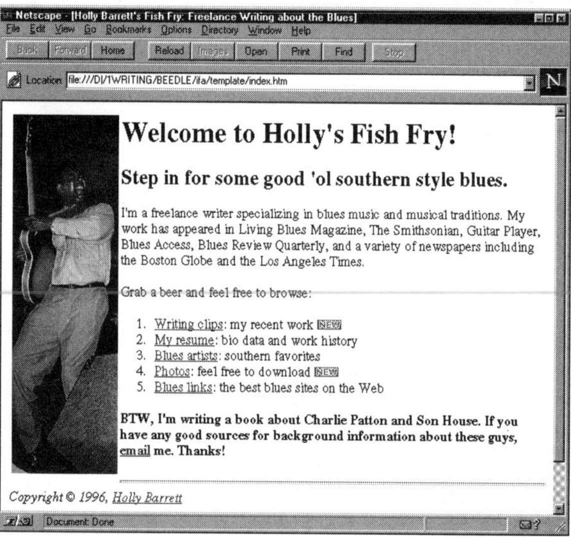

5. Add a new graphic to the end of the second **<LI>** list item, **My resume**. To do this, copy the tag **<img src="new.gif" alt="new">** from the first list item and paste it in the same location after the second list item. Your source should resemble the following:

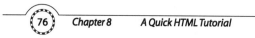

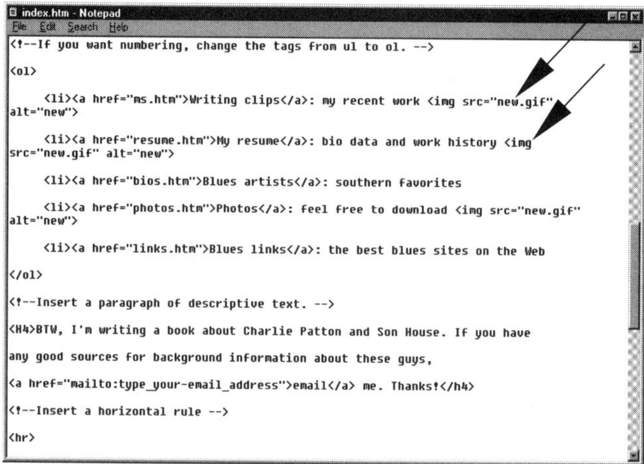

```
index.htm - Notepad
File Edit Search Help
<!--If you want numbering, change the tags from ul to ol. -->

<ol>

     <li><a href="ms.htm">Writing clips</a>: my recent work <img src="new.gif"
alt="new">

     <li><a href="resume.htm">My resume</a>: bio data and work history <img
src="new.gif" alt="new">

     <li><a href="bios.htm">Blues artists</a>: southern favorites

     <li><a href="photos.htm">Photos</a>: feel free to download <img src="new.gif"
alt="new">

     <li><a href="links.htm">Blues links</a>: the best blues sites on the Web

</ol>

<!--Insert a paragraph of descriptive text. -->

<H4>BTW, I'm writing a book about Charlie Patton and Son House. If you have

any good sources for background information about these guys,

<a href="mailto:type_your-email_address">email</a> me. Thanks!</h4>

<!--Insert a horizontal rule -->

<hr>
```

6. Save the document, switch to the browser window, and view the updated document. Your screen should resemble the following:

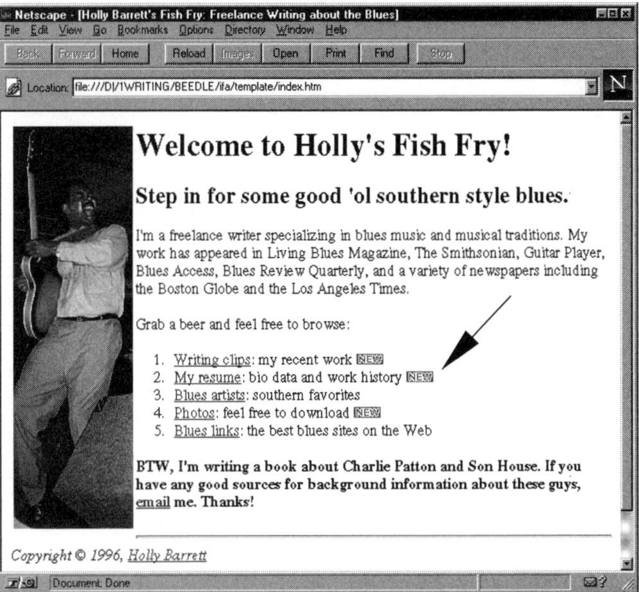

Adding Links

The Fish Fry site is already designed with a series of primary internal pages that you can edit at will. However, you might want to add more pages to your site, increasing its depth and quality. In this exercise, you'll edit a document, create a new internal document, and link the two documents appropriately.

1. In the browser, click the **Writing Clips** link on the home page. This displays the Writing Samples page. Look in the Location text box to see the filename of the current Web page—**ms.htm**. Your screen should resemble the following:

2. Switch to the text editor and open **templates/ms.htm**. For consistency, change all references from Dan Blow to your name. This includes changing the references inside the **<TITLE>**, **<H3>**, and **<ADDRESS>** elements. The text file should resemble the following:

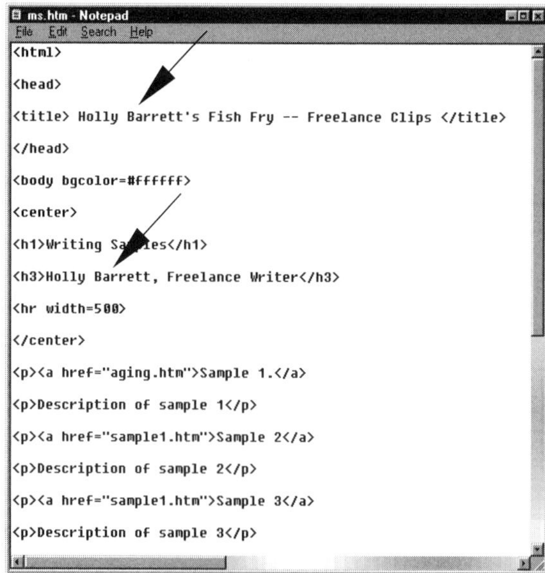

3. Save the document, switch to the browser window, and view the updated document. Your screen should resemble the following:

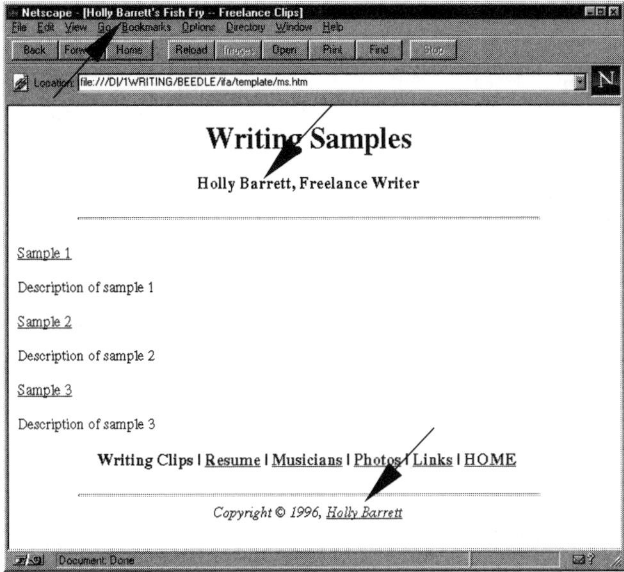

Note that the Writing Samples page contains three placeholder links. Each Sample link jumps to the placeholder page, **sample1.htm**. To create a second sample page (assuming you'll have more than one clip to display), you would simply save **sample1.htm** under a new name and then edit it as appropriate.

4. First, you'll personalize the generic **sample1.htm**. Switch to the text editor and open **template/sample1.htm**. Change all references from Dan Blow to your name (inside the **<TITLE>**, **<H3>**, and **<ADDRESS>** elements). Then save the document, switch to the browser window and view the updated document. Your screen should resemble the following:

logical (soft format)
Logical tags specify how text should be used, but allow the browser to define the appearance of the font. Browsers may render two different logical tags in the same font. For example, the **<STRONG>...</STRONG>** container is bold in some browsers and bold italic in others.

physical (hard format)
Physical tags tell the browser exactly how to display the text. Not all browsers can render all physical tags. For example, the **<B>...</B>** container tells the browser to make the enclosed text bold. The browser will comply if it can translate the tags.

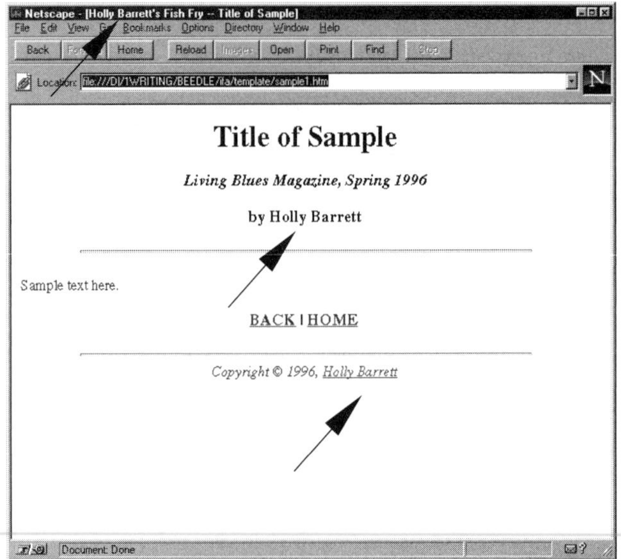

5. Now you'll edit the document and save it under a new name. Switch to the text editor and replace the **<H1>** heading text, **Title of Sample**, with **Aging without Getting Old**. Also replace the **<TITLE>** text, **Title of Sample**, with **Aging Sample**.

6. Replace the **<H3>** heading text, **Living Blues Magazine,Spring 1996**, with **Golden Years Magazine, June 1995**. Notice the physical font style tags **<I>...</I>** indicating that the enclosed text should be italicized. *Physical* and *logical style* tags are demonstrated in the following figure:

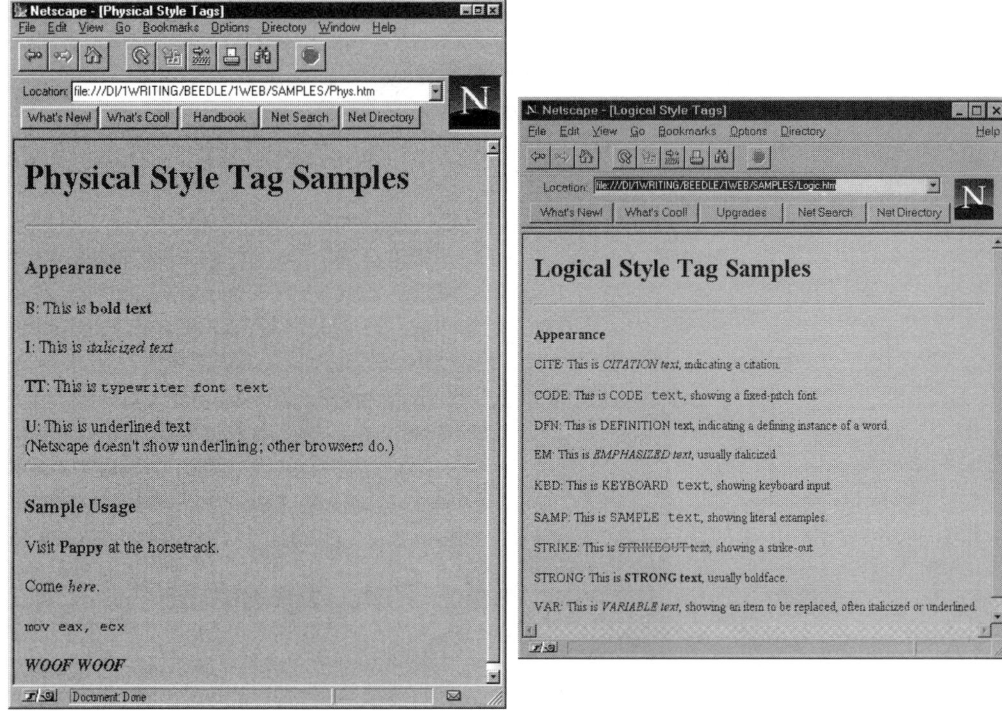

Figure 8.1 *Physical and Logical Font Style Tags*

Note: Most HTML tags are logical. Logical style tags dictate font emphasis without specifying the exact way a document should look. In keeping with the HTML philosophy, this allows each browser to render the font style based on its own capabilities. Consistency is assured. If you assign a physical style tag and the browser can't comply, it'll substitute another font or style with sometimes unattractive or inconsistent results.

7. Insert the following text to replace **Sample text here**.

   <p>"Retirement," complained Ernest Hemingway," Adding Links**is the ugliest word in the English language."**

   <p>When Hemingway uttered those discouraging words, he was talking about more than just retiring from work. He gave voice to a damaging opinion that has until recently been accepted as fact: that aging is a frightening process of physical and mental decay.

Your source should resemble the following:

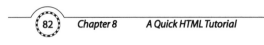

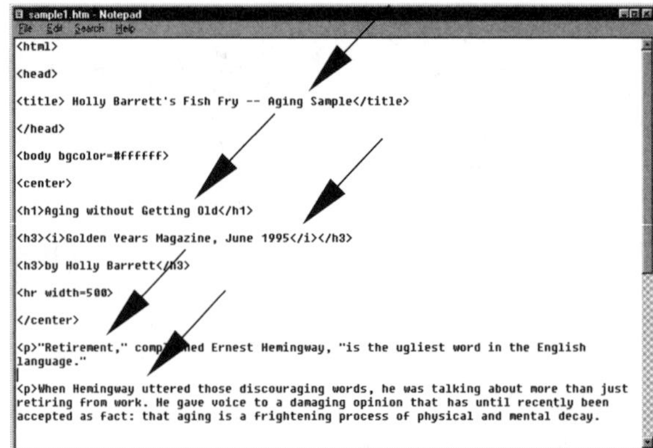

```
<html>

<head>

<title> Holly Barrett's Fish Fry -- Aging Sample</title>

</head>

<body bgcolor=#FFFFFF>

<center>

<h1>Aging without Getting Old</h1>

<h3><i>Golden Years Magazine, June 1995</i></h3>

<h3>by Holly Barrett</h3>

<hr width=500>

</center>

<p>"Retirement," complained Ernest Hemingway, "is the ugliest word in the English language."

<p>When Hemingway uttered those discouraging words, he was talking about more than just retiring from work. He gave voice to a damaging opinion that has until recently been accepted as fact: that aging is a frightening process of physical and mental decay.
```

8. Save the document as **aging.htm**, switch to the browser window, and open the document under its new name. Your screen should resemble the following:

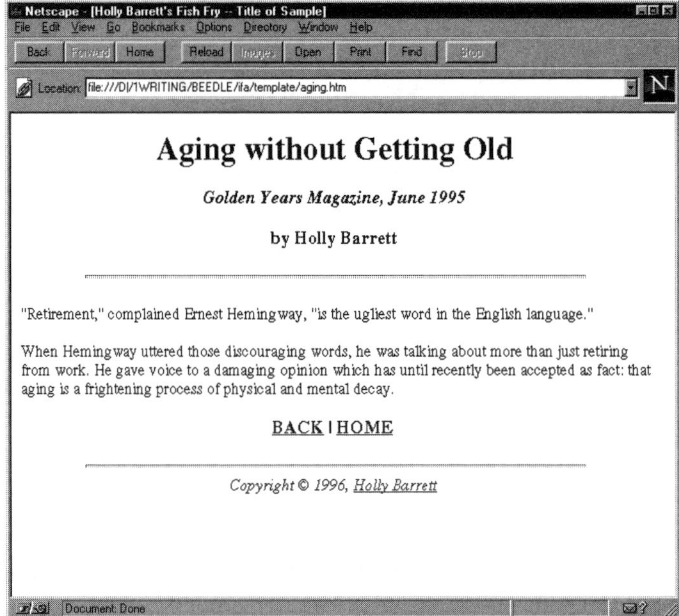

Note: You may want to add additional information about the article, such as word count, references, and so on. This is a very simple example.

9. Now you'll point the link on the Writing Samples page to your new Web page, **aging.htm**. In the browser, click the Back link to return to the Writing Samples page.

10. Switch to the text editor and open **ms.htm**. Replace the Sample 1 link and description with the following:

    <p><a href="aging.htm">Aging without Getting Old.</a>

    <p>An upbeat article exploring three foolproof ways to stay young no matter what the calendar says.</p>

    Note: The end tag **</P>** isn't necessary unless you add an **ALIGN=CENTER/ LEFT/RIGHT** attribute to the **<P>** tag. In some browsers **</P>** adds a little extra white space after the element.

    Your source should resemble the following:

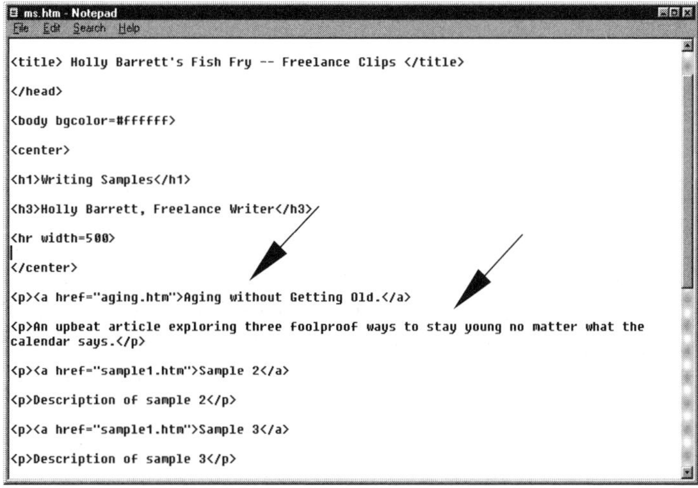

```
ms.htm - Notepad
File  Edit  Search  Help
<title> Holly Barrett's Fish Fry -- Freelance Clips </title>
</head>
<body bgcolor=#ffffff>
<center>
<h1>Writing Samples</h1>
<h3>Holly Barrett, Freelance Writer</h3>
<hr width=500>
</center>
<p><a href="aging.htm">Aging without Getting Old.</a>
<p>An upbeat article exploring three foolproof ways to stay young no matter what the
calendar says.</p>
<p><a href="sample1.htm">Sample 2</a>
<p>Description of sample 2</p>
<p><a href="sample1.htm">Sample 3</a>
<p>Description of sample 3</p>
```

11. Save the document, switch to the browser window, and view the updated document. Your screen should resemble the following:

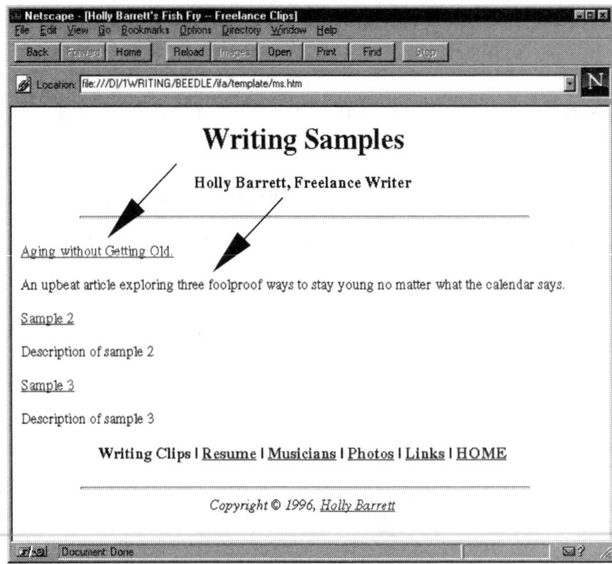

12. Click the links between the two pages to make sure they work.

Continue Editing the Site

Practice using other tags and inserting other graphics. Note that additional graphics are included in the template directory, ready to be inserted into placeholders. Try substituting other kinds of information and adding more pages. You might also include external links on some pages. The more you practice, the more confident you'll feel.

Developing Your Web Presentation

Most Web sites suffer from poor organization, ugly or clumsy enhancement, and bad content. With this as the norm, it's comparatively easy to construct a good, solid Web site that encourages repeat visits. There are two simple ways to get going:

1. Start with the home page and work your way down through the links.
2. Start with the individual "subject" pages and work your way up to the home page.

The first method works well if you know what you want on your home page. The second method works well if you don't have a sense about the overall look of your presentation, but you do know some detailed pages that you want to include. In any case, your end result probably won't look much like your original design. That's okay. It's all part of the process of Web site development.

Targeting Your Presentation

To create more than just another "This is me" stop on the Web, you must target your presentation appropriately and then design around your ideas. To target your presentation, you must define a few important Web site specifications:

1. Decide the purpose of your Web presentation.

   Web pages that try to do too much seem unfocused and haphazard. Clarify your purpose and stick to it. Is your purpose to educate? To entertain? To publicize yourself?

2. Define your potential audience.

   Knowing the audience helps to guide your writing style, your inclusions, the approach you use, even where you publicize the site. Are you trying to reach adults, teenagers, or children? Freelance writers? What are their personality traits? What are their interests? What do they want to see?

3. List the benefits people will receive by visiting your site.

   Benefits ranging from being entertained (an especially clever, interesting, or weird spot), to enjoy Web technology (an inventive use of graphics, forms, or whatever), to receiving useful information. Remember, most people will visit your site for their benefit, not yours.

Designing Your Web Site

Use the Web specifications (above) to guide the Web site design process:

1. Describe the kinds of information to be presented at your site.

   Use the Web specifications above to help guide your choices. In particular, consider the audience you want to attract. Brainstorm everything you'd like to include. Don't worry about the order of presentation, space considerations, or anything else. In the initial stages of development you need to be wide open to ideas. Too much mental editing will not only dampen your creativity, but it'll also make the Web site more difficult to create.

2. Group subjects together.

   Think hierarchically. What subjects can be grouped under other subjects? Think about your home page and what you'd like as the table of contents. If some material seems too complicated to worry about right now, just leave it alone. You don't have to do everything at once.

3. Draw (or write) a diagram of your site.

   Draw a rough flow chart. Use arrows to indicate link directions. (If all pages link to home, note it in your head; don't draw a million extra arrows.) If you don't know all your link pages or remote sites, don't worry about it. Remember that this design will develop with time. Give yourself permission to do a mediocre job. If you try to be perfect, you'll be paralyzed.

4. Define a "stretch" task.

   Think about something you might add to your Web site that will stretch your HTML capabilities. This "stretch" is a guide for your studies. It'll help broaden your Web authoring skills. If you're new to HTML, your stretch can be as simple as adding a new link. If you have some HTML experience, your stretch can be adding an imagemap (a clickable image with specific area coordinates links to other Web pages) or creating a simple form. These are subjects you can review in a hard copy tutorial or an online resource site.

Organizing Your Information

Loose or sloppy organization generates a lack of confidence in the value of your presentation. Four simple ways to organize information are:

1. *By place* (north, south, east, west; Mercury to Pluto). Destination sites and retail establishments often organize in this manner.

2. *By time* (first you do this, then this, then finally this). Sites that instruct typically structure their topics in this fashion.

3. *By comparative value or size* (important to least important, expensive to inexpensive, old to new, fast to slow, complex to simple, most favorite to least favorite). This style can fit into almost any list of topics. Most topics can be comparatively organized.

4. *By alphanumeric structure* (1–9, A–Z). This works on subjects with no geographic, time-specific, or comparative differences. Like the white pages of the phone book, indexes are often organized this way. A simple alphanumeric sort makes it easy to locate topics.

Quick-Reference Lists

The following lists will help you develop better online presentations. Many of these suggestions reference HTML tags and issues specific to the Web. This is appropriate because the Web is the primary online publishing arena.

Important: In some cases, the suggestions below will refer to HTML tags that you haven't read about in Chapters 7 and 8. The assumption is that you'll use only those recommendations that make sense to you. As your design and HTML skills develop, the other, more arcane suggestions will become meaningful. In essence, you'll grow into the following quick-reference lists.

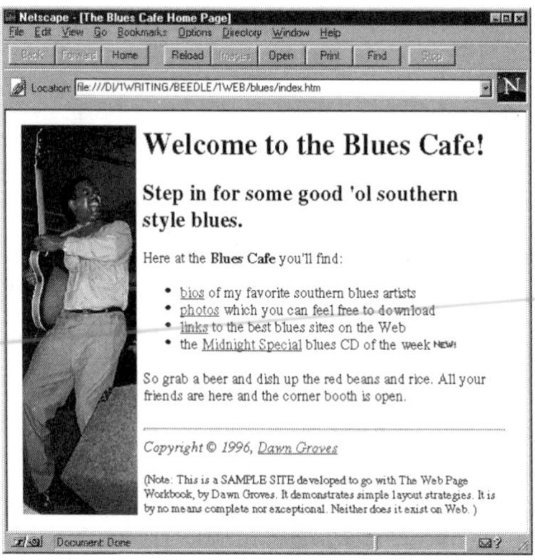

Figure 9.1 The Blues Café Home Page, an Example of How to Help Visitors Scan Your Document

To Help Visitors Scan Your Document

- Make sure your information is logically organized.
- Maintain links in easy-to-reference menu lists.
- Give links simple, descriptive names.
- Include a home page (or high-level index page) link on every page.
- If your Web page is long:

  Include a table of internal links to help readers jump through the document. Don't force your readers to scroll.

  Make sure readers can jump back to the top of the page at the end of each logical section.
- Use horizontal rules **<HR>**, white space, or subtle graphics to separate topic areas visually.
- Use the **<TITLE>** to identify the site as well as the specific content of the page (Joe's Books—Romance Top Ten; Joe's Books—Mystery Top Ten).

- Make your page transitions snappy. Unless it is necessary to the presentation, don't weigh down the opening pages of the site with time-consuming graphic downloads or text-heavy pages.

Figure 9.2 Nash Bridges Home Page, an Example of How to Add a Professional Touch

To Add a Professional Touch

- Design your presentation around a theme and specialize in only a few topics. If you include too many unrelated topics, you'll seem like a dilettante and you won't inspire confidence in the quality of your information.
- Use small, attractive graphics instead of browser-defined bullets and lines.
- Use repeating elements to create a unified look and feel on all your Web pages. For example, design a Web page footer that includes your address, a small business logo, a home page link, and a horizontal rule. Use the footer consistently on every page.
- Use icons (small graphics that look like buttons, arrows, or other navigation aids) as identifiable repeat links. For example, use repeating icons to identify home, index, previous, and next pages.
- Use "express" links to help readers bypass introductory material. Help them get right to the heart of the presentation. For example, if most visitors check the Calendar and What's New pages, make sure these links are on the home page.

- Have someone else proofread your pages for typos. They'll catch the mistakes you can't see.
- Stay contemporary. When new bells and whistles become widely available, implement them appropriately. If you reference software or products that are outdated, you lose credibility.

To Encourage Repeat Visits

- Cater to what your audience wants and expects. If the audience is children, then your writing style, layout, and graphics should be playful, bright, easy to use, and full of energy. If the audience is stockbrokers, your site should be solid, more formal, smart, and obviously well researched.
- Keep the links up-to-date and make sure your text is timely. This shows that you care about the site and that you'll keep it current. If you have to take time off from the site, let your visitors know about it.
- Include an update reference on appropriate pages (last updated: date). This tells visitors how current you really are.
- Clearly note what's new. This is characteristically accomplished on the home page by placing a link to the page(s) of new material. A small graphic of a star or the word "New" often highlights the What's New link.
- Change your site periodically. Update information, add new links, and expand your format.

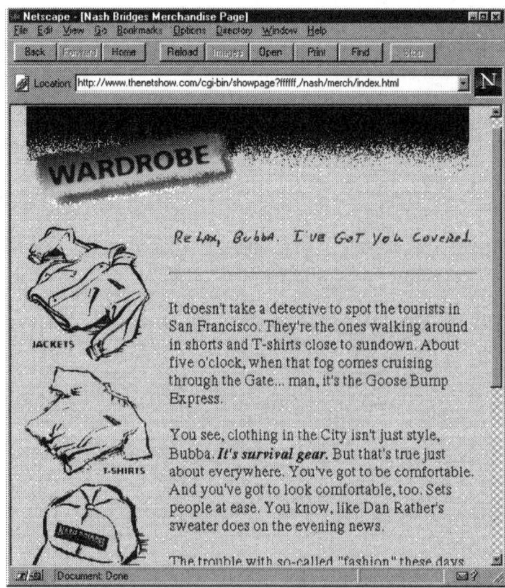

Figure 9.3 Nash Bridges Store, an Example of How to Encourage Repeat Visits

- Don't include a graphic unless there's a specific need for it.
- Make sure the graphic clearly relates to the content of the page.
- Don't burden a page with too many graphics. It's annoying to wait for a bunch of images to download.

To Use Graphics Most Effectively

- Use *thumbnail* graphics as links to bigger graphics.
- If appropriate, make your graphics *transparent* and *interlace* them.
- Offer an alternative for text-only browsers. Include an *ALT text* description of the graphic and if appropriate, design duplicate pages without graphics. Offer visitors a link to the no-graphics version of your site.

Figure 9.4 Plain Text Menu with Graphic Menu

- If possible, use JPEGs for photo-quality graphics. GIFs are fine for all other images.
- Provide low-resolution and high-resolution graphics links. A low-resolution graphic downloads faster, but doesn't look as sharp as its high-res twin. Let visitors choose which is most suitable for their browsers, monitors, and connection speeds.

thumbnail
A small portion of a larger graphic image.

transparent images
An image whose background matches the background color of a Web document. This makes the image appear to "float" on the page. Shareware programs are used to render images transparent.

interlaced images
An image that downloads as a low-resolution graphic, which then "fills in." Interlacing lets users see something quickly instead of waiting for the entire image to download. As with transparency, apply interlacing using a shareware program. You can download them from most HTML reference sites.

ALT text
Descriptive text that displays in the image location before it downloads. ALT text also displays in the image location when users disable their graphics. It tells users what should be there. ALT text is an attribute of the image **<IMG>** tag.

Writing for the Internet Audience

- Keep paragraphs and sentences short. Long sentences displayed on a computer monitor can tire and puzzle your readers. (If you're a more advanced Web page designer, use HTML tables to constrain line length. Otherwise, the text stretches into long lines of words from one edge of the browser window to the other.)
- Be concise. You must be ruthless with extra words. Anything that makes your document longer also makes more work for your Internet readership.

  Not as good:

  It has been determined that the easiest way to…

  Good:

  The easiest way to…
- Write in a friendly, conversational tone. The Internet is an informal universe. Talk to your reader. Do this by:
  - Using pronouns (I, we, you, they)
  - Using colloquial expressions on occasion (a sure thing, a rip-off, okay, etc.)
  - Using contractions (they're, you're, it's, here's, we've, I've)
  - Using simple words
  - Using second person (you) instead of third person (the reader)
  - Varying sentence length

    Example: "It's time we discussed conversational writing. I'm talking about warm, simple words and sentences—the kind of writing Dear Abby does. (And she makes big bucks at it!)"
- Avoid clichés. Especially don't use the terms *cool*, *surf*, or *information superhighway*. They've been beaten into the ground.
- Keep your adjectives to a minimum. Too many adjectives weaken your message, bloat the sentence, and add unnecessary words to the screen. Use verbs instead of adjectives and adverbs because you must hit hard and fast to keep your Internet reader's attention.

  Not as good:

  He walked quickly across the street.

  Good:

  He dashed across the street.

Not as good:

The asphalt was very hot.

Good:

The asphalt sizzled.

- Avoid sexist language. The days of the stewardess and mailman are over. Now we have the flight attendant and mail carrier. Internet audiences are often impatient with dated terminology, and sexist language will date you. To rewrite sexist text try the following:
  - Use plurals
  - Rewrite to avoid reference to gender
  - Alternate gender references
  - Use "he and she" and "his and her" (avoid he/she, his/her)
  - Create an imaginary person

Implementation Reminders

- Create a Web directory for all your Web pages and graphics. Unless your site becomes complicated or overly large, save everything in the same directory. This simplifies links because you don't have to include directory paths in the HTML link tags. It also makes it easier to transfer your site to a Web server.
- Save the site's opening document as **index.htm**. If people access your directory without specifying a page name, **index.htm** will automatically display.
- Start simple. Create basic Web pages without detailed content.
- Test each page in the browser as you create it. Save often. This make it easier to catch HTML syntax mistakes.
- Build on one or two pages at a time. Don't spread yourself thin.

Publishing an E-zine

An e-zine is an electronically distributed magazine. Typically, e-zines are online zines—zines being quirky, irreverent, small press magazines or fanzines. (The term *zine* implies that the publication is the size of half a magazine.) Zines and e-zines usually focus on specific topics, such as horror, politics, or trends. They contain targeted essays, editorials, poems, and stories usually provided by a small group of dedicated, unpaid writers. Electronic versions of *Newsweek*, *Time*, and so on, are also known as e-zines but they're in a class by themselves. If you produce one of these heavyweight publications, sometimes called an e-journal, you probably don't need to read this book.

Before the Internet became popular, most print zines maintained a relatively small, mail-order readership. But when university students discovered e-mail and FTP, a new publishing world opened up and the e-zine was born.

The first e-zines were true to their offbeat nature. Distributed via Gopher sites and archived for FTP retrieval, they contained no artistic flourishes beyond those painted by words. E-zine publishers often maintained electronic and print versions of their publications. They announced their existence via Internet newsgroups and distributed their e-zines via mailing lists. They maintained exclusivity because only a small population of users could access the Internet.

Everything changed when Tim Berners Lee developed the World Wide Web. Suddenly, pictures and sounds could be added to the electronic text, often making the e-zine more compelling than its hard copy counterpart. On the Web, e-zines came into their own. Web pages containing e-zine reference lists cropped up everywhere, the grandfather of them being John Labovitz's List of E-zines. Many e-zines now exist only in cyberspace with no print counterpart.

Like neon signs, e-zines flash in and out of Web existence. (Writing for public offering is a sobering experience.) They vary widely in scope, quality, appearance, and style. Examples of the more professional Web offerings include Word, **http://www.word.com**, Suck, **http://www.suck.com**, and Feed, **http://www.feedmag.com**.

Word (Figure 10.1) is a source of slick essays with a heavy dose of cutting-edge art. Suck (Figure 10.2) contains entertaining satire provided by a gang of renegade Wired Magazine writers. Feed is thoughtful, often political, in content.

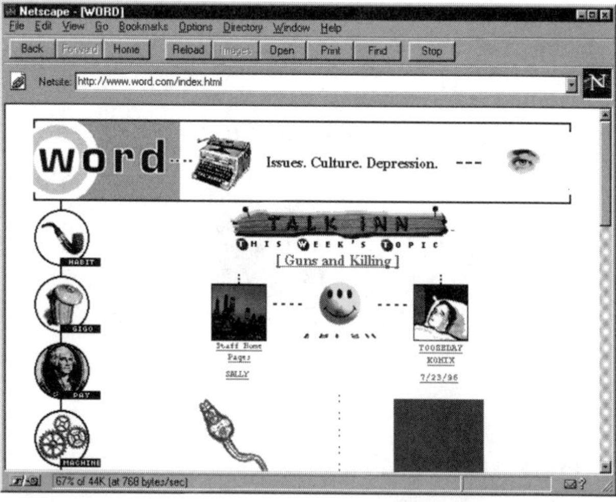

Figure 10.1 Word E-zine

Homegrown e-zines are seldom as tight as these three examples. Still, there's energy and passion behind them, and some are truly creative.

The following Web sites will connect you to enough e-zines to keep you reading for months.

John Labovitz's List of E-zines

http://www.meer.net/~johnl/e-zine-list/

The list from which all other e-zine lists spring. Organized by title and keyword.

Factsheet Five E-zine Reviews and Resources

http://www.well.com/conf/f5/f5index2.html

gopher://gopher.well.sf.ca.us/11/Publications/F5/Reviews

This is part of the Well, which is a literate online community and a great place for writers to hang out.

Zines Zines Everywhere

http://thetransom.com/chip/zines/

Resources and advice on publishing a zine electronically.

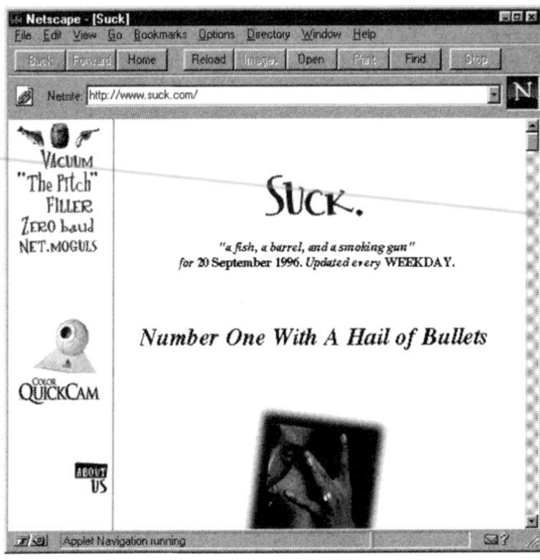

Figure 10.2 *Suck E-zine*

E-zine Benefits for Writers

E-zines are a great way to test new material or play with ideas that aren't mature enough for the hard copy world. Often rough, unconventional, and edgy, e-zines let you take chances with your writing. Hey, there's value in rubbing up against the raw side of creativity. Just don't expect your mother to approve.

> *Note:* Because of their homegrown nature, e-zine publishing credits aren't fully appreciated by the print community. So unless the e-zine that accepted your article is very high profile, don't tout it in a query letter.

If you decide to captain your own e-zine ship, the rewards go beyond testing new material. There's something stimulating—and arguably chilling—about producing a monthly or even quarterly publication. The performance pressure alone is enough to keep you hopping. (Creativity often galvanizes around deadlines.) Best of all, you're the boss. Your e-zine is a public forum for whatever you want to say. And with proper publicizing, timely content, and attention to detail, I guarantee you'll develop a loyal audience for your ideas. Producing a good e-zine can be an immensely satisfying accomplishment.

It's probably not wise to embark on an e-zine adventure if you're looking for quick bucks. Do it instead because you love your subject, because it stretches your creative muscles, because it distributes your work to an audience you wouldn't otherwise reach, because it's fun, and because it might, if you're good and lucky, lead to other sales or writing assignments.

How to Start an E-zine

So many e-zines are now available on the Internet that you need to visit e-zine-tracking sites just to keep up. The competition for readers is furious. But don't worry. If you edit your work with a razor blade and spend time publicizing your site, you'll rise above the flotsam. It just takes effort. Here are some general guidelines to help you get started:

1. Pick a topic that you're passionate about. Like all publications, online or otherwise, e-zines must have spirit. Make sure the topic lends itself to fresh material and changing content. Subjects such as politics, body piercing, UFOs, celebrities, science fiction, animals, and musical styles are all well represented in the e-zine community.

2. Read other e-zines. Find publications that cover topics of a similar nature and see how they structure their content. Learn from the mistakes of others. Use the E-zine Database Web site (Figure 10.3) to search for e-zines by subject, **http://www.dominis.com/Zines/**. On a more philosophical note, it's good to support your genre by reading other e-zines and keeping abreast of developments.

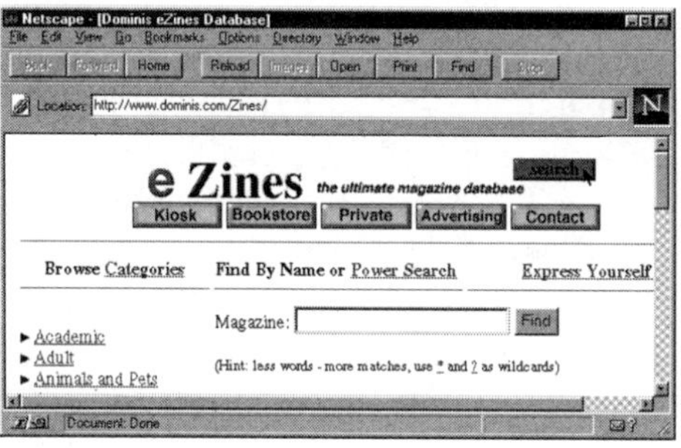

Figure 10.3 E-zine Database

3. Decide how you're going to format your e-zine. This affects the overall look of the publication, as well as your distribution and publicizing schemes. You can choose between the following formats:

a. A Web document formatted in HTML. Use HTML if your e-zine will include graphics or multimedia flourishes (see Chapters 7 and 8). Because Web site visitors will often print documents in order to read them more easily, you should avoid designing your site in colors that will print with poor contrast. (Some printers also can't handle white text on a black background.)

b. A text-only document formatted in ASCII text.. Text-only is the traditional e-zine format appropriate for distribution over nongraphic mediums such as newsgroups and mailing lists. Simply save your document as an ASCII text file in your word processor. (You can still insert the **<HTML>....</HTML>** container tags to make it Web-compliant.) Because text files are visually uninteresting, it's critical that you organize your material clearly and make your writing compelling. Use ASCII characters to create simple graphics or rules. For example:

```
/\/\/\/\/\/\/\/\/\/\/\/\/\/\/\/\/\/\/\/\/\/\/\/\/\/\/\/\/\/\
                     Welcome to
                THE FRIGHT SITE E-ZINE
   _______
      VOL 2, ISSUE 4
      SEPT 1, 1996
   _______
\/\/\/\/\/\/\/\/\/\/\/\/\/\/\/\/\/\/\/\/\/\/\/\/\/\/\/\/\/\/
```

4. Distribute your e-zine. A big advantage to electronic magazines is that you don't have the distribution costs incurred with print media. There are two primary ways to distribute e-zines: on the Web and using e-mail. Conscientious publishers will take advantage of both.

   a. The Web is a one-to-many distribution method. You upload your e-zine once and then anyone with a Web browser can view it. You can also include multimedia elements such as graphics and sound files with relative ease. Web distribution requires little technical expertise beyond learning how to generate and upload HTML files. Sometimes your provider will upload them for you, but you're limited if you can't access the files directly. Many providers will give you up to five megabytes of free server space with a cut-rate monthly fee. Even the commercial service providers are offering free space for home pages, though they may have restrictions on content and purpose.

   b. E-mail is a one-to-one method. Each person has to be e-mailed individually and there can be no graphics in the layout. An e-mail subscriber list is useful because you can keep track of your readers. If you're technically inclined, you can create an automated mailing list for subscribers. (Automated mailing lists require a special setup, so you'll need to research them. Note the URLs below.)

If you're a technically challenged e-zine publisher, you can simply announce the e-zine in a targeted newsgroup and offer to e-mail it to anyone who wants it. Although some newsgroups include full e-zines in their postings, as a rule you shouldn't send unsolicited attachments in e-mail. If a recipient isn't interested in your latest issue of Bite Me, he or she might be annoyed at having to download an attachment.

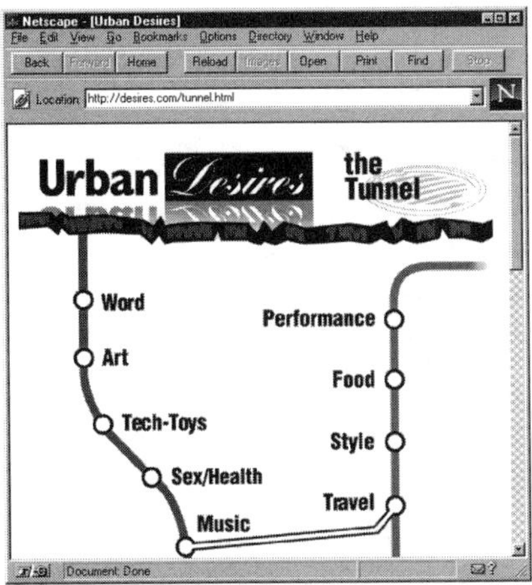

Figure 10.4 Urban Desires E-zine

5. Publicize your e-zine. You may be as contemporary and cool as Urban Desires E-zine, (Figure 10.4), but if you don't publicize your work, only a handful of people will know about it. To publicize an e-zine, follow the basic publicizing suggestions described in Chapter 14.

   a. Invite reviewers to critique your work. One or two well-placed reviews can make a big difference in your hit count. Good reviewers include John Labovitz and Factsheet Five.

   b. Don't invite reviewers to your site right away. Make sure the kinks are worked out and the typos are fixed. Let the publication age a bit, with one or two issues under your belt.

   c. Pay particular attention to the e-zine newsgroups, as this is a tried-and-true distribution network.

   d. Announce your e-zine in the newsgroups **alt.zines** and **comp.infosystems.www.announce**.

   e. Add your e-zine to the E-zine Database site, **http://www.dominis.com/Zines/**.

Traditionally, e-zines are noncommercial, hearkening back to their outlaw print zine roots. However, the Web's growing commercial nature is changing this tradition. Many e-zine publishers, especially those who publish on the Web, would gladly "sell out" to help pay the bills.

Discrete advertising is now acceptable, although most advertisers find typical e-zines too extreme to merit serious investment. Occasionally, you'll see an ad inserted by an e-zine's service provider, though this could be in barter for free server space. Earning advertising income isn't an impossible dream; high-profile e-zines such as Suck do sell ads. Just don't quit your day job (see Chapter 19).

Submitting Work to an E-zine

Query and submit to an e-zine the same way you submit to a print publication. In a nutshell, check the e-zine for submission information. If necessary, e-mail the publisher and ask for writer guidelines. Then prepare your query accordingly. E-zines should accept e-mailed queries with no problem. Be polite, respectful, and professional. You never know; the e-zine editor you e-mail today could be working for your favorite print publisher tomorrow. If you're a clueless putz, she'll remember you.

Many e-zines accept submissions, though few compensate for them. Try subscribing to an online newsletter that announces e-zines looking for contributors. Often, when e-zine publishers solicit material in a newsletter, they offer compensation. (Check genre-specific newsletters. For example, dark fiction writers will find market updates in the weekly Dark Echo newsletter connected to Dark Echo's Web site, **http://w3.gwis.com/~prlg/news.html**. Another comprehensive writer's newsletter is Inklings, which is connected to The Inkspot, **http://www.inkspot.com/~ohi/inkspot**.

As with any other submission, make sure you understand what the e-zine's audience wants. Clarify copyright issues before you turn over your article. If possible, retain your copyright and ask that the copyright notice is posted somewhere on display copy (see Chapter 19).

Publishing in Newsgroups and Mailing Lists

To publish material in a Usenet newsgroup or a mailing list, you must first find a group that suits your topic. There are more than a few sites that catalogue newsgroups and mailing lists. A popular Web location is The Directory of Scholarly and Professional E-Conferences at **http://n2h2.com/KOVACS/**. This directory includes discussion lists, Internet interest groups, Usenet newsgroups, and more. Keep in mind that new mailing lists and newsgroups are created every day.

The logistics of newsgroups and mailing lists were discussed in chapters 1 and 5; however, a few reminders are probably in order:

- Save messages you need. Postings could scroll off the list in a few days or stay up a month, depending on the update schedule and the amount of traffic in the group.
- Never quote a message without getting permission from the author. This is a copyright violation, privacy invasion, and a particularly ugly breach of netiquette.

- Read the Usenet Rules of Order in chapter 5 before posting to any newsgroup (or sending any e-mail, for that matter).
- As stated in Chapter 1, be sure to verify all newsgroup or mailing list information.

Structuring a Newsgroup Submission

When you write articles (messages) for newsgroups, remember that you can't format the text. Usenet and mailing list data are text-only ASCII files. No art, no fancy fonts. With this in mind, I have a few suggestions to help keep your newsgroup writing approachable:

1. Visually structure the document with enough white space to make it easy to read. Adding white space is as simple as hitting the **Enter** key.

2. Don't include elaborate ASCII art to make your signature (sig) fancier. Many newsreaders and mail programs can now display proportional fonts, tuning your fixed-pitch ASCII art into a chaotic mess. At most, use the asterisk key (*), hyphen (-), or equals sign (=) to create short lines that visually structure the text.

3. Try to keep lines between seventy-two and seventy-five characters long in case the recipient's program doesn't wrap text.

4. Keep paragraphs and sentences short.

5. Read the quick-reference list in the chapter 9 section, "Writing for the Internet audience."

6. If possible, avoid using too many acronyms or abbreviations. The Internet is already replete with jargon.

7. Give the same attention to the subject line of your article as you would give to the first sentence and the title. Remember, it's the subject line that readers first see in a Usenet list.

8. Use smileys :-), frowns :-(, and winks ;-) with discretion. How many times have you seen well-written books and hard copy magazine articles punctuated with emoticons?

9. Some writers employ a form of cryptic shorthand when writing Usenet documents. They deliberately misspell certain words, eschew capitalization (in a manner similar to programming commands), and leave out prepositions such as the, to, etc. This kind of writing has a short shelf life. If you want your work to stand on its own, don't play around with spelling and grammar. It makes your work seem immature and annoys most readers.

10. Keep your message sig short and to the point. Rule-of-thumb netiquette dictates that a sig shouldn't contain more than four lines, including your name, e-mail address, perhaps your phone number, and business or home page URL. Some sigs include meaningful quotes or book titles.

```
===========================================================
Joe Blow, Esq.                              joeblow@computer.com
Mighty Fine Freelancer                      http://www.blow.com/
"If you want to make God laugh, tell him your plans." —John Chancellor
```

11. If the article is long, use subheads and numbered lists to give it more structure. As with FAQs, chain a long document into one or more individual pages.

12. Proofread your article thoroughly.

13. Never write anything that you wouldn't want your mother and the United States government to read. Usenet is not a secure environment.

    Hint: For more advice, check the out the Usenet Writing Style FAQ, **http://www.cis.ohio-state.edu/hypertext/faq/usenet/usenet/writing-style/part1/faq.html**.

14. If you can't find a newsgroup that appeals to you, consider creating a new newsgroup in the **ALT** hierarchy. (Alt newsgroups are the least complicated to create.) The FAQ describing how to create an alt newsgroup is located on the Web at **http://www.math.psu.edu/barr/alt-creation-guide.html**. To receive the FAQ via e-mail, send a message to **mail-server@rtfm.mit.edu**. In the body of the message, type: **send usenet/alt.config/So_You_Want_to_Create_an_Alt_Newsgroup**.

Publishing a FAQ

FAQs (pronounced "facks") and PIPs (Periodic Informational Postings) help individuals learn about a newsgroup without burdening regular newsgroup participants with repeated questions. FAQs typically contain information about newsgroup netiquette, background, lore, jargon, and the names and e-mail addresses of moderators (if any). The document is usually organized in a question/answer format.

FAQs are ASCII (text-only, no art) documents because they are commonly posted on Usenet or made available via FTP and Gopher. Many FAQs are also available on the Web.

You may think that writing a FAQ is a poor substitute for publishing a short story or freelance article, but in fact, FAQs are sought-after reading material. Some are legendary, such as the alt.devilbunnies FAQ (Figure 11.1) at **http://www.cs.ruu.nl/wais/html/na-dir/devilbunnies-faq/part1.html**.

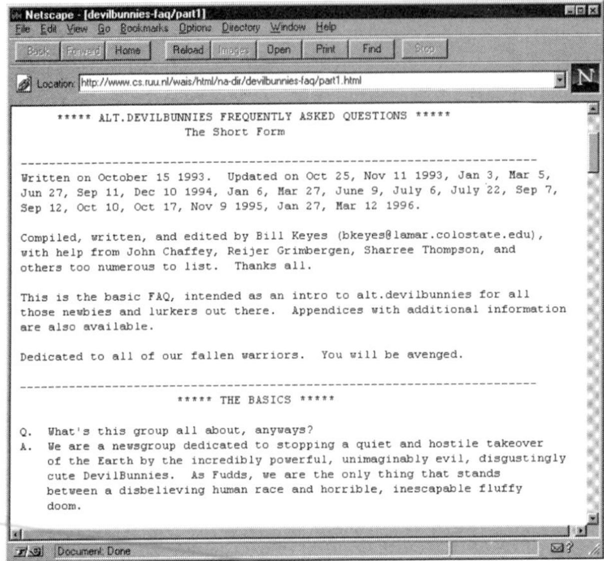

Figure 11.1 The alt.devilbunnies FAQ

Newsgroup FAQs are posted from once a week to once a month. They are dynamic documents, requiring regular maintenance and updates. Newsgroup participants often suggest additions and enhancements. As with other forms of online publishing, FAQs have evolved a somewhat standard style of presentation as well as a variety of support and distribution avenues.

With over 2500 FAQs online, many Web sites are devoted to keeping track of them and providing ways to search for specific FAQ topics. One such site is The List of Usenet FAQs, **http://www.cis.ohio-state.edu/hypertext/faq/usenet/FAQ-List.html**. Another resource is located at Oxford University, **http://www.lib.ox.ac.uk/search/search_faqs.html**. You can also visit the **news.answers** newsgroup where "nothing but the FAQs" is posted.

Before writing and publishing a FAQ, be sure to read the Infinite Ink Web site, **http://www.jazzie.com/ii/internet/faqs.html**. Of note on the Infinite Ink site are:

- *.answers submission guidelines
- Introduction to the *.answers newsgroups
- Eugene Miya's FAQ on FAQs

Here are a few hints for creating and managing FAQs:

1. Write the FAQ in your word processor, saving it as an ASCII text file. When you're ready to mail it, you can copy the text into a message and post it to the newsgroup. If you're formatting the FAQ for the Web, refer to chapter 7, How to Create a Web Page.

2. Keep the FAQ as short as possible. Reference Web sites, books, and articles without rewriting them. If the document seems cumbersome, break it into more than one page (message).

3. If the FAQ is complex, or more than one page, include an outline of the subject matter at the top of the opening page. This helps the reader skip to topics of interest.

4. FAQ subject lines should be simple and self-documenting. If you have a multipage FAQ, be sure the subject lines make it easy to navigate through the entire presentation. For example: **alt.lizardlove I, general care; alt.lizardlove II, species; alt.lizardlove III, home habitat.**

5. Keep the writing tight, clean, and jargon free. FAQs are meant to be read by people who are learning about your topic, not those who already know it. If jargon and acronyms are commonly used in your newsgroup, add a glossary at the end of the FAQ.

6. Limit line lengths from seventy-two to seventy-five characters. This is because some people don't have automatic wordwrap in their editors and some newsreaders simply don't wrap text. If the text line is over seventy-five characters, it runs past the right edge of the screen window. To help you determine line length, use a fixed-pitch font such as Courier and set your margins to conform to the number of characters you prefer.

7. Avoid including graphic attachments or ASCII art (as with e-zine headers). These are unnecessary in a FAQ. If you reference graphics, make them available via FTP or display them in a Web page.

8. Keep the article sig line simple and unobtrusive. Long, complex, or self-serving sigs have no place in a FAQ.

9. Structure your FAQ in a manner that best communicates the information. According to Eugene Miya, one of the originators of the FAQ concept, there are three ways to organize a FAQ:

   a. Question/answer, question/answer

   b. Summary of topic, then question/answer, question/answer

   c. All answers, no questions

10. Join the faq-maintainers mailing list to keep up with the latest trends and distribution networks. E-mail **faq-maintainers-request@consensus.com** with **subscribe** or **subscribe digest** in the subject line and nothing in the body of the message. (The word *digest* tells the mailing program to send a group of postings in a single e-mail message instead of sending each message individually.)

crosspost
To post to more than one newsgroup. FAQs are often crossposted to the news.answers newsgroup in addition to their own newsgroups.

11. E-mail your FAQ to **news-answers@mit.edu**. This assures that it will be archived by major index sites and *crossposted* to **news.answers**.

12. The best posting timetable is subject to debate. If you're posting a FAQ in a newsgroup, don't do it more than once a week. (Even once a week is too often for many newsgroups.) If the FAQ is broken into multiple documents, you may want to post portions of it daily, chained together by subject lines.

13. FAQ distribution can be as simple as e-mailing a document (message) to the newsgroup, or as complex as maintaining FTP, Usenet, and Web versions of the FAQ with a mailing program managing the periodic posting. Check Infinite Ink's site for more information about automating the distribution of your FAQ.

The Writer's Guide to the Internet
Chapter
12

Writing Hypertext Fiction

Hypertext fiction uses links to expand a linear story into a nonlinear, multiple-path narrative. Instead of keeping an A-to-B-to-C format, hypertext offers readers the opportunity to dive into previously unaddressed aspects of the story and jump around in the plot.

Author and teacher Robert Kendall describes hypertext fiction in his essay "Writing for the New Millenium: The Birth of Electronic Literature," **http://ourworld.compuserve.com:80/homepages/rkendall/pw1.htm**. "The new electronic literature breaks the bonds of linearity and stasis imposed by paper. In digital form, a story can draw readers into its world by giving them a role in shaping it, letting them choose which narrative thread to follow, which new situation or character to explore."

When you read hypertext fiction, you take side trips that often parallel the plot. Ideally, you return to the main theme with greater involvement and enthusiasm. Some writers believe that hypertext fiction embodies the true interactivity of the Web. The reader makes choices, follows hunches, tries different paths. There's nothing passive about a good hypertext novel.

The biggest obstacle to the widespread acceptance of electronic books and magazines is currently the primitive state of the technology for reading them. Staring at today's computer screen just doesn't have the same attraction as curling up with a good book. Many Web enthusiasts claim that the audience they're writing for is coming of age in a few years. This is especially true with the developing technology that simulcasts information with television shows. When a TV show is combined with background information and the option of interacting with other watchers, the user literally must be able to process more than one or two screens of information concurrently. Young viewers who grow up with this technology will already be "trained" to manage the input, whereas older folks may not have the same mental muscles developed.

In spite of questions regarding the presentation and acceptance of online storytelling, fiction offerings on the Web are growing at a phenomenal rate. Sites are popping up with weekly stories, novellas, ongoing soap operas, and even television tie-ins. A site I helped to develop used hypertext fiction "webisodes" as prequels feeding into the current week's television show teaser.

The story structure was conservative in terms of hypertext. Readers helped the main character (Nash Bridges) solve a mystery by making a decision based on clues provided in the story. Each webisode had up to three endings with the wrong choice resulting in disaster and the "right" choice leading into the TV show (Figure 12.1).

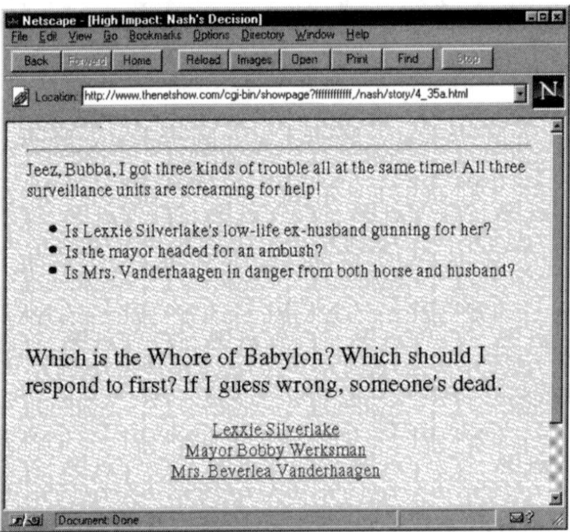

Figure 12.1 Nash Bridges Webisodes

The webisodes were created by screenwriter John Groves, who subscribes to the "short pages and quick downloads" style of presentation. Other hypertext fiction sites ask the reader to scroll through a longer Web page that often contains many images. Still other hypertext stories employ few graphics but lots of text, emulating the look of a novel instead of a picture book.

If you're thinking about writing a hypertext fiction novel or series of stories, you should consider the following issues:

- Targeting audience preferences. Determine your target audience preferences and use them to guide your writing and Web design style. For example, the cybersoap The Spot caters to a Melrose Place audience with big graphics of young, sexy characters, soap opera story lines, and lots of melodrama. The Nash Bridges TV series Web site attracts viewers who want to get closer to the show's main character, played by Don Johnson. As such, the site is filled with photos of the actor and plenty of background information.
- Techno-props. Though most site developers are keenly interested in displaying the latest techno-toys and software upgrades, hypertext fiction doesn't currently require high-end technology. As the Web evolves and technical bells and whistles become less obtrusive, they will no doubt be woven into the storytelling process.
- Platform technology. Design your Web site for the most commonly used browsers and computers. If you add story options that only a few computer platforms can access, you're ignoring much of your potential audience. If users have slow modems or busy Internet connections, you'll lose them with long downloads.
- Story structure. Most current hypertext fiction is a single plot with a variety of paths that always lead back to the core story. If you plan to complicate matters with multiple plots and narrative decisions, make sure you don't overload your reader with too many link options per page. Links can easily add confusion instead of clarifying relationships and providing background.

Further helpful hints include:

- Study other fiction sites. Get a feel for how you want to present your fiction. Explore features such as high-end (versus low-end) graphics, fancy technology, variable page sizes, and increased site complexity before you decide whether to include them in your presentation.
- Start simple. Because the very nature of hypertext fiction can lead to confusing story elements, start with a simple plot line and keep it simple throughout. Unless the style of your fiction literally depends on many links and a variety of alternative narrative paths, you should keep the choices down to three or fewer per screen in the body of the page.
- Write well and appropriately for the Internet audience. John Groves sums it up by saying, "Brevity and a punchy writing style are more important for the Net than for print. Internet users seem to have limited patience and short attention spans."

Robert Kendall adds, "Tackling this new breed of writing is now little more difficult or risky than trying one's hand at any other unfamiliar genre—and it should be regarded as a new genre, not a potential replacement for traditional forms of literature. Like any distinctive medium, it requires first-time practitioners to rethink some elements of their craft to use it effectively. It can also demand some artistic readjustment as the hypertext author learns to relinquish to the reader some control over the final form of the work. This doesn't mean giving up responsibility for the structure of the writing or somehow losing authorial claim to it. If anything, the structural responsibility increases, for the work must maintain coherence in the many possible permutations it can undergo."

Some hypertext fiction is published on CD-ROM, but the primary distribution system seems to be the Web. To learn more about this fascinating Web publishing format, visit Robert Kendall's site, **http://ourworld.compuserve.com:80/homepages/rkendall/**, or Hyperizons: Theory and Technique of Hypertext Fiction, **http://www.duke.edu/~mshumate/hyperfic.html** (Figure 12.2).

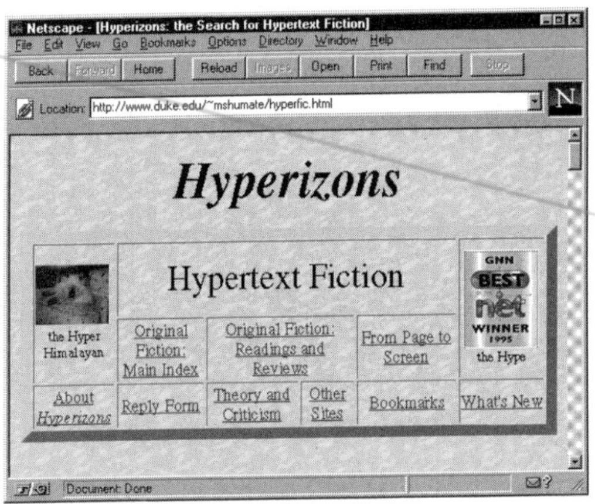

Figure 12.2 Hyperizons

Another good site is managed by author Stuart Moulthrop, **http://raven.ubalt.edu/staff/moulthrop/**, who also teaches design for electronic environments in the Institute for Language, Technology, and Communications Design at the University of Baltimore. His site contains sample hypertext fiction, excellent design and development links, and other interesting resources (Figure 12.3).

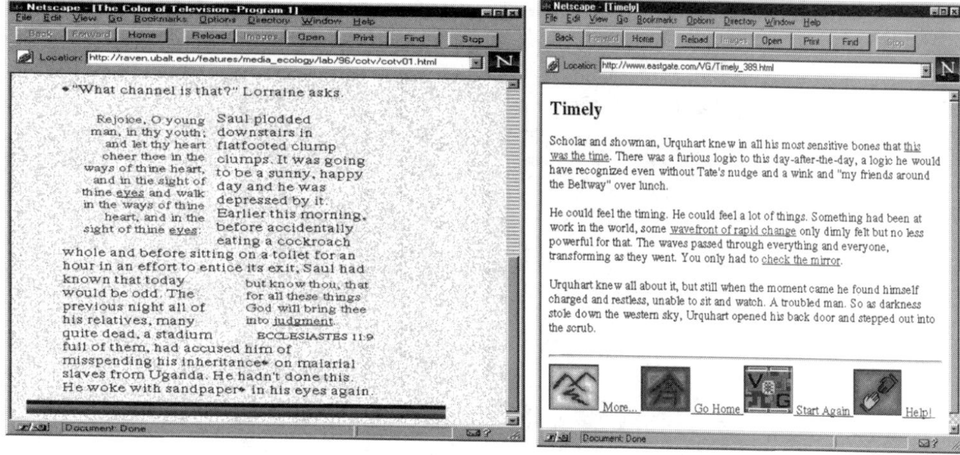

Figure 12.3 The Color of Television and Victory Garden by Stuart Moulthrop

The following additional resources will provide you with ample background and guidance in writing hypertext fiction.

Eastgate Systems

http://www.eastgate.com/

Publishers of hypertext fiction (hypermedia in general) on CD-ROM. Catalogue, writing samples, and ordering information available.

Hyperizons: Theory and Technique of Hypertext Fiction

http://www.duke.edu/~mshumate/hyperfic.html

An e-zine of hypertext stories, references, and links. Comprehensive list of books and online resources that discuss hypertext theory and practice.

Hyperreality

http://www.geocities.com/Athens/1114/writers.html

Good hypertext links and a lot of attitude. Read the article "In Defense of Hypertext Fiction."

StoryWeb

http://www.storyweb.com/

Reviews and links to the best and worst narrative on the Web. All genres.

Writing for the New Millenium: The Birth of Electronic Literature, by Robert Kendall

http://ourworld.compuserve.com:80/homepages/rkendall/pw1.htm

An excellent essay about hypertext fiction. This site also includes many good links to related hypertext resources and sites.

"Written on the Web," by Carolyn Guyer, from Feed E-zine

http://www.feedmag.com/95.09guyer/95.09guyer.html

A summary of hypertext fiction as well as an annotated bibliography of hypertext works.

Yahoo Search Directory Category

http://www.yahoo.com/Arts/Humanities/Literature/Electronic_Literature/Hypertext_Literature/

The ever-expanding list of hypertext fiction categories in the Yahoo search directory.

alt.hypertext

A newsgroup dedicated to hypertext fiction.

Writing for the Web

Most writers will tell you that it doesn't matter whether you publish your material in hard copy or online. The end result should still be a well-organized, clean, tight presentation of ideas. Still, there are issues unique to the online world, and writers who ignore them are punished by poor reviews and meager audiences.

This chapter is titled "Writing for the Web" because that's where most online publishing occurs. Only the Web offers the richness, accessibility, and raw distribution potential that define it as an end and not a means.

User Technology and Expertise

When you write a book, you seldom worry about the brand of chair in which your reader will be sitting. But this is exactly the kind of concern you must address when writing for the Web. Specifically, you must consider not only the reader's technical setup, but also his or her level of expertise. For example, if I construct a dynamite Web site that uses sexy features such as *animations*, then I'm assuming that visitors will own the hardware and software necessary to

animations
Just like everything else on the Web, animation is evolving. It started as simply downloading a series of graphics, one after the other, giving the appearance of movement on the screen. Then Macromedia developed a plug-in program called Shockwave, **http://www.macromedia.com/shockwave/**, that lets you "play" complex animated sequences created in Macromedia Director, a multimedia development application. Sites that use Shockwave animations are categorized as "shocked."

enjoy them. If my site depends on these features, I effectively cancel out a large share of my potential audience. On the flip side, the Web is so vast and disorganized that cliquish exclusivity may give me an edge. Sexy enhancements and additions can help you snag a listing in well-traveled resource lists such as Netscape's What's Cool. In the online world, new and special technology attracts people. It also repels them. You have to decide if the time required to develop and enjoy your high-tech work is appropriate to your topic.

What about computer platform? If your site targets college kids, you might want to create an alternative, text-only version of the material so that students on a UNIX connection don't have to deal with graphics they can't see.

What about modem speed? If your site is high-end and you're designing for graphics professionals, you might assume that they have fast Internet access. This gives you the freedom to create a graphics-rich document requiring hefty bandwidth. On the other hand, if you're designing for Joe Anyone, you'll want to keep download time to a minimum. No big graphics.

Another consideration is user expertise. New users often don't understand even simple navigation techniques such as clicking Back buttons or clearing forms, and can't grasp what it really means to download a file and save it to disk. In another five years, this probably won't be the case, but there is still an enormous population of individuals who haven't used the Internet. If you're providing information or stories to those folks, you should subtly explain how to do certain things. For example, if I offer a list of short stories or art for download, I might include a Web link *Help* that users can click to receive extra advice. Moving helpful advice to a linked page keeps the primary page size smaller and doesn't annoy more experienced users. If you're providing information to people who are already skilled (for example, you're selling content to companies or individuals who specialize in software), then writing basic instructions would brand you as ignorant of your audience.

A good practice for most sites is to provide a FAQ (Frequently Asked Questions) link. In the FAQ, you can easily address potential concerns. Besides, you can finally respond to a user's e-mail by simply writing "RTF" (Read The FAQ). Another way of handling this issue is to provide a "Hints" page (Figure 13.1), especially if visitors obtain optimal viewing by setting certain defaults or sizing their browser windows appropriately. Just don't expect people actually to follow your suggestions.

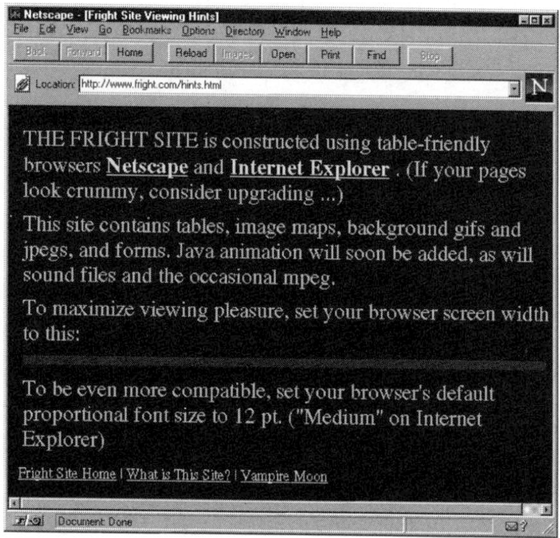

Figure 13.1 Helpful Hints Web Page

Monitor Issues

Even though good writing follows the same basic rules no matter what the display medium, there are issues unique to the computer. Bottom line, it's physically more tiring to read a computer screen than to read a book. This has to do with the location of the light source, the resolution of the screen display, and the reader's comfort level with the display medium, reading style, and document layout and design.

Light Source

The monitor's light source comes from inside the cathode ray tube (CRT). The light shines from behind the screen into your eyes, as with a light table. This differs from a book or newspaper that reflects light from a source usually located above or behind you. Unless books are translucent or come with little headlights, they don't shine into your eyes.

The light from the computer becomes visually tiresome, especially if you're trying to recognize and interpret small, detailed images such as letters in a sentence. This is one reason why people often print articles they find on the Internet, instead of staring at the monitor and attempting to read the articles on-screen.

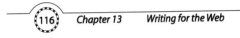

Monitor Resolution

Low-resolution monitors are extremely difficult to read for any length of time because the text is so unclear and the display quality of images is so rough. Anything that forces you to work harder to resolve letters and words will naturally tire your eyes. Fortunately, monitors now come with high-resolution displays, but even the best monitor resolution can't hold a candle to a quality magazine page.

Comfort Level

Reading is a mental skill bolstered by positive associations. The positive associations—assuming you like to read—include the satisfaction of holding the book, becoming delightfully immersed in content, and being stimulated by the ideas presented. Most people have the skill to stay focused on a monitor just as they would with a book or magazine, but they haven't kindled the positive associations that make them want to stick with it. Monitor reading doesn't have the cozy, home-and-hearth feel of a good novel and a soft couch.

Reading Style

Documents punctuated with hypertext links encourage people to graze over topics without delving deeply into any of them. It's just too easy to click away to something new. If a site presents too much effort or requires more than a cursory visit, people think, "I'll come back when I have more time to spend here," and off they go. As much as I dislike the cliché of "surfing the Web," it accurately describes the mind-set of most wired folks. Visitors will sample sites instead of exploring them in depth. This doesn't mean that online readers don't actually read the sites they visit. Many do. But more commonly, they'll nibble briefly and move on to the next morsel.

Visuals

Visuals include the length of each line of text, the size and type of screen font used, the number and type of graphics, navigation aids, and added elements such as scrolling or blinking text (ouch!), font colors, animations, and other display-oriented structures. If any of these areas are carelessly managed, the document's basic readability is at risk. When readability suffers, visitors click away.

Topic Timeliness

Online documents go stale quickly. That is, when new material isn't added, links aren't updated, and topics lose their timeliness, the entire site appears staid. This is death online. Sites that become dusty are not only doomed to quick drop-in visits, but the site developers are likely to receive complaints about it. Online audiences aren't shy about communicating their opinions. I have personal experience with this; I took long vacations from two of my sites and began receiving loud, bitter complaints from regulars. When users enjoy a site, they take emotional ownership of it. Everybody's happy until the site manager lets it go fallow for a period of time, or even worse, shuts it down.

Design Presentation

Online publications must be especially well organized because visitors don't always enter on page 1. Unless the site has security protection, visitors can type the URL for any page and enter. This is akin to entering a house from the bedroom window instead of the front door. Also, search engines often list many pages of a site instead of just the opening page, again permitting users to enter a site at any point of the presentation. This presents unique navigation problems as well as structural demands. You can't always assume that the reader reached page 3 from its logical parents, pages 1 and 2.

Organization

Let's use a book metaphor (Figure 13.2) to help visualize how Web pages can be organized. Think of the home page as the introduction and table of contents (links). From each item in the table of contents, you jump to a "chapter" page. Most chapter pages link to appropriate "topic" pages. Some topic pages may be linked to each other, forming linear relationships. Other topic pages may contain only links to remote Web sites. If your presentation is more complex, you can insert "section" pages between the home page and the chapter pages, or insert "subtopic" pages.

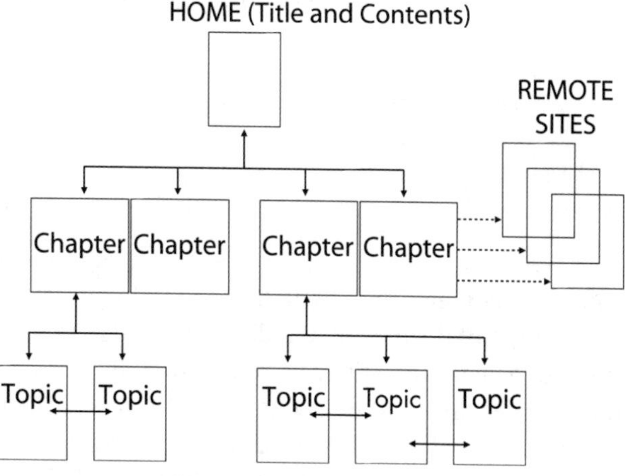

Figure 13.2 Hierarchical and Linear Organization

As with a book, people can "open" your presentation arbitrarily from any page. But unlike the pages of a book, each Web page should stand alone. You should provide descriptive links on every page guiding visitors back to a logical chapter or home page. By making the **<TITLE>** descriptive of the contents as well as presentation (International Writers Consortium—Tips for Web Writers) and by including your address at the bottom of each page, you can help orient your visitors quickly.

This is a simplified description of a typical Web presentation. There are many ways to organize Web pages. The point is to keep the relationships between pages as uncomplicated and logical as possible (Figure 13.3). This will not only help visitors to use your site, but it'll also make it easier for you to maintain and upgrade it.

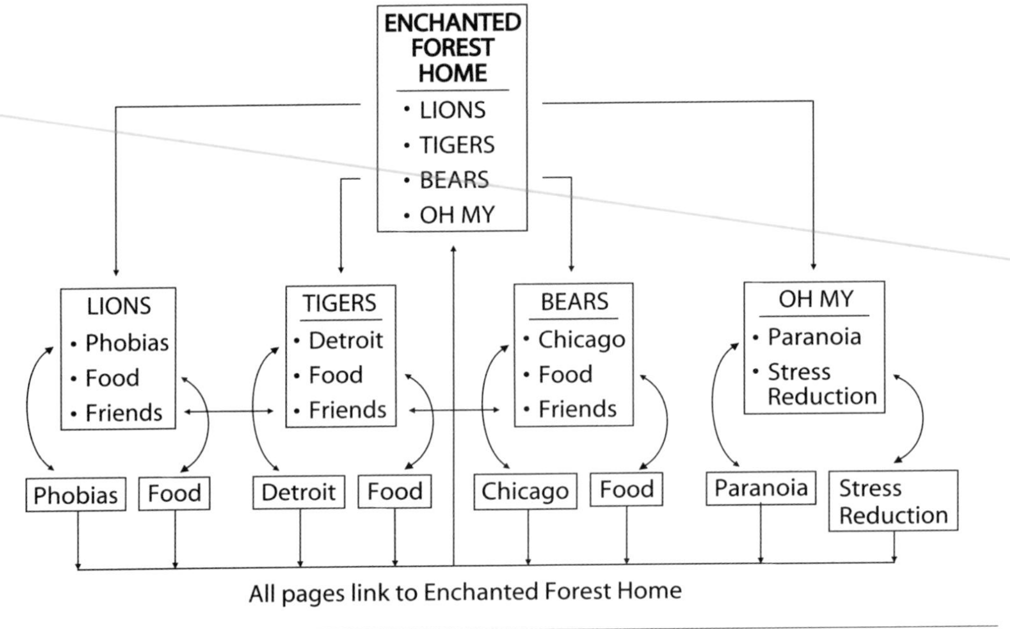

Figure 13.3 Example Web Site

Layout

A final concern with online documents deals with the layout. In most screen documents, lines of text run from the left margin of the display window all the way to the right margin. This is fine if your window is sized to view ten to fifteen words across. But most people read with their windows maximized to view as much of the document as possible. The results are long lines that pack a lot of text on a screen and prove unpleasant to read. You can actually lose your place between the end of one sentence and the beginning of the next. (This is why you sometimes read the same sentence over and over again.)

Other layout concerns mirror those discussed under "Monitor Issues" above. Color, font size, and graphic choices all make a big difference to the readership. No matter how good the content, if the storefront looks bad or users can't find their way from one room to the next, your site will sink into electronic oblivion.

Quality Composition

Despite countless attempts to prove otherwise, the fact remains that orderly content, picture-perfect presentation and high-tech wizardry will never make up for bad writing. When you produce an electronic document, you should write your material, cut at least half of it, rewrite it a few more times, and cut it again. Think of your document as a good, homemade stew. Let it simmer for a few days. Maybe even freeze it and come back to it in a week or so. Then reinvent it. These are writing basics; most of us know the drill. But when publishing is so logistically simple (just upload it), it's tempting to serve the stew before it's ready. Or even worse, serve bad stew.

As **misc.writing** newsgroup participant Wendy Chatley Green states, "Online publications must do more than hold a reader's interest; they must also keep that reader planted in a chair and glued to a screen. Spiffy graphics and adept use of color will catch my eye, but only substance will keep me staring at my monitor or flipping through a printout."

Basic Recommendations

The following recommendations summarize a few simple ways to compensate for the challenges outlined above. Once you've read these suggestions, check the "Helpful Hints" quick-reference lists at the end of Chapter 9 for more detailed, often HTML-specific suggestions.

> *Important:* If a suggestion refers to an HTML-related topic that you don't understand, don't worry about it. As you learn more HTML, you can reread the suggestions that were previously beyond your skill level. They'll suddenly make a lot more sense.

- Keep graphic files as small as possible to minimize long downloads.
- Make sure the color difference between the browser background and the text is good and strong.
- If the document is text heavy, resist the temptation to use black as a background and white as a text color. Even though black is a relief to the eyes, the contrast is too bright for extended reading. Imagine following a flashlight in a pitch-black room. The flashlight is clearly visible, but if you have to continue looking at it, your eyes will become tired.

- Use a soft background such as eggshell, soft gray, or even white. Subtle earth tones evoke a sense of elegance and maturity. White is almost never wrong. It gives your page a little class. It also prints cleanly and clearly for those folks who prefer to print what they see.
- Because we know that visitors often browse sites instead of reading them at length, online publications should include some form of topic list in the opening page presentation. At the very least, the topic list will promote interesting aspects of the site, encouraging visitors to return. The Lead Story Web site (Figure 13.4) is a good example of this.

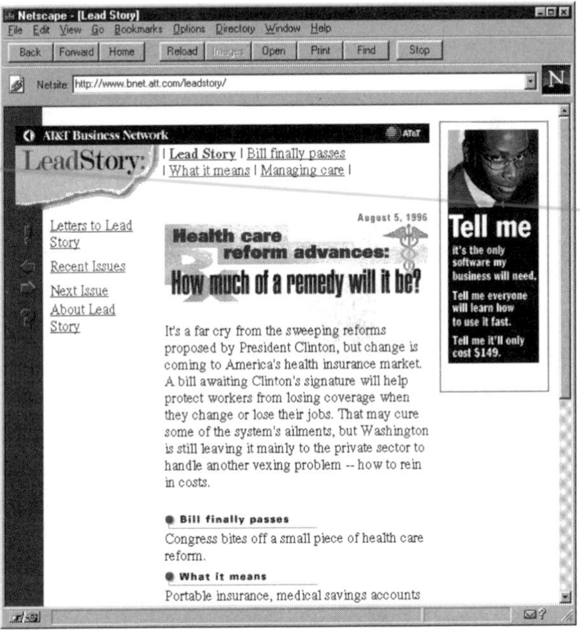

Figure 13.4 Lead Story Home Page

- Keep links, titles, and navigation symbols as self-documenting as possible. In the old days of the Web, cleverness was valued because it made the site appear to be cool and contemporary. But these "cleverisms" and unusual navigation icons confused visitors instead of helping them. They also became stale quickly. Current design trends value clarity and ease-of-use over jargon and excessive innovation.
- A table of contents should be clearly linked and repeated in some logical form on most of the pages internal to the site. This forces you to organize the material for easy navigation and helps visitors move through the site from any entry point.

- Use visual clues and creative headings to engage readers in your material. You want to catch them with your content. Think of your site as a well-done newsletter. Effective newsletters tend to use a variety of subheadings, flourishes, bulleted lists, and call-out text to provide readers with plenty of drop-in points.
- Controlling line length on the Web is relatively easy, though brutal. You can either insert line break tags **
** at the end of each line or use HTML *tables* to confine the text in specified table cells. The text then wraps naturally at the right and left borders of the table cell, regardless of the browser window size. This provides some control, but it's no guarantee. Users can always increase or decrease the default font sizes in their browsers, sending your carefully-orchestrated Web page into layout hell.

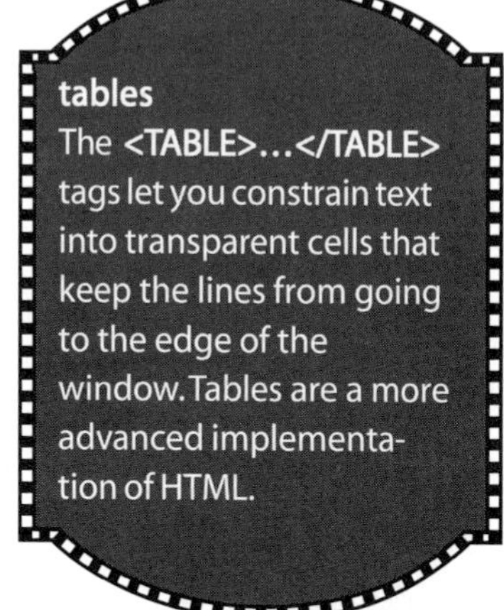

tables
The <TABLE>...</TABLE> tags let you constrain text into transparent cells that keep the lines from going to the edge of the window. Tables are a more advanced implementation of HTML.

- Stylize your site to fit into a category that search directories can easily catalogue. For example, if you publish a variety of small articles or stories on a semiregular basis, you might want to classify yourself as an e-zine. If you're providing market data or how-to information, you might call yourself an online newsletter. If your site is mainly a comprehensive resources and link list, then you might classify yourself as an index.
- Copy the layout of someone else's site. As you copy the layout (*not content!*), you begin to change and modify it to suit your tastes. You really aren't copying anymore; your own style emerges. Some sites, in fact, bank on being known as copies. Do a search in Yahoo for parodies and you'll find that many parody sites exist on the Web.

Adding Graphics, Audio, and Video Files

When the Web was young, big graphics were everywhere. Most sites flaunted huge opening images and complex navigation button bars. Graphic artists designed amazing visuals with little understanding of download time. The screams of frustrated users caught in death-spiral downloads could be heard for miles around.

Today, the trend is to be much more conservative with art. File sizes are smaller and many good sites use comparatively few images. Often Web travelers simply turn off graphics as a browser display option to prevent exhaustive downloads from commencing.

Some Web presentations demand a quantity of large images. For example, sites connected to television shows, celebrities, and movies need a lot of art. Clothing stores and other shopping areas include bigger graphics, as do travel destination sites. In these cases, visitors generally expect big graphics and don't resent them. Often, these sites display thumbnail versions of the images, letting you click on the small graphic to invoke the bigger version.

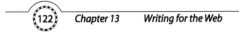

Other multimedia enhancements such as audio and video files also fall into the "long download" category. (See Appendix D for details on audio and video enhancements.) As with big graphics, audio and video files can be interesting, but they don't make or break a site. It's always the written content that tips the scales.

Use your head. If you're marketing musical arrangements, you'd be silly not to include audio clips. If you're promoting a TV show or a training series, video clips would be a good enhancement. If you're a graphic artist displaying your portfolio, big graphics are appropriate. But not having audio, video, and graphic additions shouldn't prevent you from creating a solid site that sells your work. You're a writer; your words are your business. If you make them count, the other adornments won't matter as much.

Make the Best of It

Writers often lament the short attention spans of online travelers. But this is the inevitable backwash of a generation weaned on television. Right or wrong, TV must continually top itself in order to maintain the attention of its passive, chronically-numb audience. Audiences are trained to require strong stimulation and immediate gratification. Attention spans shorten as remote controls click through the hundreds of TV channels now available. And unfortunately, the Web is a medium that can reinforce this hit-and-run mentality.

Maybe things will change. Maybe monitors will become more like books, people will learn patience and attention skills, and jumping from one topic to the next won't be the standard mode of online travel. But currently, if you want visitors to stick around your site, you must use the distribution medium effectively. Don't "dumb down" your work; rather, be sensitive to the way people use the Internet and present your content in a manner that makes the best use of it.

Promoting Your Publication

On the Web, promotion is everything. If you don't promote your site, no one will find it. You must contact resource lists, search engines, site directories, and site reviewers, letting them know about your new showcase. If you have the cash, you can pay a publicity company anywhere from $200 to $1000 to do your promotional work for you. But you're smarter to do it yourself because: 1) it's cheaper, and 2) you get to know the publishing arena. If you're interested in taking advantage of the Internet, you should know the turf.

Before announcing yourself to cyberspace, write a twenty-word paragraph summarizing your site and save it as a text file (straight text, no formatting) named **publicity.txt**. This document will be your record of who you contacted and what you wrote. When you visit a site or search engine to publicize your Web presentation, copy the site's URL into **publicity.txt** and date it. Add comments if you like. Then copy the twenty-word paragraph from the document into the requisite form or e-mail message. This will make the process go faster and it'll minimize ugly typos. If you change the wording of the paragraph or add to it, paste a copy of the edited paragraph next to its URL in **publicity.txt**. You may be able to expand your paragraph on occasion but most sites will want it as brief as possible. Some sites may ask you to format your

URL in HTML. For example, instead of writing **Visit Cats'N Bats!**, you'd write **Visit <a href="http://www.domain.com/catbat/">Cats 'N Bats</a>!**

Here are a few suggestions to help galvanize your promotional efforts:

1. Include your Web URL (and e-mail address) on all business stationery and correspondence.

2. List your URL with every free Internet search engine, list, and catalogue you can find. (Many good locations are listed below.) This may take you a few hours, but the increased visibility is well worth the time.

   Note: Carefully read each list's submission rules and regulations before posting your site.

3. Because many site administrators have backlogs of URLs to add, you may find a delay in getting listed. For this reason, some folks begin advertising their sites a few days to two weeks before they're actually ready. They put up placeholder pages with "under construction" notices. The only glitch is that when users hit an "under construction" notice, they might not return when it's ready to go. The solution is to make your site a valuable place to visit, even though it isn't officially open for business. Give early visitors a sense of what's coming, and make them want to return when all the deck chairs are arranged.

4. If you have an advertising budget, consider investing in a few high-traffic spots. Yahoo is a good example of an immensely popular Web site that charges for some (not all) of its promotional placement.

5. Check Usenet and include appropriate announcements to targeted newsgroups. (Make *sure* the group is amenable to the information you want to share. If the group is moderated, ask permission before advertising. Otherwise, you risk getting flamed.)

6. Visit **http://www.yahoo.com/Computers_and_Internet/Internet/World_Wide_Web/Announcement_Services/** to get a list of free announcement service Web sites (Figure 14.1).

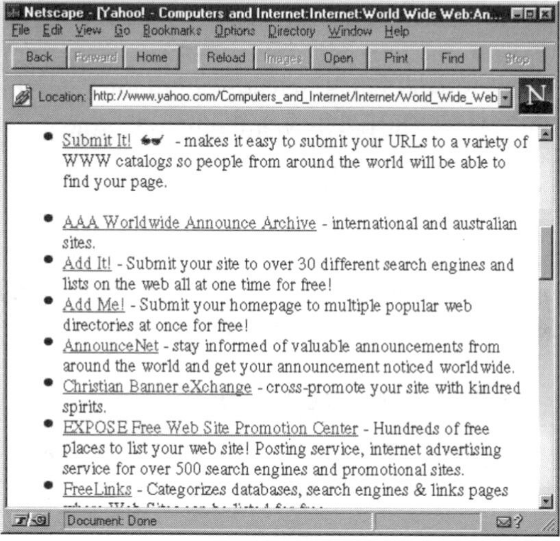

Figure 14.1 *Yahoo Search Directory: Announcement Services*

7. Check your local city/county publications. Many newspapers and journals include weekly columns listing interesting new URLs.

8. E-mail Internet magazines such as Internet World, Internet Underground (Figure 14.2), NewMedia, Wired, and Mondo 2000. When you contact a busy magazine, it is helpful to read previous issues and target a specific editor who fits your topic.

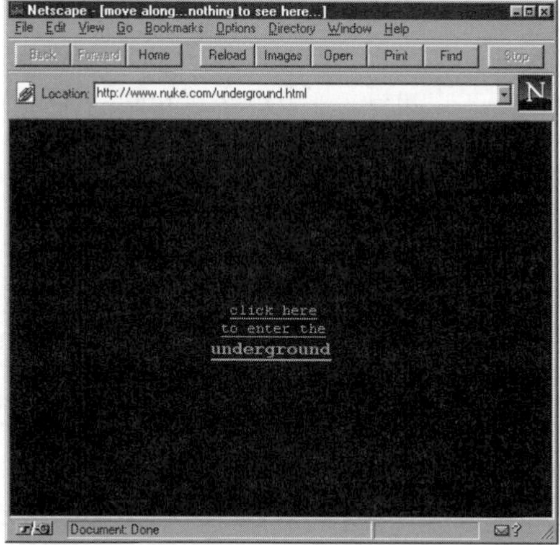

Figure 14.2 *Internet Underground Magazine*

8. Search in Yahoo or Alta Vista for "Site of the Day." Submit your URL to the many sites that offer awards and publicity for sites they deem best, worst, silliest, prettiest, or whatever. If your site is especially interesting or unique, get someone to recommend it to Cool Site of the Day at **http://www.infi.net/cool.html**.

9. Monitor your site's traffic. Check with your service provider on how to do this.

10. Quickly announce your site to multiple major WWW catalogues via sites such as, Submit It!, **http://www.submit-it.com/** (Figure 14.3), Postmaster, **http://www.netcreations.com/postmaster/index.html**, and Add It, **http://www.liquidimaging.com/submit**.

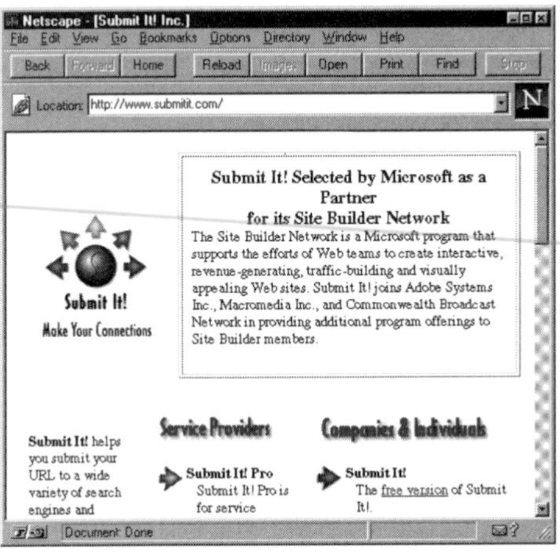

Figure 14.3 Submit It!

What follows is a list of good locations for Web page promotion and announcements. Some of them may overlap. (Remember, these URLs might be different by the time you're ready to promote yourself. And there will be many more ways to get the word out than are listed here.)

- E-mail an announcement, **net-happenings@is.internic.net** and **www-announce @info.cern.ch**
- Directory of Directories, maintained by Internic (for a small fee you can post a limited entry); send e-mail to **admin@ds.internic.net**
- Web Launch, (a pricey but very high-traffic place to get noticed), **http://www.yahoo.com/docs/pr/launchform.html**
- Mother of all BBSs, **http://wwwmbb.cs.colorado.edu/~mcbryan/bb/summary.html**
- The Huge List, **http://thehugelist.com/**
- Open Market's Commercial Sites Index, **http://www.directory.net/dir/submit.cgi**

- New Internet Knowledge System, e-mail **javiani@rns.com** for noncommercial entries.
- WWW Virtual Library, **http://www.w3.org/pub/DataSources/bySubject/Maintainers.html**
- CERN's WWW Server List, **http://www.w3.org/pub/DataSources/WWW/Geographical_generation/new.html**
- NCSA's What's New, **http://www.ncsa.uiuc.edu/SDG/Software/Mosaic/Docs/whats-new-form.html**
- Register with individual search databases:
    - Lycos, **http://www.lycos.com/addasite.html**
    - ALIWEB, **http://web.nexor.co.uk/public/aliweb/doc/registering.html**
    - WWW Worm, **http://guano.cs.colorado.edu/home/mcbryan/WWWWadd.html**
    - InfoSeek Corporation Server, **http://www.infoseek.com**. If you think your site is cool, e-mail **cool@infoseek.com**
    - WebCrawler, **http://webcrawler.com/WebCrawler/SubmitURLS.html**
    - Excite, **http://www.excite.com**
    - Alta Vista, **http://www.altavista.digital.com/**
    - Yahoo, **http://www.yahoo.com/**
    - Hotbot, **http://www.hotbot.com/**
- Nerdworld Index, **http://www.nerdworld.com/users/dstein/index.html**
- iMall Classified Ads, (insert a free classified ad), **http://www.imall.com/homepage.html**
- Opentext, **http://index.opentext.net/main/submitURL.html**
- The Inter.Net: A listing of home pages, **http://the-inter.net/www/future21/html.html**
- Galaxy Annotations, **http://galaxy.einet.net/cgi-bin/annotate**
- New Riders Yellow Pages, **http://www.mcp.com/newriders/wwwyp/submit.html**
- The Whole Internet Catalog, **http://www.gnn.com**
- Spider's Pick of the Day, **http://gagme.wwa.com/~boba/**
- Starting Point, **http://www.stpt.com/util/submit.html**

Doing Research Online

An ancient Chinese curse says, "May you live in interesting times." No phrase so succinctly captures the promise and peril of Internet research. Wandering through repositories of information, you're at once dizzy with possibilities and overwhelmed by the sheer volume of material. An expedient online research project can quickly develop into a grand time-waster, something you must continually defend to coworkers, clients, even family. ("I'm not wasting time. I *wanted* to learn about yodeling.")

Today, the Web alone contains over twenty million pages of information scattered in computers around the globe. Gopher sites, Usenet newsgroups, and FTP archives add tens of thousands more pages of data. And don't forget about the exceptional resources available from commercial service providers such as America Online (AOL), CompuServe, Microsoft Network (MSN), and Prodigy.

Writers can easily get lost in this labyrinth of data. It's like meandering through an enormous used bookstore or library without the benefit of a card catalogue. Many interesting items can be uncovered, but it is hardly an efficient process. Fortunately, *Web search sites* are growing smarter and easier to use by the week (see Chapter 17). Now, even a Net novice can conduct a fairly organized, successful online search with little preparation (see Chapter 16).

Most online research is conducted in a straightforward manner. It usually involves accessing an electronic index and entering a search word or phrase into an online form. For example, if you were researching an article about whales, you'd enter the term *whale* into the form. The program that reads the term produces a list of resources (books, articles, clickable Web site links, newsgroups, and so on) from its database. Some of the resources will be appropriate to your needs; others will be repetitive or unnecessary. The more clearly you refine the search topic, the more targeted will be your results. The following paragraphs discuss how to refine a topic using *Boolean operators*.

Web search sites
Sites dedicated to cataloguing and indexing the wealth of information available on the Web. In some cases search sites also index other parts of the Internet, such as Gopherspace and Usenet. Some sites employ "robot" programs to travel the Internet, combing for new documents. Other sites require users to submit their document names and addresses to the database.

Boolean operators
Words that help you define search topics more clearly by eliminating certain terms from the search scan or by specifying particular phrases and groups of adjacent words. Common Boolean operators are OR, AND, and WITH.

Narrow Your Search with Boolean Operators

Online searches can produce enormous numbers of references. A single search engine can generate literally thousands of site listings and Usenet references. To narrow your search and increase the likelihood that you'll receive useful results, you must eliminate certain keywords or more clearly define particular groups of words and phrases. For example, if you're researching training tips for the Boston Marathon you can either search for **Boston Marathon** or you can refine the search by entering **Boston WITH Marathon AND training OR preparation**. The **AND**, **WITH**, and **OR** are known as Boolean operators.

Nontechnical people get nervous when "Boolean" is mentioned. The term hearkens back to Boolean logic and those frustrating high school math classes. But there are two good reasons you should learn about Boolean operators: 1) Most search engines use Boolean logic to refine search queries, and 2) Boolean operators are easy to comprehend and a cinch to use.

Important: Check the syntax of the Boolean operators for each search engine you use. Usually there's a button labeled "Advanced" (Figure 15.1) or something similar.

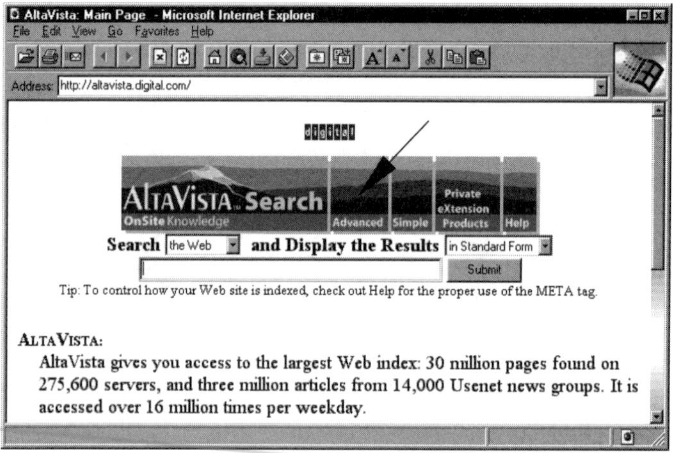

Figure 15.1 Alta Vista Search Form and Option Buttons

Search engines often have preferences for the symbols or words used as Booleans. For example, when eliminating a word from a search, some sites use **NOT** and other sites prefer a minus sign (–). Here's a quick list of the most commonly-used Boolean operators:

AND (Find Me This and That)

Keywords joined by a Boolean **AND** will return pages containing the "**AND**-ed" terms. For example, searching for video **AND** Quicktime will return pages containing both words. Beware, however, that the two words don't have to be contiguous. This is the default for most search engines. You might search for:

- **tornadoes AND Kansas**
- **Boston AND marathon AND 1995**
- **dogs AND grooming**

OR (Find Me This or That)

Keywords joined by a Boolean **OR** will return pages containing only one of the "**OR**-ed" terms. **OR** helps you locate terms with multiple spellings (**online OR on-line**) and subjects with more than one name (**Beelzebub OR Lucifer**). Using **OR** typically increases the number of hits you can expect. You could search for:

- **California OR Oregon**
- **Bosnia OR Yugoslavia**
- **headache OR migraine**

NOT (Find Me This, But Not if It's with That)

Keywords joined by a Boolean **NOT** will exclude pages containing the "**NOT**-ed" term or phrase. **NOT** helps you eliminate irrelevant information (**jazz NOT Dixieland**) and narrow your search category (**cars NOT new**). **NOT** is especially useful when you've executed a search that dumps a bucket of irrelevant links on your screen. Some search engines use a minus sign (–) instead of the word NOT.

- **PC NOT 286**
- **Paris NOT Texas**
- **Washington – D.C.**

WITH or ADJ (Find Me the Word Combination "This and That")

Keywords joined by a Boolean **WITH** or **ADJ** will return pages containing both words found as a unit. This is helpful when you're looking for phrases (**cosmetic WITH surgery**) and names (**Dawn WITH Groves**). The Boolean operator **ADJ** (adjacent) is sometimes used in place of **WITH**. Some search protocols substitute plus signs (+) for **WITH** or enclose words in quotation marks.

> *Note:* If you're looking for an exact match of a phrase containing words such as *the, if, and, it, be, if, for, are, as,* and so on; considering using a search engine that doesn't throw them out, either Alta Vista or Open Text (see Chapter 17).

- **Homer WITH Simpson**
- **olympics ADJ 1996**
- **HTML + author**
- **"the cat in the hat"**

Grouping Search Terms and Operators (Find Me This and This, Excluding That or That)

The more skillfully you construct your searches, the more targeted your results will be. By combining different operators, you can execute advanced searches that eliminate a slew of irrelevancies. Use parentheses to group your subjects together:

- **(cosmetic AND surgery) NOT (mastectomy OR augmentation)**
- **(Tom AND Cruise) NOT (Cocktail OR Risky)**

Note that although Tom Cruise made a film called Risky Business, the search only needs to exclude Risky because Business will almost always follow it.

Searching Usenet

Usenet newsgroups are a good source of story leads and ideas. They can also shed light on opinion-oriented pieces, especially controversial topics. Because Usenet is a discussion forum and not a news feed, all research should be verified. If you quote an article or message, you must first secure permission to do so from its author.

Some Web search sites let you select whether or not to include Usenet in the search parameters. Yahoo, InfoSeek, and Alta Vista all offer optional Usenet searches. But the mother of Usenet research is Deja News, **http://www.dejanews.com/**, a database of almost everything posted in Usenet since early 1995 (Figure 15.2).

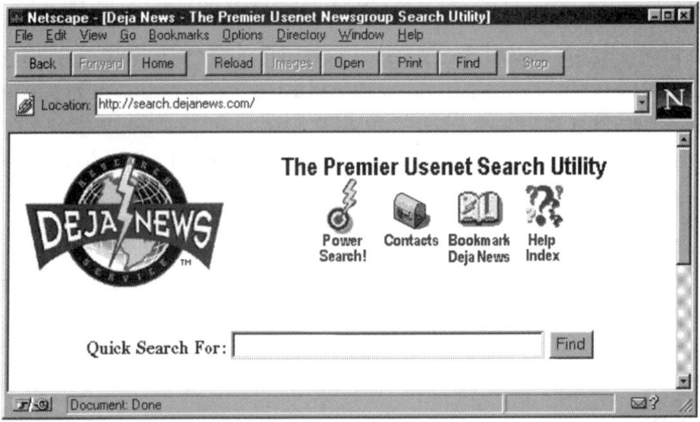

Figure 15.2 Deja News

Deja News lets you mine the Usenet universe by entering a keyword into the search engine and retrieving a list of all Usenet articles containing the keyword. Articles are sorted by keyword frequency, conversation thread, author, or posting date (Figure 15.3). You can even click the author's name to display statistics on Usenet articles originating from a particular e-mail address. Articles with a file size of over four kilobytes (such as FAQs) are broken into segments.

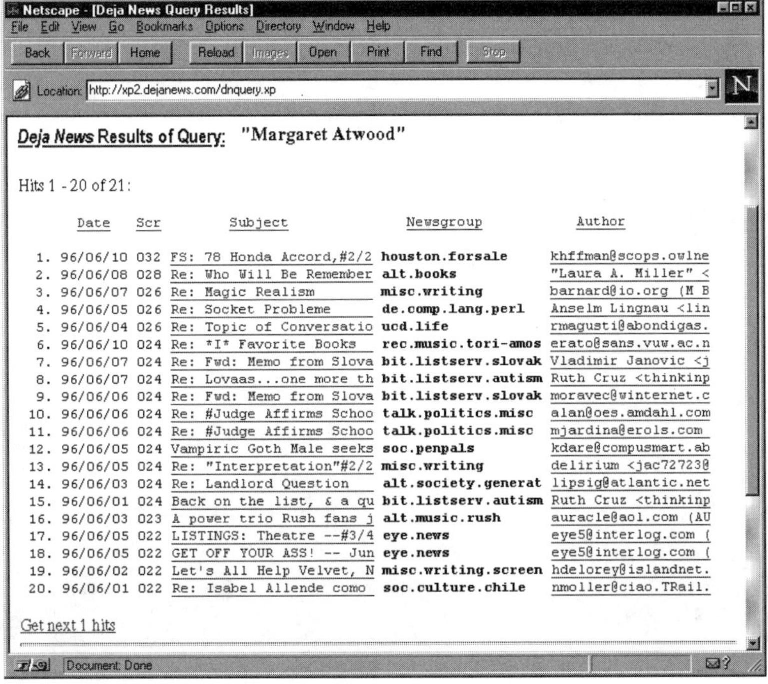

Figure 15.3 *Deja News Search Results*

The ability to search through Usenet raises serious questions about privacy. Many newsgroups contain conversation threads that reveal personal information. Deja News will exclude these personal postings from its database if the sender typed **x-no-archive: yes** as the *first line* of the message body text, or if the message contains the X-Header, **x-no-archive: yes**.

Gopher
A menu-oriented program that provides access to text-only documents and services on the Internet (no graphics). A Gopher *client* is the program you use locally to dig through remote files distributed over the network of Gopher servers. A Gopher *server* is the software that responds to your inquiries and "serves up" data to be downloaded to your computer.

Gopherspace
The thousands of computers and archived files that run on Gopher servers.

Searching Gopherspace

Some writers look to *Gopherspace* for a hearty helping of excellent research resources. *Gopher*, the tool that navigates Gopherspace, is usually available from your service provider. Web browsers can also access most of Gopherspace, making it especially easy to move back and forth from the Web to a Gopher server.

Gopher's value lies in the quality of materials it catalogues. *Gopherspace* is based in academia and so contains countless technical reports, studies, theses, doctoral dissertations, library and newspaper archives, complete reference works, etc.

If you belong to a commercial online service such as AOL, you'll probably find easy access to Gopher (Figure 15.4).

Figure 15.4 Gopher in AOL

If you don't go through a commercial online service, you'll find that your Web browser travels easily to a Gopher site when you type in the correct address (Figure 15.5). For example, to access the University of Minnesota Gopher, type **gopher://gopher2.tc.umn.edu/** in the Web browser location text box. (Gopher URLs look different because they start with **gopher://** instead of **http://**.) Generally, each Gopher site provides menu access to Gophers around the world in case your connection drags. You can also search Gopherspace via a few of the Web search sites such as Lycos.

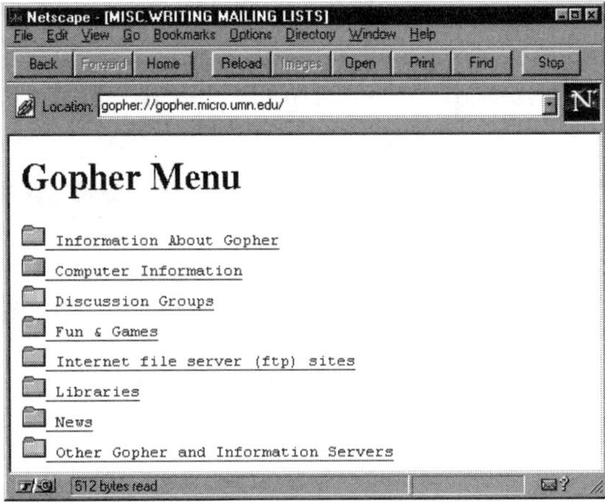

Figure 15.5 *Gopher Site Via the Web*

> *Note:* To narrow your Gopherspace search even further, you can employ the Veronica search utility. Veronica was so named because of another search tool called Archie. These names come from the Archie and Veronica comic strip. After the fact, Veronica came to stand for Very Easy Rodent-Oriented Netwide Index to Computerized Archives.

Veronica searches menu and/or document titles in Gopherspace, returning a list of links for you to peruse. Using Veronica is much more efficient than simply clicking through Gopher menus hoping to find something useful. Veronica is easy to access from almost any Gopher site because you'll see menus that say things like "Search Using Veronica" and "How to Use Veronica FAQ" (Figure 15.6).

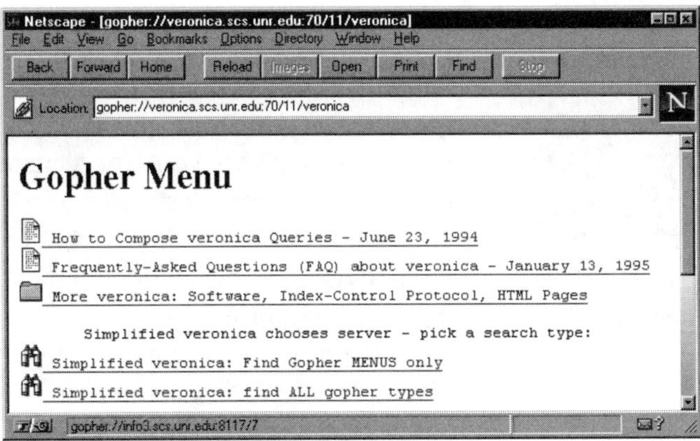

Figure 15.6 *Gopher Site with Veronica Menus*

When you click a Veronica menu option, you can read about structuring your search (quite similar to Web searches with Boolean operators). It's important to read the supplementary articles, because when you view the Veronica query page, it may have very little documentation on it (Figure 15.7).

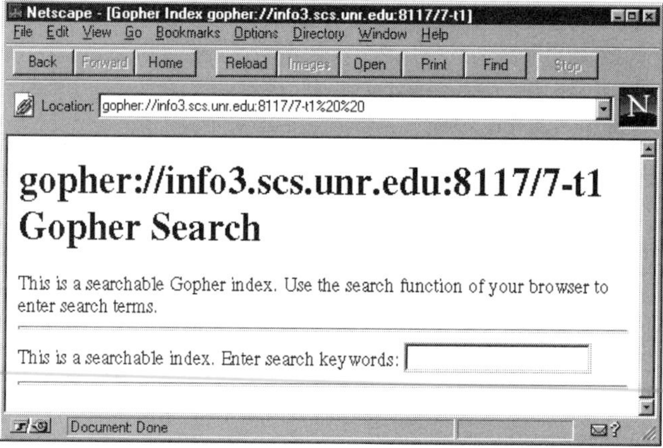

Figure 15.7 Veronica Search Engine

Note: If you read helpful documents or FAQs before executing a Veronica search, you may have to use the **Back** button on your browser to return to the menu page containing the link to the Veronica query page.

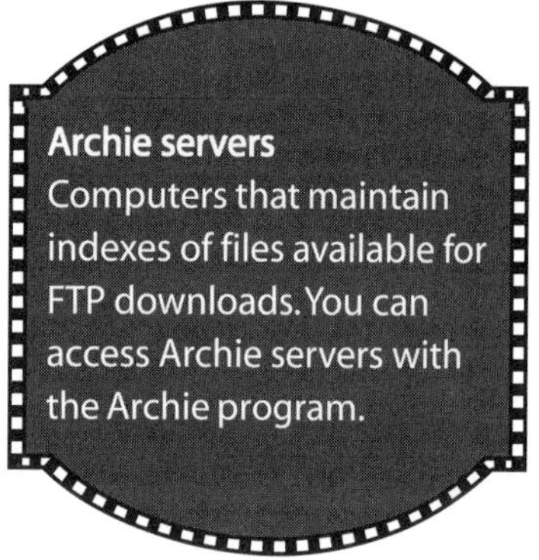

Archie servers
Computers that maintain indexes of files available for FTP downloads. You can access Archie servers with the Archie program.

Searching FTP Sites

If you already know the name of the file you want to download, try locating it using *Archie*—a search program that scans FTP databases for specific files. Archie uses your search keyword (the filename) to scan indexes of over 2.5 million files stored at more than 1500 FTP sites. Once you locate the file, you can use an FTP program to retrieve it. Or, without employing FTP, you can try searching for a Web site that makes the file available. The results of an Archie search range from simple to complex, depending on the search topic and the search parameters you select.

Archie used to be accessible only through Telnet. Now there are several Archie forms located on the Web. Start with Archieplex, **http://www.lerc.nasa.gov/archieplex/doc/form.html**, a form-driven site out of NASA (Figure 15.8).

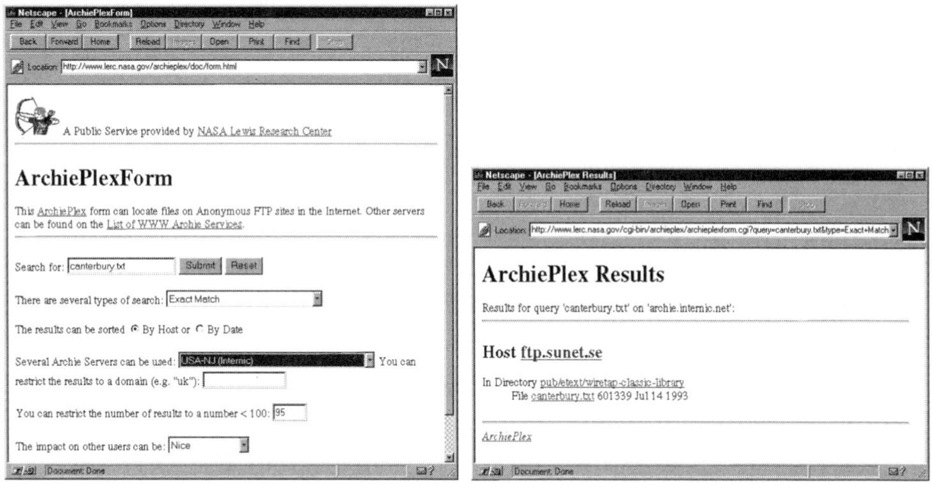

Figure 15.8 *Archieplex from NASA*

Archie forms are easy to use; simply enter the name of the file and select a server from the drop-down list. If the form offers other parameters such as search impact, leave the default values in place. (The "nice" option in the search impact list keeps you from taking processing power away from the server's other activities.) Archie servers sometimes receive up to 50,000 queries a day, so they can be somewhat slow. You may need to visit a couple of servers before you locate your file.

Many researchers no longer rely on Archie because most companies that provide downloadable files also maintain Web pages. You can often find information about a file or program more easily using a Web search site such as HotBot or MetaCrawler (see Chapter 17).

To visit Archie servers both on and off the Web, check out the List of WWW Archie Servers, **http://pubweb.nexor.co.uk/public/archie/servers.html**.

Using Commercial Online Services for Research

Commercial online services typically have well-stocked reference areas containing a library of standard free reference texts, mainstream search engines, and fee-based research databases. Information retrieval companies such as IQuest contract with the commercial provider to offer their services to subscribers. Some services are useful and less expensive, but currently, most fee-based commercial provider databases are too expensive to be a steady resource for freelance writers.

If you're a research hound, it behooves you to visit some of the commercial services to explore their databases. All services offer some form of incentive to subscribe, usually a free trial to learn more about their communities. You can mine the archives of AOL, MSN, and CompuServe for days without coming up for air. For example, AOL is known for its easy interface. AOL also maintains a reference chat area where you can ask questions of a live reference expert. (Other providers may also offer this: I just haven't checked them out.) CompuServe is known for its professional bent, attracting cream-of-the-crop forum moderators and contributors. Their reference forums are equally impressive. Prodigy and MSN are also full of great reference sources and text.

If you already subscribe to a commercial service, then by all means nose through their reference desks and hit all the freebies. But if you don't subscribe, it shouldn't affect the quality of your online research unless the topic is very specific to a database that only a particular service offers.

How to Conduct a Search

Good online research is more than simply entering a keyword into a search engine. It involves structuring the search for the best possible results and avoiding the pitfalls of distraction and disorganization. So much material can be returned from searches that without an effective, efficient, and orderly approach, you'll drown in oceans of marginally-useful data.

Be Effective

The following suggestions will help you construct and execute effective searches, regardless of the tool you use:

1. Determine the subject.

   Get a feel for the target arena by starting with a simple topic. You may need to poke around a little, just to see how your topic area tends to be referenced. For example, if you're doing research on commercial honeybees, you might use a Web search tool to look up the word *bee*. This should yield a large list of hits including things like the *Sacramento Bee*, beekeeping, and the Bee Gees. You might then choose to refine your search to the phrase *beekeeping*, but you should avoid restricting yourself too much. Try a variety of related phrases such as *apiculture* or *honey*. As you continue searching, beware of seductive time bandits. In other words, don't get lost reading about the Bee Gees—augh!—just because *bee* is in the title.

2. Select the search tool.

   Every search tool accesses its own database of information. To select the best tool, consider the search topic, the available resources, the database index structure and update schedule, and even the time of day. For example, if you're searching during heavy traffic hours, you may need to use a less popular site in order to gain access. If you know the database won't be updated for another three weeks, you might want to schedule another search at that time. Until you have a lot of experience (and understanding) about the strengths and weaknesses of individual search tools, you should probably sample a variety of sites. You can also save some time by making a few logical decisions before executing a search. For example:

   - If you're looking for a file and you know its name, you might try using Archie (see Chapter 15) to locate an FTP site. If you don't know the file name, you could use Veronica (see Chapter 15) or one of the Web search tools to zero in on information about the file subject.
   - If you're looking for a software upgrade or something directly related to a company, try searching for the company name on the Web. The company home page will probably guide you to the information you need. Most companies use their name in their URL. Try entering **http://www.*companyname*.com** into the location text box in your browser.
   - If you're researching a paper, you should probably check for related newsgroup subjects (see Chapter 5).

3. Execute the search.

   Make sure you're using the search options available in the tool. (If you don't know them, read the search documentation and help screens.) If the tool lets you specify words, phrases, or dates, be sure to include them. Keep in mind that 100 search hits are of little value when most of them are outdated references to the same file. Accept that sometimes you'll retrieve useless information or the same information twice. This is the minor price you pay for the convenience of searching online.

4. Keep track of details.

   Because the robot programs that scan the Internet for database updates may only cycle through the entire database archive every few weeks (or less), you should consider executing the same search at a later date to see if anything new is available. Try maintaining a simple record of your searches, including the date of the search and the tool selected, any significant keywords used to refine the search, and pertinent comments about what you found. Keep in mind that there can be a lag between when events occur and when related information is posted on the Internet.

5. Reader beware.

   Some information sources are clearly reliable—the Library of Congress, the Smithsonian, *The Writer's Guide to the Internet* (if I do say so myself). You may need to verify by e-mailing the author or publisher or by cross-checking to see if similar information is posted elsewhere. This is especially true regarding data cited in newsgroups where opinion and exaggeration run rampant. If you find a particularly juicy bit of information that you want to build into a feature story, make darn sure the news is accurate or include some sort of disclaimer in your work.

Be Efficient

No matter how prepared you are for your search, you can always use a few tricks to be even more efficient. Try some of these:

1. Connect to local servers and search at odd hours.

   Local servers may provide quicker access times, although you need to keep in mind the peak access hours. On weekdays, peak access is usually 7:00 A.M. to 9:00 A.M., 11:30 A.M. to 1:30 P.M., and 4:00 P.M. to 6:00 P.M. These are hours when working folks usually check their computers for messages and do a little Web browsing. Surprisingly, weekends aren't as busy because many people use computers in the workplace, not at home.

2. Stay focused.

   Search only for the topic of interest. If you don't stay on target, you'll lose valuable time with little to show for it. If you see something really interesting, jot it down and promise yourself you'll go back to it after you've completed your work.

3. Keep the search tool instructions handy.

   Search tools are deceptively simple. It's tempting to stab blindly into cyberspace hoping for a hit. However, a little advance reading will help you construct a better search that yields more satisfying results. Read the search documentation, keep it handy, and use the tool intelligently. You'll fare better in the long run. (See the section in Chapter 15 on Boolean operators.)

4. Don't limit yourself to one Web search site.

   Be willing to use more than one search site regularly, because they all have different databases and different ways of storing information.

5. Move beyond the Web.

   Because Web is simple and flashy, it's easy to get lazy and forget about non-Web regions such as Gopherspace. Remember that even though the Web does access these other arenas, it doesn't always do it as effectively as a tool designed specifically for the resource. As you become more skilled, you may want to use a program specifically designed for Gopher.

6. Keep a hotlist of useful sites that index or collect interesting information.

   Let's face it. When you're rushed, it's more efficient to scan a large, well-organized information clearinghouse than to traipse through a million tiny lists hoping for a hit. Fortunately, there are a variety of excellent data collectives such as the Gopher Jewels menu and John December's list of essential resources, **http://www.december.com/cmc/info/**. There are also many other repositories on the Web: Global Network Navigator, the Library of Congress, and so on. Chapters 20–22 list many fine resource sites.

7. Plan time to experiment.

   Planned breaks will circumvent the tendency to mess around when you're supposed to be getting in and getting out. They'll also significantly expand your search horizons as well as your skill level. Try investigating new databases and comparing search tools. Use different Boolean operators (**OR** instead of **AND**) to observe the changes in search result.

8. Don't forget about the library.

   Online research is fantastic, but it hasn't replaced the library (yet). To be truly thorough, use offline as well as online resources.

Be Organized

Once you have a research document on the screen, you must decide if you're going to save it or move to the next page. It's tempting to try to print or save every document that's moderately useful. But the dark side to saving or printing research material is that it skirts the edge of copyright infringement. Theoretically, whenever you save a file to disk or print a hard copy, you're generating a tangible replica of the item—a form that can be copied and distributed. (This is usually done innocently with the intention to seek permission from the source if the reference is cited.) To be on the safe side, toss documents when they are no longer useful. And even though a lot of research copying falls into the category of fair use, you should still e-mail the data source to explain what you're doing. This courtesy not only keeps everything aboveboard, but it also maintains a standard behavior that respects copyrighted materials.

Searching online can quickly turn the most conservative researcher into a major data hog. Folders on disk swell with miscellaneous data. Hard copy file folders groan from pages of printouts. Much of this information you'll never really need. So as you look over a document, ask yourself if you absolutely must have this item. If there's any question in your mind, don't save it. You can always come back to it later. Furthermore, be ruthless with yourself when it comes to printing. It's easy to print pages and pages of information without really needing them. As a rule of thumb, save the document to disk and think about printing it later on. Try to read it on-screen without wasting paper.

Create a Topic Outline

The challenge in any research project is to keep the growing coffers of information organized for easy accessibility. To ward off problems, create a folder (directory) structure on your hard disk before you gather any data. This structure should roughly mirror the outline of the piece you're writing. It can be as general or detailed as you like, and it can evolve as your project progresses. Hard copy file folders should mirror the structure on disk. You want everything to be organized in the same manner.

For example, if I'm researching an article about orca killer whales living off the coast of British Columbia, I'll create the following folder structure on my hard disk:

- British Columbia
- Famous whales
- Behavior
  - Swimming
  - Socialization
  - Feeding
  - Breeding
- Vocalization
  - Dialect
  - Recording
- Capture
  - Procedures
  - Aquariums
  - Politics
- Temporary
- Ideas
- Publicity

Each of these topics translates into a folder. The subtopics become subfolders. As I locate documents in my searches, I save them to the appropriate folders. Data that don't immediately fit into a category are saved in the Temporary folder and classified later in the day when I'm offline. Interesting documents that might work for another project are saved in the Ideas folder. Advertising and publicity information is saved in the Publicity folder.

Many writers in newsgroups and mailing lists tout the use of InfoSelect (Figure 16.1). InfoSelect 3.0 (**http://www.miclog.com**)is an adaptable Personal Information Manager (PIM) that minimizes time spent storing, organizing, and finding the countless bits of information you need every day. It works especially well for writers because it provides a variety of ways to organize data into outlines, search and sort quickly, manipulate text, print data, build databases, convert between data types, perform mail-merges, and much more. You can also use InfoSelect to schedule single and recurring events and reminders. A trial version of InfoSelect is located on the CD that accompanies this book.

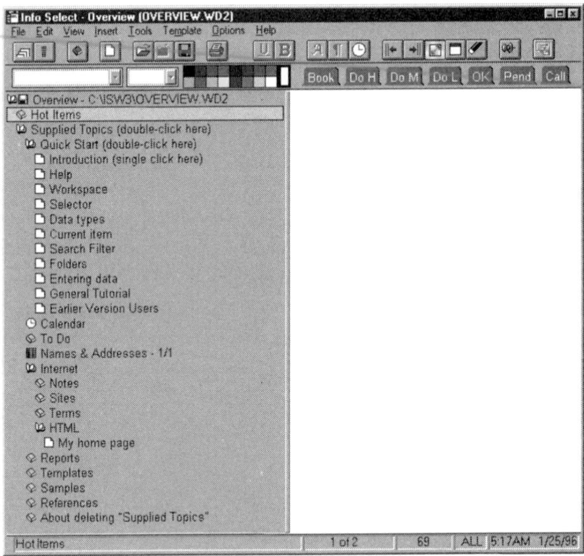

Figure 16.1 InfoSelect

Print if You Must

To print any document displayed in your browser, simply click the Print button, menu command, or function key. Be sure to check your hard copy as it prints; some Web pages print poorly due to color contrast problems.

To print the Web page source (the HTML document complete with tags) instead of the Web page in its browser display form, select the Source command from the View menu. When the source is displayed either in the Web browser window or in a text editor such as Notepad, you can print it directly or save it for later retrieval. In the case that you want to strip out the HTML, the source can be edited in your word processor or you can speed things up with a shareware program such as HTMLcon, **http:///www.crl.com/~mikekell**.

Citing Your Results

The problem with referencing virtual documentation is that it can quickly disappear from cyberspace. Unlike material in the library, virtual documents can be removed from databases at the Webmaster's descretion. This is why you should print or at least save to disk documents that may be cited in your research work. Remember to inform the author of your intentions and remove the document when you no longer need it.

Cite the Original

Credible Internet documentation often has an original hard copy counterpart. If possible, cite the hard copy instead of the Net address. The hard copy is usually the primary source; secondary versions are often abridged.

If you do cite a virtual reference, either contact its author to reconfirm the information or locate a moderator or Webmaster to help establish its source. If you can't find a source to confirm, then check the facts with other experts and note that they were consulted. If the text simply can't be confirmed, then make sure you indicate its status as opinion or hearsay.

Cite it Properly

Because the Internet is still relatively new as a reference resource, the manner in which references are documented hasn't been standardized. Many electronic style guides base their decisions on the Modern Language Association (MLA) and American Psychological Association (APA). Two especially good online guides are *Beyond the MLA Handbook: Documenting Electronic Sources on the Internet*, by Andrew Harnack and Gene Kleppinger (**http://falcon.eku.edu/honors/beyond-mla**), and the *MLA-Style Citations of Electronic Sources* by Janice R. Walker (**http://www.cas.usf.edu/english/walker/mla.html**).

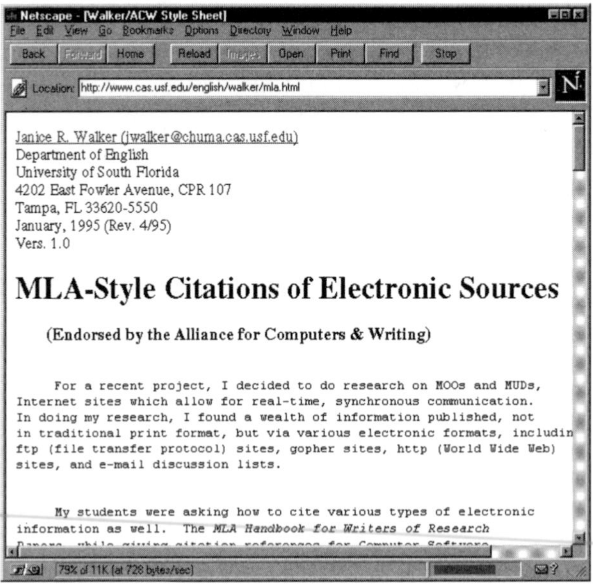

Figure 16.2 *The MLA-Style Citations of Electronic Sources*

The following sample citations are based on *The MLA-Style Citations of Electronic Sources* (Figure 16.2), which the Alliance for Computers and Writing has endorsed:

E-mail, Listserv, and Newslist Citations

Author. "Subject line." Address of list or name of newsgroup (date of access). Personal e-mail does not require the sender's e-mail address.

Fubar, Amy S. "Cetacean dialects in B.C." whales.orca.sci (20 Dec. 1994).

Barrett, David. "General Hospital Rules Cyberspace." Personal e-mail (22 Jan. 1996).

FTP

Author. "Document Title." FTP address and full path (Date of publication).

Jones, Millard. "Outside the Envelope." ftp.mhld.edu pub/papers/outenv-96 (4 Dec. 1996).

Gopher

Author. "Full title of work." Print publication information (if any), full Gopher path (date of access).

Groves, G.P. "Pugly the Ugly Seal." Published in *Kid's Tales*, 7 Nov. 1993. gopher / University of Koeln/stories in Education/Selected Papers/Kid's Tales (5 Dec. 1994).

Synchronous Communications (Chat, IRC, etc.)

Speaker(s). Type of communication (e.g., Personal Interview). Access address (date of communication).

Cat2000 (Sue Miller), Mightymouse (Blanche Arnold). Personal Interview. telnet world.sensemedia.net 1234 (30 Oct. 1996).

HTML Writing Class, Level 1. Tables and Frames discussion group. AOL Writers Club Chat Room, (3 Aug. 1995).

Telnet

Author. "Full title of work." Full Telnet address and access instructions (date of access).

Sparks, Eleanor. "Bats in the Belfry: A Guide to Constructing a Bat House." *EcoNews*, 8 June 1992. telnet nas.skycat.com 8888, @go #11832, press 21(18 Mar. 1993).

World Wide Web

Author. "Full title of work." Full URL (date of access).

Barrett, Holly. "Adoption from China FAQ." http://www.ccs.neu.edu/home/lpb/chinafaq.html (9 July 1996).

Other Sources for Standards and Styles

The American Society of Indexers

http://www.well.com/user/asi/

Excellent reference lists and articles about indexing, reference sites, and much more. Includes membership information and—no surprise—a thorough index of the site.

The CopyEditing Style FAQ

http://www.rt66.com/~telp/sfindex.htm

Style and usage Q&A culled from the copyediting-l mailing list. Lots of good advice.

Electronic Style: A Guide to Citing Electronic Information

http://www.uvm.edu/~xli/reference/estyles.html

A popular reference on college campuses that includes styles for the APA and MLA. Written by Xia Li and Nancy Crane.

The Elements of E-Text Style

http://wiretap.spies.com/ftp.items/Library/Classic/estyle.txt

The Elements of Style for electronic text. A must-read site.

MLA-Style Citations of Electronic Sources

http://www.cas.usf.edu/english/walker/mla.html

Janice Walker's style guidelines for citing electronic information sources. Endorsed by the Alliance for Computers & Writing.

Style Guide for Online Hypertext

http://www.w3.org/hypertext/WWW/Provider/Style/

Tim Berners-Lee (creator of the Web) discusses hypertext style.

Yale Center for Advanced Instructional Media Style Guide

http://info.med.yale.edu/caim/StyleManual_Top.HTML

An example of Yale's comprehensive style guide for online communications.

Web Search Sites

Free Web search sites have become a mainstay of Internet navigation. Most Web travelers visit one or two of them on a regular basis. On a surface level, search sites all tend to operate in much the same manner; you type a word or phrase into a text box, click a **Submit** button, and wait for a display of clickable links that match your entry. Search sites differ from each other in: 1) the Internet regions they encompass—any combination of the Web, Usenet, FTP, and Gopher, 2) their levels of friendliness and accessibility, 3) their syntax for simple to advanced queries, 4) the manner in which they catalogue information, 5) the frequency with which they update their databases, and 6) the speed at which they perform their tasks. (Many search sites claim to be exceptionally fast, but it's difficult to judge speed over the Internet because unrelated factors such as message traffic and line noise can bog down a connection.)

Search sites can be loosely categorized as *directories* or *indexes*, although some sites combine features of both.

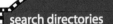

search directories
These search sites (usually Web sites) organize information by subject classification, general to specific. A typical subject classification hierarchy would be Arts and Entertainment:Television:Sitcoms. Some directories also rate (cool, five stars, etc.) the sites that they catalogue.

search indexes
These search sites organize information by keyword, displaying results of the search based on how many times the keyword showed up in the document or title.

Directories

Directories are easy to understand and use because you can browse by subject classification. Some directories organize documents in comprehensive subject hierarchies such as *Arts:Computer Generated:Artists:Personal Exhibits.* Other sites are less comprehensive, using more generalized categories such as Entertainment and the Internet. Directories often require you to submit your document address and description for inclusion in their databases. For this reason they can be somewhat limited in scope. In some cases, directory editors rate the submissions for inclusion in specialized lists (cool, mature audiences, four stars).

Executing a directory search can yield a variety of results. For example, if you search for *writing* through all of the Yahoo Directory, your results will include individual sites under diverse categories such as *Arts:Artists:Collectives*, and *Arts:Computer Generated:Artists:Personal Exhibits.* You'll also display all the categories that include the word *writing* in their descriptions, such as *Business and Economy:Employment:Resumes:Resume Writing Tips*, and *Arts:Humanities:Literature:Genres:Nonfiction:Travel Writing*. Figure 17.1 shows the results of a Yahoo search on *Margaret Atwood.*

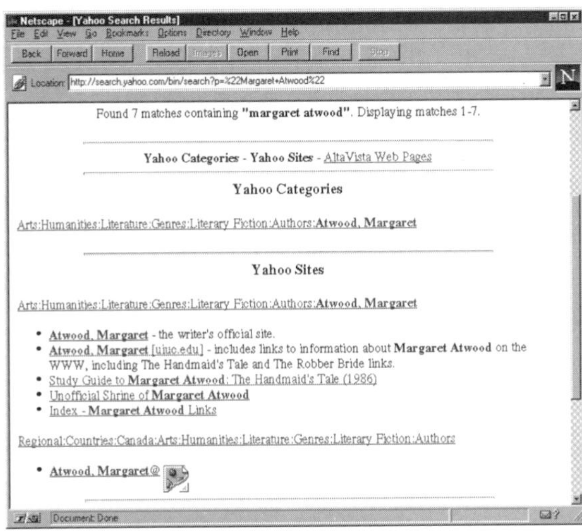

Figure 17.1 Search Directory Results

The following paragraphs list some of the high-profile search directories currently active on the Web.

A2Z

http://a2z.lycos.com/

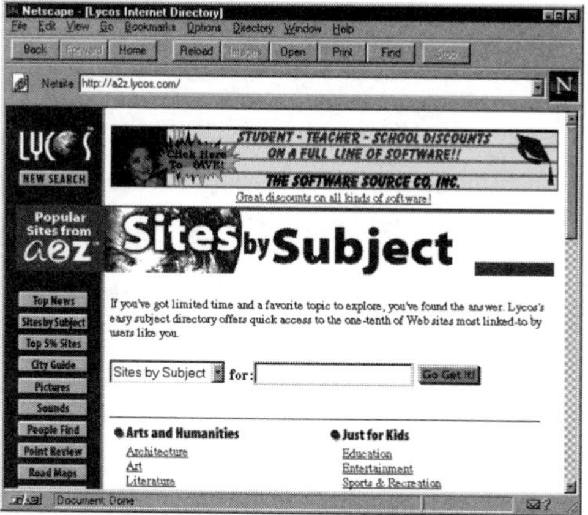

Figure 17.2 A2Z Directory

Begun in February 1996, the Lycos-run A2Z Directory (Figure 17.2) lists the most popular Web sites, as estimated by the Lycos *search index*. There is no way to submit a site to the A2Z Directory.

Excite NetDirectory

http://www.excite.com/Subject

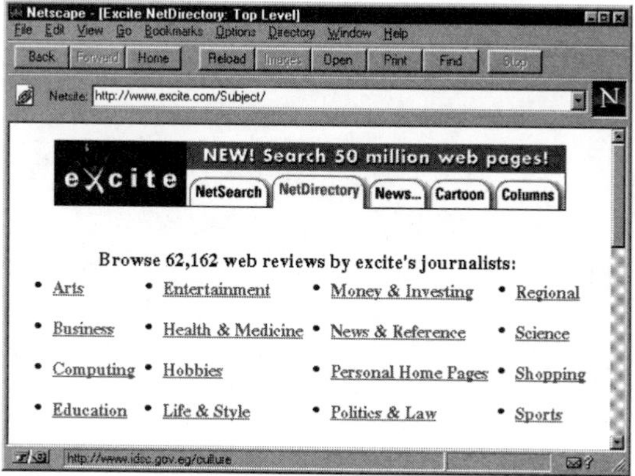

Figure 17.3 Excite NetDirectory

NetDirectory (Figure 17.3) is a catalog of over sixty thousand reviewed sites available from the Excite home page. Reviewers record their opinions about the sites they visit. They may also review sites based on submission.

Magellan

http://www.mckinley.com/

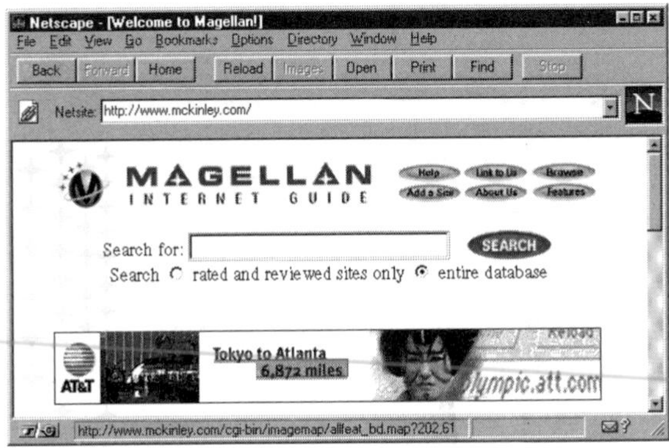

Figure 17.4 Magellan Search Directory

Magellan (Figure 17.4) is a directory and rating service that includes Web sites, FTP and Gopher servers, Usenet, and Telnet sessions. Reviewers rate sites with one to four stars, four stars being the best by Magellan standards. "Green Light" sites are suitable for all age groups. A nice feature of Magellan is that you can search for topics by rating. For example, you might search for sites that rate two stars or better and contain the word "Spam."

Point

http://www.pointcom.com/

Figure 17.5 Point Search Directory

Point (Figure 17.5) is a directory and a rating service. Point's claim to fame is that it includes only the top five percent of all Web sites in its directory (the top five percent being a subjective decision made by Point reviewers). Whenever you see the Top Five Percent logo displayed at a Web site, it's a Point winner.

WebCrawler Select

http://www.webcrawler.com/

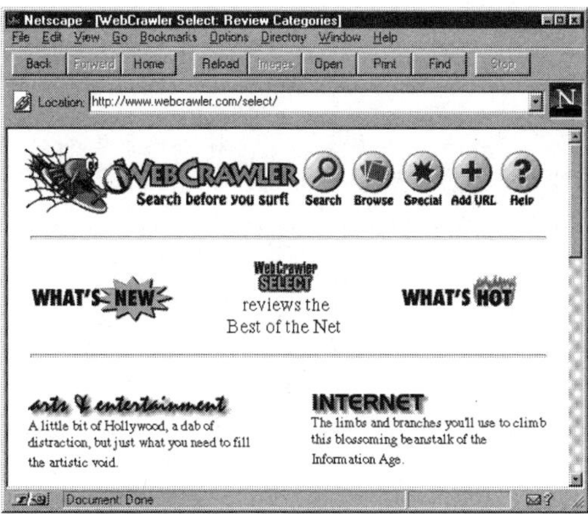

Figure 17.6 WebCrawler Select Search Directory

WebCrawler Select (Figure 17.6) contains sites gleaned from those submitted to the Global Network Navigator (GNN), **http://www.ora.com**, NCSA What's New page. The quality of sites in this directory is quite good. You can access it from the WebCrawler search page by clicking the Browse button.

Yahoo

http://www.yahoo.com/

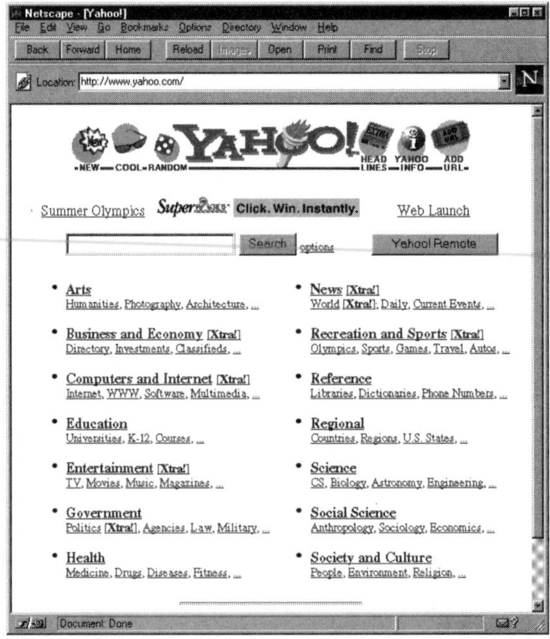

Figure 17.7 Yahoo Search Directory

Having been around since late 1994, Yahoo (Figure 17.7) is the most famous directory on the Web. It lists more than 200,000 Web sites under 20,000 categories, includes optional Usenet search capabilities, and includes a kids' directory called Yahooligans. You can search for a word through all of Yahoo's categories and site descriptions, or narrow down your search by subject. Yahoo makes it especially easy to conduct a more advanced search by offering a clickable screen of options. This lets you control the context around your search, yielding satisfying, understandable results.

Search Indexes

Search indexes don't typically maintain classification hierarchies as do directories. The results aren't organized by subject; rather, they're often listed by the number of *keywords* present in the document. (This is why you'll see some home pages containing one or two paragraphs of repeated phrases or keywords. It's a crude way to show up as one of the first sites in a search index list.) Figure 17.8 shows the results of an Alta Vista search on *Margaret Atwood*.

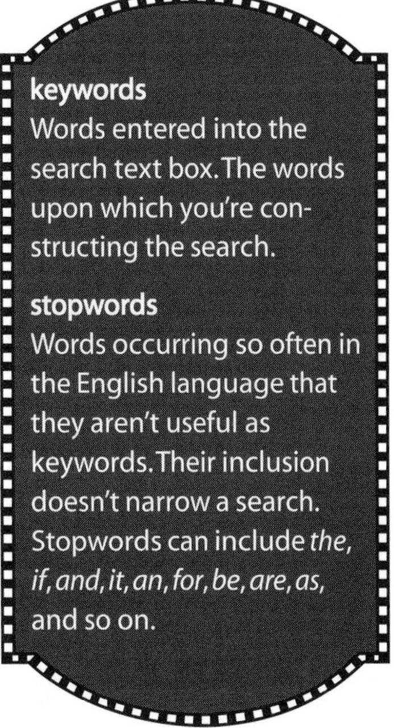

keywords
Words entered into the search text box. The words upon which you're constructing the search.

stopwords
Words occurring so often in the English language that they aren't useful as keywords. Their inclusion doesn't narrow a search. Stopwords can include *the, if, and, it, an, for, be, are, as,* and so on.

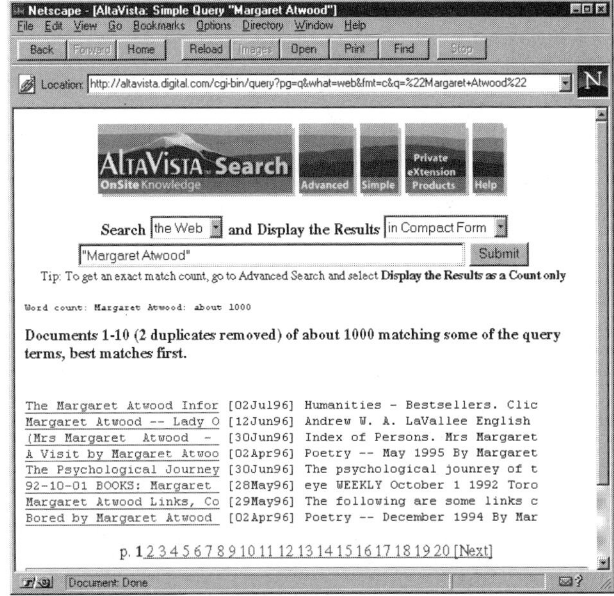

Figure 17.8 Alta Vista Search Index Results

Opinions vary about the best index to use. Most researchers experiment with any or all of the sites listed below (not a comprehensive list; by the time of publication there will be more). Remember that it's a good idea to use more than one search index because they cover different territories and update themselves at different times. You'll get some overlap, but you may also find new gems.

The following paragraphs list some of the high-profile search indexes currently active on the Web:

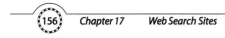

Alta Vista

http://www.altavista.digital.com/

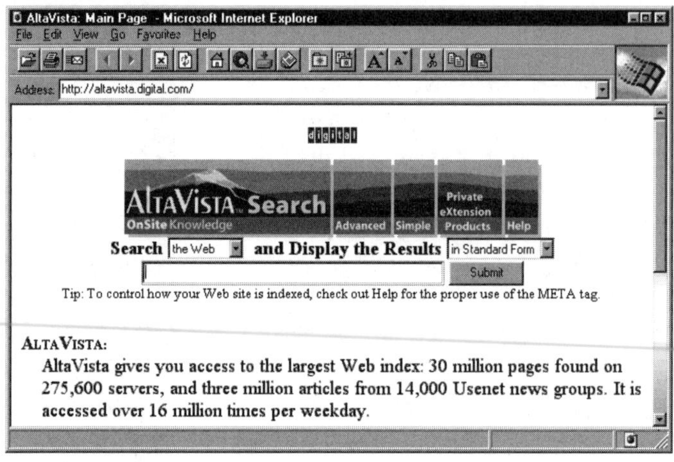

Figure 17.9 Alta Vista Search Index

Alta Vista (Figure 17.9) is run by Digital Equipment Corporation (DEC). It touts the largest Web index with a catalogue of over thirty million Web pages and 14,000 Usenet newsgroups. Like Open Text, Alta Vista doesn't throw out stopwords, making it easier to match titles containing words such as *to*, *as*, *the*, and *if*. Alta Vista's results include listing how many matches it found for each keyword you typed. It also thoughtfully refrains from clearing your keywords or phrases from the submission field after a search is conducted. This helps you refine your search because you can see what you previously entered and edit it appropriately. Alta Vista's comprehensive database and excellent advanced search options make it a superb choice for conducting searches.

Excite Netsearch

http://www.excite.com/

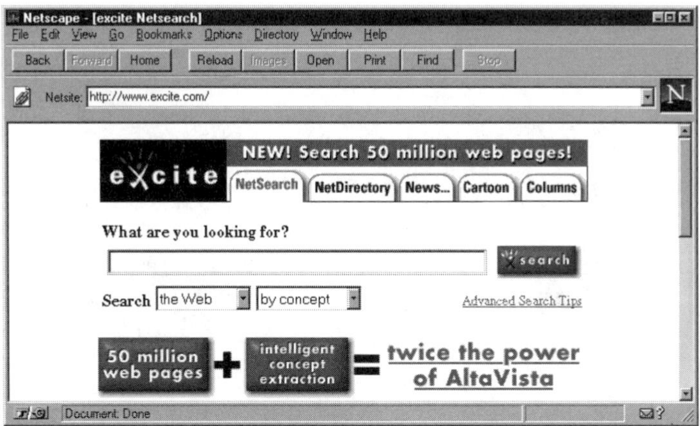

Figure 17.10 Excite Search Index

Launched in late 1995, Excite (Figure 17.10) is a smart, user-friendly database that indexes the Web, over ten thousand Usenet groups, and Usenet classified ads from the past two weeks. Excite's *search engine*, Netsearch, provides optional, concept-based searches, meaning that in addition to finding exact matches to your keywords, Netsearch also locates pages *related* to your keywords. For example, if you search for the word *film*, Netsearch will also find *movie*. Highly touted with lots of advertising bucks invested, Excite provides good results in minimal time.

search engine
Programs that retrieve and index online documents in a manner that you, the user, can peruse. Often called "robots" or "spiders," search engines comb the Internet day and night, updating searchable catalogues of information. Search directories and indexes use search engines.

HotBot

http://www.hotbot.com/

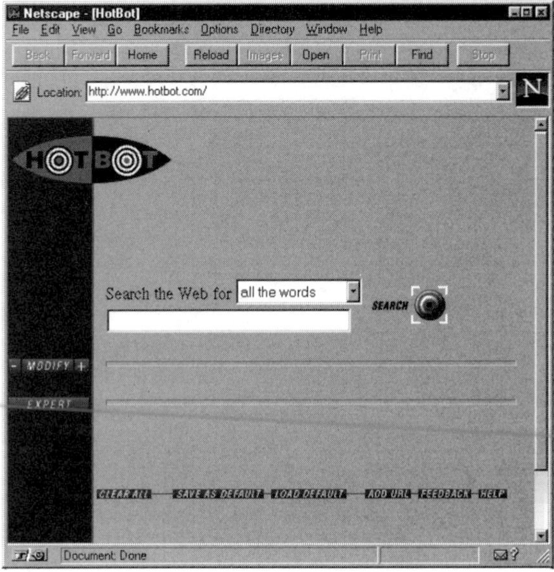

Figure 17.11 HotBot

HotBot (Figure 17.11) combines the latest search engine technology with a customizable interface. The user selects an area to search (newsgroups, the Web, Gopher) and then narrows the search with one or more parameters, such as keyword, date, geographic location, and Internet domain or file type. Even better, HotBot saves the search parameters and results for the user to retrieve at a later time. HotBot is the result of a union between HotWired Ventures LLC (a subsidiary of Wired) and Inktomi Corp.

InfoSeek

http://guide.infoseek.com/

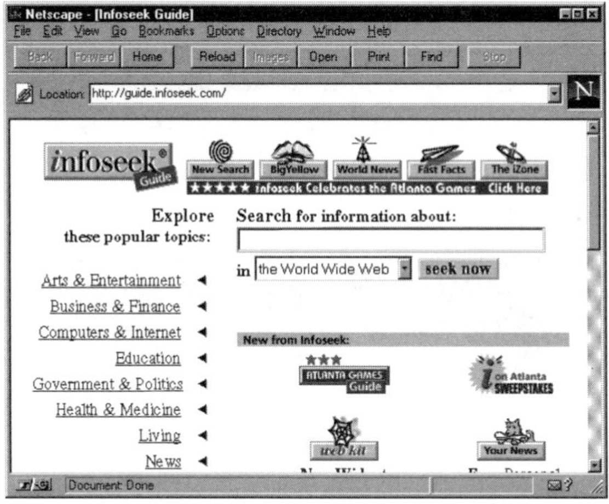

Figure 17.12 InfoSeek Search Index

InfoSeek (Figure 17.12) lets you specify a variety of search areas including the Web, Usenet, a directory of company names, recent news stories, and Web FAQs. You can also search for e-mail addresses. InfoSeek is fast, easy to use, and limits you to no more than 100 hits. Results are grouped by relevance with each listed site containing a link to similar types of pages. InfoSeek's Usenet results are particularly helpful because InfoSeek provides a link to the newsgroup as well as to the individual posting. Articles posted in multiple newsgroups are listed only once with links to all the source groups. For more hits as well as access to the exclusive InfoSeek database, you'll need to register for the fee-based InfoSeek Professional service.

Inktomi

http://inktomi.cs.berkeley.edu/

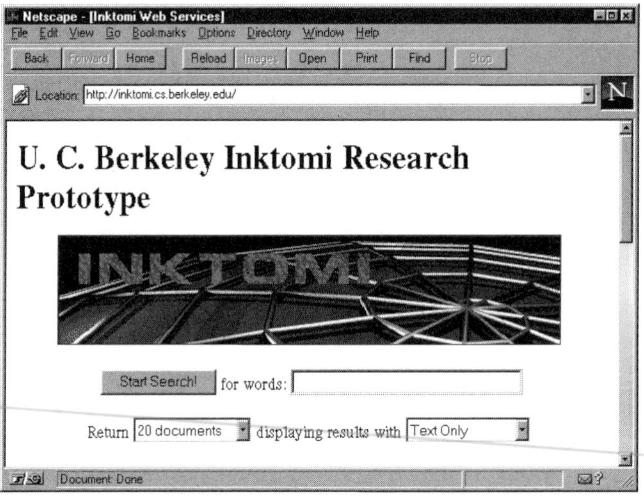

Figure 17.13 Inktomi Search Index

Inktomi (Figure 17.13) is named after a mythical spider of the Plains Indians. An experiment in cost-effective *hive* computing (networking a bunch of workstations together and sharing the workload between them), Inktomi is a prototype with a lot of promise. Inktomi's claims to fame are its hardware configuration, simple interface, and the breadth of its Web database. Results are ranked by keyword significance and hit count. You can specify the level of detail but your results will never include summaries or abstracts of the sites. Inktomi returns up to 100 hits with impressive speed. A full-featured commercial version may be up and running by the time this book is published.

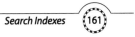

Lycos

http://www.lycos.com/

Figure 17.14 Lycos Search Index

Lycos (Figure 17.14) is one of the oldest and strongest search engines. It indexes the Web, FTP archives, Gopherspace, and also includes binary files such as JPEG and GIF graphics, .wav sound files, and video files. Sizewise, Lycos isn't the biggest search database anymore. But it still provides effective keyword searches and ranks the results in order of relevance. It also indicates how many terms in your search expression were successfully matched and lets you customize your matching threshold (two to seven matches). Even though Lycos doesn't index stopwords, it tells you which stopwords were ignored when the search was executed. Lycos also runs the A2Z directory and the Point rating service.

Opentext

http://www.opentext.com/

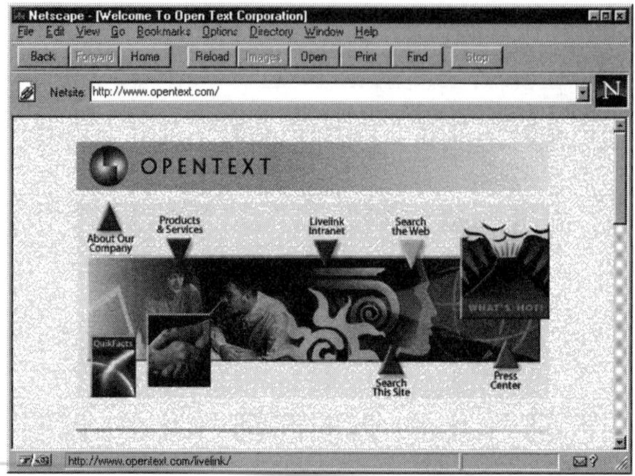

Figure 17.15 Open Text Search Index

Open Text (Figure 17.15) indexes every word on every Web page it finds. (Most other search engines drop the stopwords such as *and*, *the*, *at*, *it*, and *of*.) It's simple to refine a search using Open Text. Pop-up menus let you specify the part of the document you want to search—page summary, title, first heading, URL, hyperlink, or anywhere on the page. The results of your search are scored, with the highest score (the most keyword matches) topping the list.

WebCrawler

http://www.webcrawler.com/

Figure 17.16 WebCrawler Search Index

Owned by AOL, WebCrawler (Figure 17.16) was born in early 1995. Its layout is clear and uncomplicated and caters to newbies. The online help is especially interesting and useful. WebCrawler indexes only Web documents. The scored results of your search can be displayed as titles or they can include page summaries and URLs. Searches are limited to 100 hits. WebCrawler also keeps a running list of the twenty-five most popular sites (according to the number of hits it registers) and is associated with the WebCrawler Select directory.

Using Metasearch Sites

Instead of attaching yourself to one or two search sites, you might consider visiting a one-page-does-it-all site. There are a number of *metasearch sites*, each with its own limitations and strengths. At the time of this writing, the best of the bunch appears to be MetaCrawler, **http://metacrawler.cs.washington.edu:8080/index.html**.

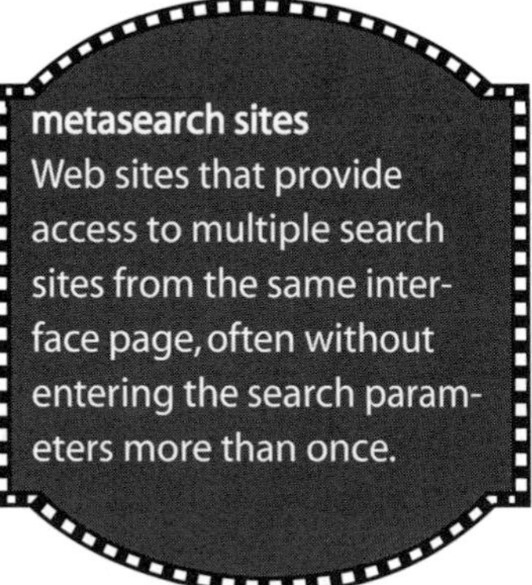

metasearch sites
Web sites that provide access to multiple search sites from the same interface page, often without entering the search parameters more than once.

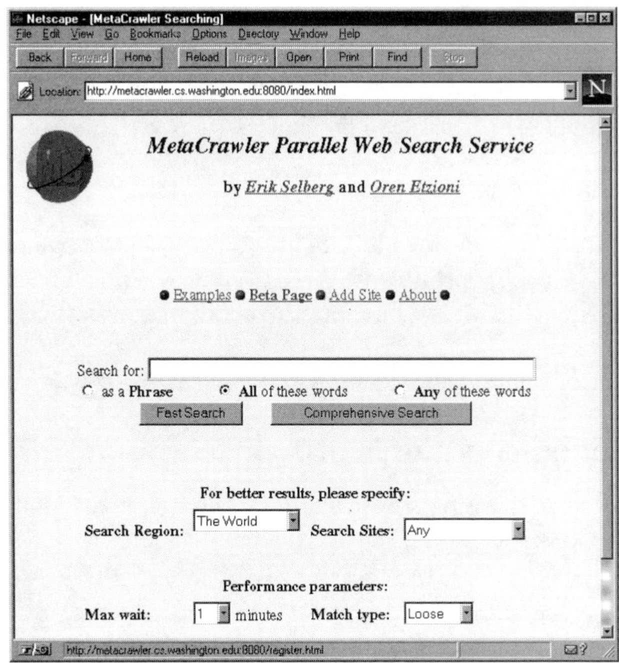

Figure 17.17 MetaCrawler

MetaCrawler (Figure 17.17) provides the most useful results with the least redundancy. It requires only one search entry, which is then fed to a variety of search sites, including Inktomi, InfoSeek Guide, and Lycos. MetaCrawler also eliminates invalid and outdated URLs.

Searches are easily customized in MetaCrawler. You can narrow the parameters with simple operators: 1) "+" before the term means that the word must be included in the document text, 2) "–" means that a word must not be included, and 3) "()" indicate phrases and word combinations. MetaCrawler also lets you specify geographic area, domain, and wait time.

Check Yahoo's All-in-One search pages hierarchy for more metasearch sites. Here are a few:

- Allinone Search Page: **http://www.albany.net**
- EZ-Find: **http://www.theriver.com/**
- Find-It: **http://www.itools.com/**
- The Internet Sleuth: **http://www.isleuth.com/**
- LinkSearch: **http://where.com/ls/LinkSearch.html**
- SavvySearch: **http://www.cs.colostate.edu/~dreiling/smartform.html**
- Starting Point: **http://www.stpt.com**
- Web Search Simple Search: **http://www.web-search.com**

Quick-Reference Searching List

Want to find something fast? Check the following topic areas:

To Find a Company

Using any search engine, type the name of the company between the "**http://www.**" and the "**.com**". This is a commonly accepted way to create a domain name. Most companies or products with domains will use the **http://www.companyname.com** syntax.

Use the InterNIC Whois database, **http://www.internic.net/wp/whois.html**.

To Find Information about Animals

Petscape Online: **http://www.petscape.com**. A resource about all kinds of pets, including a comprehensive link list. Watch out for the graphics on the opening pages. They're pretty, but they're big.

To Learn about Copyright

The Copyright Page: **http://www.benedict.com/**. Details, case histories, and facts about copyright. Forms for registering copyrights via the Web.

To Find an E-mail Address

InfoSeek: **http://guide.infoseek.com/**.

Netscape People Search: **http://home.netscape.com/home/internet-white-pages.html**.

To Find Legal Information

Legal Information Institute: **http://www.law.cornell.edu/lii.table.html**. "Integrates both the Gopher-based and the WWW-based offerings of the Legal Information Institute (LII), Cornell Law School. Includes links to other relevant legal materials on the LII's Gopher server and elsewhere on the Internet."

To Find a Zip Code

USPS: **http://www.usps.gov/ncsc/**. Where else but the United States Postal Service site?

To Find a FAQ

Visit Oxford University and use their FAQ search engine, **http://www.lib.ox.ac.uk/search/search_faqs.html**.

To Find a Cartoon or Print Comic

United Media: **http://www.unitedmedia.com/**. This is home to a comprehensive collection of contemporary comic art.

To Find an Index of Indexes for Locating Things

Scoop Cybersleuth's Internet Guide: **http://www.evansville.net/courier/scoop/**. Cybersleuth lists government offices, political information, demographic data, news, and every other kind of information.

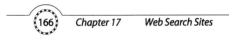

To Find a List of Specialty Directories

Promophobia: **http://www.interbiznet.com/ibn/specialdirs.html**. A list of directories and indexes specializing in topics such as gardening, travel, skiing, and more. This list isn't comprehensive, but it's a good place to start.

To Find Information or Support Relating to a Medical Condition or Disability

The Ability Website: **http://www.ability.org.uk/azindex.html**. An A to Z list of Web sites, indexes, and newsgroups specializing in a variety of medical conditions.

To Find a Federal Government Resource

Federal Web Locator: **http://www.law.vill.edu/Fed-Agency/fedwebloc.html**.

To Find Out How Your Senators and Representatives Voted

http://pathfinder.com/cgi-bin/congress-votes. Enter your zip code and check your reps voting record. Part of Time Magazine on the Web.

Electronic Interviews

Most interviews are conducted over the phone or in person. With the advent of the electronic age, however, interviews can be conducted via e-mail or in text-based conferences known as chats. (Videoconferencing is technically possible, but the cost and logistics are still prohibitive.)

E-mail Interviews

E-mail is the easiest electronic interview to conduct because it allows you to prepare your questions in advance and e-mail them at your leisure. In turn, the recipient has time to craft responses that are well thought out and, hopefully, clearly written. E-mail interviews don't demand synchronous schedules, they save money on long-distance phone calls (which can make a big difference when expenses aren't paid), and they make it especially easy to quote your subject accurately.

E-mail interviews work best when questions are specific and you know what you want. Time shouldn't be a big concern, although you should always let interviewees know how long they have to respond. After receiving the e-mail response, you may need to continue the interview by clarifying information and if necessary, asking more questions. Freelance writer Michele Picozzi finds that e-mail interviews work well when she writes 1200- to 1800-word pieces for trade publications. She says, "E-mail interviews are great timesavers. The success of an e-mail interview depends on how focused the writer is in asking the necessary questions, and the willingness of the subject to answer in a written and somewhat anonymous format."

Picozzi conducts a "pre-e-mail interview," where she includes a general idea about the questions she'll ask and makes sure that the e-mail format is acceptable to the potential interviewee. She notes, "If I get a positive response, I'll e-mail about six to eight main questions, sometimes less if I know they require lengthy replies. I think it's important not to bombard the subject and to let the person know when you need a response. Sometimes I follow up with a phone call."

E-mail interviews aren't always appropriate. If the interview material is too comprehensive, e-mail can be taxing. Asking more than ten questions makes the interview resemble an essay exam—not good. If your article is supposed to showcase the personality of your subject, e-mail may be limiting. Most important, your subject must work well with the interview format. (Some people don't like to type, or feel that e-mail contact is too constrained.)

Conducting an E-mail Interview

Conducting an e-mail interview requires the same attention to detail and research as any other form of interview. Just because you can do it in your birthday suit doesn't mean you shouldn't be a professional. The basics are the same as for other types of interviews: 1) prepare intelligent, thoughtful questions that will elicit the kind of information you're looking for, 2) deliver the questions in a respectful manner and a logical sequence, 3) keep an accurate record of the proceedings, and 4) thank the interviewee for his or her time. Beyond these basics, however, there are a few extra considerations to keep in mind when it comes to e-mail:

1. Do your homework. Make sure the individual you'll be contacting is a thoughtful choice. Internet writer Wendy Chatley Green of the **misc.writing** newsgroup states, "I ignore any e-mail interviews that are sent scatter-shot across the Net or are obviously someone's desperate attempt to duck work. Asking questions of strangers is not a substitute for research."

2. Always ask permission to conduct the interview before sending it. In your query, summarize what you'll be asking and if appropriate, tell the individual why you've selected them as an interview subject. If the e-mail is a cold call, you should also briefly explain your background to help legitimize the intrusion. Note that e-mail provides limited layout options—no formatting or special characters. You won't see

italics, quotation marks, or other enhancements. I used the following e-mail interview query as I developed this book:

```
Dear Adam,
I'm writing a book, The Author's Guide to the Internet,
(Franklin, Beedle and Associates), which should be on the
bookshelves by fall of this year. I'm interviewing (via e-mail)
writers and editors about writing for an online audience,
finding paid employment using the Net, publishing on the Web,
using the Net for research and skill development, and so on.
Without question, your expert opinions would be of great
interest to me and my potential readership.
If you'd be willing to respond to my e-mail interview, I'll
credit you properly and ask permission to use direct quotes.
Thank you for your time and attention, Adam. Regardless of
your response, best wishes for your continued success.
Respectfully,
Dawn Groves
dawng@skycat.com
work: 333-444-5555
fax: 444-555-6666
```

3. Send the interview as part of the e-mail text—a simple ASCII text file. Don't generate the interview in Word for Windows and then include it as an attached file. An attachment formatted with a word processor or some other application assumes that the recipient is willing to jump through a few extra hoops to read, save, and return the interview. You're also assuming that the recipient's e-mail program will translate the attachment correctly (which is not always the case).

4. By including the interview as part of the e-mail message, you simplify the recipient's workload considerably. The subject opens the message, generates a reply message that includes your original text, and inserts answers into the reply. Then boom, it's sent back to you. No fuss, no muss.

5. Because the e-mail interview is ASCII text, you can't format it. But you should still take the time to structure the interview visually with enough white space and navigation aids to make it easy to read. And it goes without saying that typos should be corrected.

6. I used the following e-mail interview in doing the research for this book. You don't have to duplicate this exact style, but you can see that it's fairly easy to navigate despite the lack of formatting.

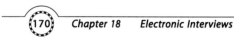

   Note: Check the Usenet Rules of Order in Chapter 5, to remind yourself of e-mail netiquette.

```
Dear Adam,
Thanks for being willing to respond to the following e-mail
interview.
These questions relate to my upcoming book, The Author's Guide
to the Internet, which will be published by Franklin, Beedle
and Associates, Inc.
Please feel free to elaborate on your response as much as you
like; your input is valuable and appreciated. I'll credit you
in my acknowledgments and if I quote your material directly,
I'll send you an e-mail requesting permission.
When you return this e-mail, please spell your name as you
would like it referenced in print. I would appreciate receiv-
ing the response within two weeks. If you have any questions,
feel free to call me at 333-444-5555.

=====INTERVIEW QUESTIONS=====

  1. How do you think writers can benefit from the Internet?
     Support? Skill improvement? Promotion? Publishing oppor-
     tunities? Please elaborate.
  2. Is there a difference in writing for the Web versus
     writing for print media? If so, what do you think the
     difference(s) is (are)?
  3. What do you dislike about online publications? What makes
     you want to click away from them?
  4. How do you feel about e-mail interviews?
  5. Do you have any favorite sites that epitomize good Web
     writing style?
  6. Is there anything else you'd like to add? Comments about
     your genre? Gripes? Rude noises? Additional references?
=============================
```

```
Thank you, Adam, for your time and trouble. If you know of
other online writers who'd have interesting opinions about any
of the above issues, please tell me and I'll contact them
directly.
Looking forward to your responses.
Cordially,
Dawn Groves
dawng@skycat.com
333-444-5555 (work)
333-555-6666 (fax)
```

Make the interview as easy on the recipient as possible, because e-mail interviews require more work from the interviewees than other types of interviews. It helps to keep questions short and clear. Don't ask more than ten questions (and that's pushing the envelope). If you reference material that the recipient has written or said, be sure to cite its source. Try to anticipate any questions the recipient might have, and answer them before they're asked.

5. Once you complete your project, e-mail the interviewee an update note. If appropriate, explain where the piece is available. This isn't a requirement, but it's a thoughtful gesture and generates goodwill.

Interview Structure

A good basic structure for a formal ASCII text e-mail interview is as follows:

1. Greeting.
2. Brief reminder of what the interview is for.
3. Brief instructions, including how and when to respond, and how to contact you. Be sure to include a phone number and possibly a street address to formalize the interaction.
4. ASCII line marking the start of the interview: `======`.
5. Numbered questions forming the body of the interview.
6. ASCII line marking the end of the interview: `======`.
7. Closing.

Keep in mind that your interview doesn't need to be this structured. If you only ask a couple of questions and you've established a good rapport with the interviewee, there's plenty of room for a more casual approach. I've been interviewed in a casual style by many individuals and have never had any trouble with it. But if the interview is longer or is being widely distributed, it's often easier to structure it clearly. You can then send the same e-mail to any number of individuals—easily deleting or adding questions as appropriate.

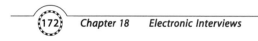

Chat Interviews

Chats are online conversations conducted in real time. They require your subjects not only to think on their feet, but also to type immediately what they're thinking. Chat sessions have developed a certain notoriety because of their associations with anonymous online erotic encounters and relationship "chat rooms." In fact, chats are similar to the notes you sent back and forth in junior high school, except that instead of slipping handwritten messages to your geometry buddy, you're typing those messages into a chat window and sending them to your buddy sitting in front of the computer in a distant city. Because chats are real-time conversations, they can be a lot of fun and often give you a good feel for the personality of the individual you're interviewing. The immediacy of chat preserves some of the spontaneity lost in e-mail, but the lag time between what you type and what the respondent types can be distracting. Lag time increases if your connection is slow or one of you doesn't type quickly. For this reason, chat interviews are best conducted with interviewees who have had chats before and feel comfortable with the format.

Like e-mail interviews, chats can generate a written transcript of everything that transpires. But because spelling and punctuation take a back seat to getting the text on the screen and sent, editing will always be necessary. Logistically, chats are more challenging than e-mail interviews because they must be prearranged so that both parties will be online at the same time and electronically connected to the same chat area. Oftentimes, taped phone calls are more practical and easier to arrange.

Commercial online service providers advertise moderated chats featuring celebrities, authors, pundits, or any expert du jour. These online talk shows are much more complicated than a simple two-person chat connection because more than one person can participate in the interview (sometimes hundreds of people will be tuned in), necessitating online moderators and traffic managers. (Let's talk stress.) Chances are, you won't be conducting moderated chats unless you specifically volunteer to do so.

Conducting a Chat Interview

It's easy to conduct an interview using an online service such as America Online (AOL) or Prodigy, provided you're both subscribers. For example, in AOL, you enter the People Connection area, name a private room, and then let your interviewee (and whoever else you want) know the private room name and the scheduled meeting time. Show up a little early to enter your private room and when your attendees enter the People Connection, they need only type the name of the private room in order to enter it. Participants—especially you—should be sure to choose Logging from the File menu to generate a complete transcript of the meeting. Prodigy, Microsoft Network (MSN), and CompuServe have their own chat structures, but the functions are similar.

If you're monitoring questions from visitors as you conduct the interview, open a second chat room for visitors only. It's a good idea to assign one or two individuals to help you monitor questions. The interview itself should be conducted in a room without access to visitors. This way you can manage the flow of questions to the interviewee.

Chat conducted on the Internet is known as Internet Relay Chat (IRC). It is a little more complex because it requires specialized software and a familiarity with the IRC command structure. In most cases, your potential interviewees won't be prepared to do an IRC interview. More likely they'll be connected to a commercial provider. To explore the possibilities of IRC, visit the mIRC home page, **http://www.mirc.co.uk**.

Chat Structure

Because a chat is really just a typed conversation, prepare your typed questions ahead of time so you can simply cut and paste them into the chat text box. This helps minimize typos and makes conversing much easier on the wrists. If you're unfamiliar with chats, practice with a friend before going live. You may also need to offer a little pre-chat practice time to the interviewee if the interview is open to the public. If you are managing visitor questions, refer visitors to a page containing simplified rules. Direct visitors to a chat room separate from the actual interview.

A good basic structure for a typical chat interview is as follows:

1. Greeting (to both the interviewee and the visitors if the chat is public).

2. Brief introduction if the chat is public.

3. Begin the chat by cutting and pasting prepared questions into the chat text box. If possible, refrain from interrupting the interviewee in the middle of a thought.

4. If the chat is public, periodically break the interview to interject questions from the audience. Allow only one or two questions at a time before you return to the scripted interview. This offers a smooth balance between visitor questions and the issues you especially want to cover.

5. End the chat with thanks and an offer to e-mail or make available to your guest the logged copy of the conversation. Chat interviews shouldn't be longer than one hour (the shorter the better) because they demand such intense concentration.

6. Send an e-mail message later in the day, once again thanking the interviewee for participating in the chat.

Income and Copyright

There are plenty of ways to make money with your writing, but the Internet isn't likely to be your primary conduit—not this year anyway. Concerns about copyright, value of work, and quality assurance are currently dampening the income-drawing potential of electronically published works. That being said, there's a great deal of interest in finding ways to earn income from online sites. Until recently, advertising has been the main form of income for most electronic sites. Fortunately, other forms of income are quickly developing for writers:

- The new tracking and royalty distribution systems will make an enormous difference to writers who self-publish electronically.
- Digital payment systems are becoming easier to use, more reliable, and more secure.
- Web advertising is on the rise due to better tracking and customer database software.

Making Money

At present, few online publications pay much for freelance copy. It's a buyer's market and e-zines usually have plenty of staff writers to fill their literary coffers. Hard copy magazines often electronically redistribute articles with little or no compensation to the writer. Lower-end and specialty e-zines sometimes pay small amounts, but more likely you'll be paid in exposure and gratitude.

Fortunately, this trend is changing. Professional writers' organizations are exerting considerable pressure on publishing houses to pay for hard copy work redistributed in cyberspace. (See Protecting Copyright later in this chapter.) High-end electronic journals such as Slate (Figure 19.1) are setting new standards by valuing the electronic media and paying for quality writing.

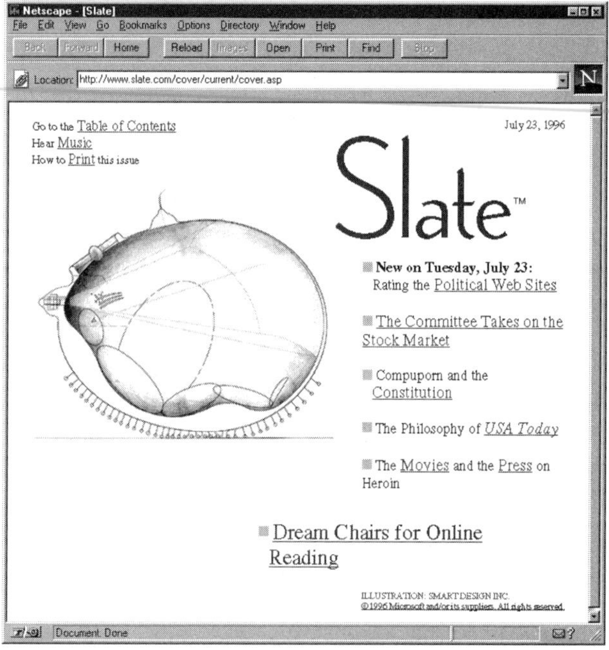

Figure 19.1 Slate Electronic Journal

Even if you don't get paid for publishing your work online, you'll quickly discover that the Internet is a great resource for networking with potential clients and finding writing assignments of all kinds. Professional positions are advertised in a variety of subscriber newsletters. Many writers, myself included, have received lucrative opportunities via Internet connections and registries. The trick is to establish an Internet presence (usually with a Web site and/or contributions to other sites), to stay sharp regarding online writer's markets and industry news (usually by visiting or subscribing to an industry newsletter site), and to use the Internet on a regular basis.

For a brief rundown on the paying markets, check the Market Information Page at **http://www.inkspot.com/~ohi/inkspot/marketinfo.html**. If you're a published freelancer, check the classifieds at Editor & Publisher Magazine, **http://www.mediainfo.com/ephome/class/classhtm/class.htm**. Some of the top newspaper home pages are listed at The Career Path Web site, **http://www.careerpath.com/info.html**. And last but not least, visit Scrivenery Magazine for writer-related support, ideas, training, and updates, **http://www.lit-arts.com/scriven/scriven.htm**.

To find general career advice and job databases, visit CareerMosaic, **http://www.careermosaic.com:80/**, a fine site run by one of the largest recruitment advertising and human resources communications agencies in the world. Also drop by The Monster Board, **http://www.monster.com/home.html**, and The Internet Career Connection, **http://iccweb.com**.

Royalties and Micropayments

The Association of Journalists and Authors (ASJA), the National Writers Union (NWU), the Authors Guild of America (AGA), and virtually every other writers organization in the United States are all struggling to define what worth should be credited to electronic distribution of copyrighted works. Equally complex are issues surrounding the distribution of electronic royalties.

Fortunately, the mechanics are now in place to ease the burden of tracking and dispensing potentially repeated payments of very small sums, thanks to two nonprofit organizations. These organizations are designed to serve writers and publishers in the same manner as the American Society of Composers and Publishers (ASCAP) serves the music industry.

Publications Rights Clearinghouse

Formed in early 1996, the Publications Rights Clearinghouse (PRC) (Figure 19.2) is essentially a new division of the NWU. The NWU represents nearly 4500 writers in all genres. Dedicated to collecting and distributing royalties for uses of some subsidiary rights (such as electronic use of freelance articles), PRC hopes to create a copyright model for the electronic database industry.

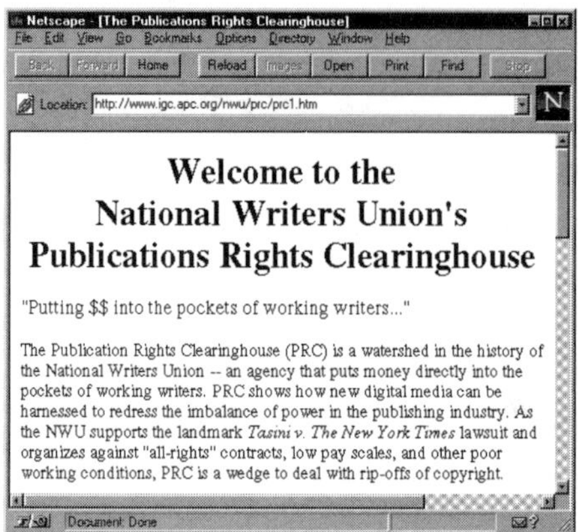

Figure 19.2 The Publications Rights Clearinghouse

PRC distributes works via the UnCover Company, which deems itself "the largest magazine and journal article database in the world." Writers can participate in PRC for a fee of $20. For more information on enrollment in the PRC, visit the PRC Web site at **http://www.igc.apc.org/nwu/prc/prc1.htm**. Contact Irvin Muchnick, NWU, 337 17th St., Suite 101, Oakland, CA 94612; phone: (510) 839-0110; fax: (510) 839-6097; e-mail: **irv@nwu.org**.

The Authors Registry

Formed in 1995, the Authors Registry (Figure 19.3) is not associated with a specific organization. Instead, it is a broadly based agency endorsed by numerous writers organizations and literary agencies representing more than 50,000 authors.

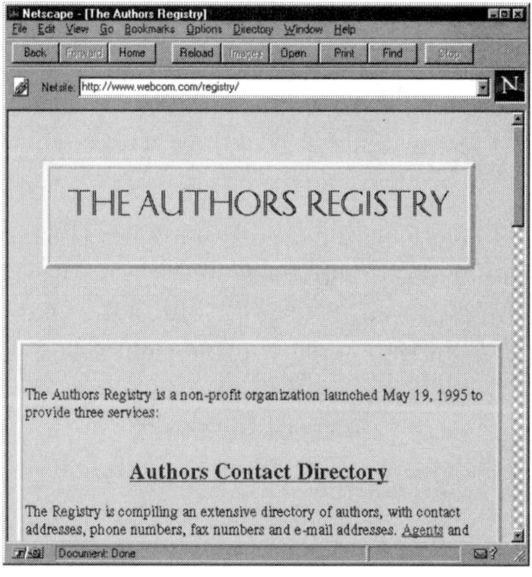

Figure 19.3 The Authors Registry Web Site

Its Web site says: "The Registry plans to collect money from publishers, database producers and reprint services and distribute the funds to authors whose works are being used. Registry representatives are in active discussions with periodical publishers as well as several of the larger article resellers. We hope to begin collecting and distributing moneys in the near future. Payment methods and any administrative expenses will be determined in these and subsequent discussions."

Members and clients of the writers groups and literary agencies that have signed on to the Authors Registry are eligible to enroll without charge. Unaffiliated writers may join as individuals for $10. For more information, contact the Authors Registry at (212) 563-6920, send e-mail to **registry@interport.net**, or visit their Web site at **http://www.webcom.com/registry/**.

Regardless of how royalties are distributed, they'll likely be garnered via online *micropayments*. The site or registry typically takes a cut of the transaction payment and after expenses are covered, the writer is paid. If enough transactions occur, the micropayments add up.

Few micropayment systems are currently in place because it's still unclear how Web audiences will react to them. To see a pay-per-download site in action, visit Mind's Eye Fiction, **http://tale.com/** (Figure 19.4). Mind's Eye publishes hypertext fiction with a money-back guarantee. Visitors can choose from three different micropayment systems.

micropayment
Tiny fees, often under $1.00, charged to a credit card or a site-specific subscription account. Micropayments are especially interesting to writers and artists whose works are downloaded countless times. Each download constitutes a transaction secured via some form of electronic debit system.

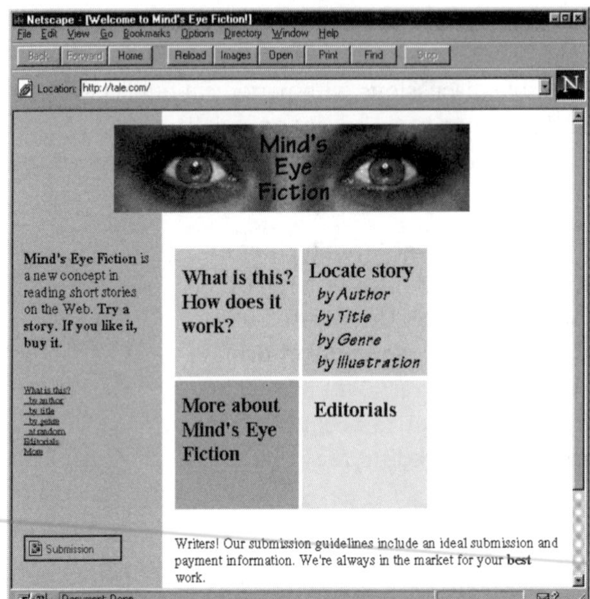

Figure 19.4 Mind's Eye Fiction

Advertising and Sponsorships

Industry pundits claim that in three years the Web will be a market worth five billion dollars. Advertisers are lining up to mine the riches of cyberspace, but until recently technology hasn't been in place to prove that their dollars are actually tapping into the mother lode. (See Database Development later in this chapter).

On the Web, the terms *advertising* and *sponsoring* are often used interchangeably. An advertiser pays a fee for a strategically placed banner ad containing a brief, action-oriented message and a link to the advertiser's home page. Online advertising fees are calculated in a manner similar to print and television ads; that is, monthly fees are determined per thousand "impressions" (visits to the page containing the ad). If you're a site such as ESPNET SportZone, which garners over 370,000 visits a day, these revenues add up quickly.

Sadly, most writers won't create Web sites that can match the visitor count of ESPNET SportZone. And the database technology that attracts advertisers also requires technical expertise to implement and maintain. (Unless you have a knack for programming, you'll need a lot of advice. Check the HTML Writers Guild Web site at **http://guild.infovav.se/**.) The bottom line is if you can find a company to sponsor your Web site, consider it a coup. You may not get rich but at least you'll get some expenses covered.

Smaller sites often use an older form of grass-roots advertising: reciprocal links. If you include their URLs on your Web site, they'll return the favor. This system hangs over from the Internet's early years when users freely shared information without financial overtones. The problem is that unless you're a resource hub, a long list of URLs may make you appear indiscriminate. Like too many words, too many URLs can sometimes weaken your presentation.

Database Development

Database software is coming of age for online businesses. Here's a hot topic that's on the upswing. In the Web's youth, gathering information was a slow, cumbersome process viewed with outright hostility. Web travelers balked at online forms asking for personal information such as name, age, computer platform, and e-mail address. Today, users are less suspicious because commercial sites and registration forms have become commonplace. Netizens seem willing to log into regularly visited sites (Figure 19.5) and fill in requisite forms, provided they receive value such as a customized presentation or an opportunity to win a prize. The gathered information can then be used to target potential advertisers.

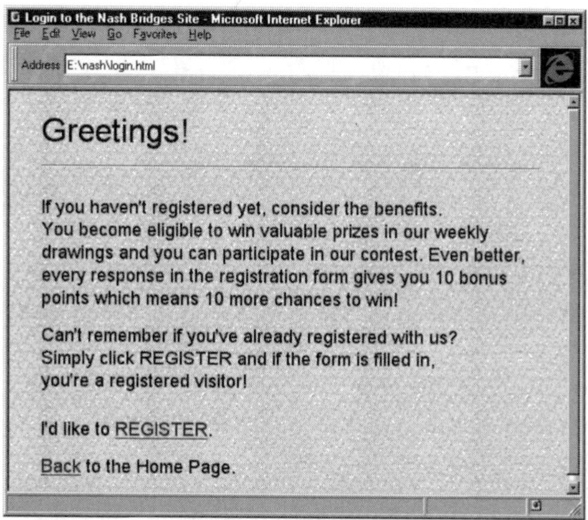

Figure 19.5 Database Log-in Form

Purists may blanch, but the fact is, storing information about visitors (i.e., customers) is a hot button to potential sponsors. Visitor data also helps Web developers craft sites that respond to the needs and preferences of the users. In the spirit of fair play, most sites ask permission to sell your name to other companies. If you check no, your name supposedly stays where it is.

Databases require technical expertise. If you're already computer savvy and you want to play with databases, research the topic "database" at a site such as webreference.com, **http://webreference.com/html/validation.html** or Yahoo. If you're not technical, talk to your service provider about database implementation and management costs. (A warning: it won't be cheap.)

Subscription Fees

Free for now, some e-zines are banking on eventual subscription fees. But don't look for dollar signs. To date, subscription fees are unwelcome on the Internet. Except in rare circumstances, no one charges for registration or subscription. Even high-end e-zines don't charge for subscriptions, though they plan on doing so in the future. These fees would probably be handled as credit card charges. If and when they do start charging, you can bet that they'll deliver substantial bang for the buck, much more than what you might be able to provide as a single individual.

To learn more about online commerce as it affects writers, read the NWU paper "Digital Cash and Other Online Payment Systems for Writers," **http://www.igc.apc.org/nwu/docs/e-money.htm**.

Protecting Copyright

Copyright law dictates that writers are entitled to payment when their works are reused, unless they turn those rights over to a publisher. Until the Internet came along, copyright issues remained fairly consistent and predictable, with many court cases backing up decisions and standards. But electronic publishing and distribution have generated a frenzy of activity in writers' organizations and publishing conglomerates as everyone attempts to determine the value and scope of electronic copyright protection. Publishers strive to combine new technology with traditional first publication and reprint rights; writers struggle to define the dollar value of new technology rights if indeed they are to be given up.

The problem of value extends to the number of changes deemed necessary in order for a written work to be redistributed over an electronic medium. If the piece remains unchanged except for the means of distribution, rightfully the author should receive more money than if the piece requires substantial revision. The NWU has stated that publishers who accept submissions for online publication without making editorial changes are actually functioning as distributors. Lower production costs for distribution mean that writers should receive 50 percent of the proceeds from these projects. Currently, most writers receive little to no payment at all.

The NWU, the ASJA, the Authors Guild, and the Society of Professional Journalists (SPJ) all champion appropriate compensation for new technology rights. For example, the SPJ's 1995 convention supported a resolution that "condemns efforts to deny freelancers the legitimate secondary rights to their work and commits itself to closely monitor proposed guidelines for the National Information Infrastructure as it pertains to freelance journalists and copyright protection in cyberspace and keep members informed of developments."

In the United States, copyright protection is secured for an original work as soon as the work is fixed in a tangible form. This tangible form could be paper, tape, disk, or any form that can be copied and distributed. Because everything on the Internet is on disk at one time or another, roughly speaking, you can consider most everything on the Internet copyright protected. The exceptions would be titles, names, short phrases, slogans, ideas, facts, blank forms, familiar symbols, variations in typography, color of lettering, lists of ingredients, and works consisting entirely of information that is common property and contains no original authorship.

The length of copyright is as follows (from the Copyright Website):

Pre 1978 (published):

The copyright expires seventy-five years from the date of publication (if the copyright was renewed).

Pre 1978 (created, but not published):

The copyright will expire on December 31, 2002.

1978 to present (copyright owned by an individual):

The copyright will last for the life of the author, plus an additional fifty years.

1978 to present (copyright owned by employer or author):

The copyright will last 75 years from the date of publication, or 100 years from the date of creation, whichever occurs first.

A work is protected by copyright when it is fixed in tangible form. For example, when a song is recorded, it is fixed; when a dance is videotaped or a Web page is saved, it is fixed. Broad categories subject to copyright protection include literary works (also software); musical and dramatic works; pantomime and choreography; pictorial, graphic, and sculptural works; audiovisual and sound recordings; and architectural works.

As you publish your works online, keep in mind the following copyright guidelines:

1. Include a copyright notification on the page. (For works first published after March 1, 1989, it isn't necessary to display the copyright symbol © in order to secure copyright, but most writers are encouraged to do so regardless.)

2. The copyright notice should be placed at the bottom of the page in a small, easily readable font. It should include as a minimum, the name of the copyright holder, the year, and the phrase "All Rights Reserved." (If your copyright statement is more complex, you may want to include a copyright link at the bottom of the page with the copyright information placed on its own Web page.) Always include an e-mail link in case someone wants permission to reference or use materials on your site.

The following two examples are both adequate (underlined text indicates a link):

Copyright © Col. G. P. Groves, U. S. M. C. Ret., 1996. All Rights Reserved.

Copyright © Holly Barrett, 1996. All Rights Reserved. All materials contained in this Web site are protected by copyright and shall not be used for any purpose whatsoever other than private, noncommercial viewing purposes. No part of this site may be reproduced in any manner without written permission from Holly Barrett.

3. Legally, copyright notification must include the word copyright or the © symbol. On Web pages, it's a good idea to include both because not all browsers can read the HTML tag that inserts a copyright symbol into the document.

4. If the work is especially unique or important, consider formally registering it with the Copyright Office. This establishes a public record of your copyright, which you can then use in legal claims and lawsuits. To register, send $20 (per application) along with a nonreturnable copy of the work and a completed application form to the Registrar of Copyrights, Copyright Office, Library of Congress, Washington, D.C. 20559.

   If you have questions about copyright protection, visit the Copyright Website, **http://www.benedict.com/** (Figure 19.6). It is an excellent resource for the basics of copyright as they relate to online works. It also explains how to fill in copyright registration forms. Also read "Copyright Registration for Freelance Writers: Why and How to Register Your Articles," available at ASJA's Web site, **http://www.asja.org/cwpage.htm**.

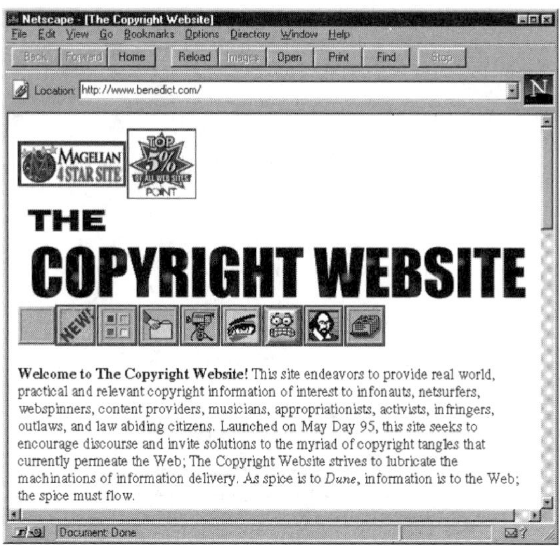

Figure 19.6 The Copyright Website

For further information about copyright issues, subscribe to the ASJA Contracts Watch Newsletter. This newsletter is periodically mailed to inform subscribers of important changes to writers' contracts and landmark legal cases that define the arena. To subscribe, e-mail **asja-manamger@silverquick.com** with **join asjacw-list** written in the body of the message (no subject line is necessary). Electronic publishing concerns will no doubt require major revision of the current copyright law. But until that time, writers and publishers must try to get by, attempting to fit the square peg of copyright law into the wide open circle of new technology.

Writers' Resources Online

Most writers look for specifics about their chosen genre, be it romance, technical writing, mystery, poetry, or horror and science fiction. The following list contains genre Web sites and newsgroups as well as sites of general interest to writers. There are many more sites than those listed below. Consider checking one of the major writers reference index sites, such as the WWW Virtual Library Writers Resources, **http://www.interlog.com/~ohi/www/writesource.html**. Or visit Yahoo's literature genre category with links to all the genre groups, **http://www.yahoo.com/Arts/Humanities/Literature/Genres**.

If this feels like too much information, read "Taking it Step by Step" in Chapter 3.

General Support for Writers

There are many excellent sites that support professional as well as novice writers. The following list is only a sample of what's available.

Web Sites

Infinite Ink

http://www.jazzie.com/ii/

Useful writers' references and examples.

The Inkspot

http://www.inkspot.com/~ohi/inkspot/

One of the most popular and useful writer sites on the Web. Well organized and maintained, it has links and guidance on just about any topic related to the writer's craft. This is a site worth marking. Home of Inklings newsletter.

Midwest Book Review

http://www.execpc.com/~mbr/bookwatch/mrb/

An excellent, comprehensive site for writers and booklovers alike. Everything from resource to genre updates to reviews to Web page advice.

The misc.writing Web Site

http://vanbc.wimsey.com/~sdkwok/mwrit.html

Writing-related links and references to the misc.writing newsgroup. The misc.writing and freelance FAQs are especially useful to new writers.

Papyrus

http://www.readersndex.com/papyrus/

From the site: "A quarterly magazine that features craft-oriented columns on writing that are inspirational, practical and easy for the beginning writer. In addition, we provide a marketplace column where writers will find specific guidelines for submitting to other publishers, along with a news and notes column for information on black writers and their works and activities."

Scrivenery: A Writer's Journal

http://www.lit-arts.com/scriven/scriven.htm

An excellent e-zine with helpful articles, skill builders, and lifestyle and market information.

The Writers Edge

http://www.nashville.net/~edge/

Excellent resource list for all genres. Lists of agents, writers, conferences, and contests. Marketing information, newsgroups, guidelines, groups, workshops, and much more.

The WritePage

http://www.writepage.com/

Newsletter for readers and writers of genre fiction: science fiction, romance novels, historical novels, murder mysteries, techno-thrillers, weird tales, and more.

Mailing Lists and Newsgroups

Inklings

Inklings is a free electronic newsletter for writers published every two to three weeks. It includes new resources for writers on the net, market information, writers' tips, interviews, and useful articles. To subscribe, send e-mail to **majordomo@samurai.com** with **subscribe inklings** (nothing else) in the message body.

misc.writing

A newsgroup that provides a forum for discussion of writing in all its forms—scholarly, technical, journalistic, artistic, and day-to-day communication.

rec.arts.books

A newsgroup for writers and book-lovers. Includes discussions about various books, questions about book genres, announcements of new electronic bookstores, and other book-oriented news.

rec.arts.prose, alt.prose

Both newsgroups cater to original fiction and nonfiction composition. Writers can post their works, soliciting critique and discussion from newsgroup participants.

Standards and Practices

Electronic style guidelines are still evolving. The following sites will give you good, clear advice.

Web Sites

The American Society of Indexers

http://www.well.com/user/asi/

Excellent reference lists and articles about indexing, reference sites, and much more. Includes membership information and—no surprise—a thorough index of the site.

The CopyEditing Style FAQ

http://www.rt66.com/~telp/sfindex.htm

Style and usage Q/A culled from the copyediting-l mailing list. Lots of good advice.

The Editorial Eye

http://www.eei-alex.com/eye/

A newsletter that includes a variety of useful articles on writing style, untangling Web jargon, copyediting practices, and more.

Electronic Style: A Guide to Citing Electronic Information

http://www.uvm.edu/~xli/reference/estyles.html

A popular reference on college campuses that includes styles for the APA and MLA. Written by Xia Li and Nancy Crane.

The Elements of E-Text Style

http://wiretap.spies.com/ftp.items/Library/Classic/estyle.txt

The Elements of Style for electronic text. A must-read site.

MLA-Style Citations of Electronic Sources

http://www.cas.usf.edu/english/walker/mla.html

Janice Walker's style guidelines for citing electronic information sources. Endorsed by the Alliance for Computers and Writing.

Style Guide for Online Hypertext

http://www.w3.org/hypertext/WWW/Provider/Style/

Tim Berners-Lee (father of the Web) discusses hypertext style.

Yale Center for Advanced Instructional Media Style Guide

http://info.med.yale.edu/caim/StyleManual_Top.html

An example of Yale's comprehensive style guide for online communications.

Mailing Lists and Newsgroups

alt.usage.english

bit.listserv.words-l

copyediting-l

misc.education.language.english

Writers' Associations

Most writers' associations are establishing a strong presence on the Web. Their sites typically provide requisite membership information, but many also include comprehensive links and market information.

Web Sites

The Alliance for Computers and Writing

http://english.ttu.edu/acw/

An association of teachers and researchers interested in using computer technologies and networks to improve their classroom writing instruction.

See **American Society of Indexers** under **Standards and Practices**.

American Society of Journalists and Authors

http://www.asja.org/

The leading organization of professional nonfiction writers. Includes membership information, the ASJA Contracts Watch newsletter, and good articles about freelancing, e-rights, and so on.

Associations for Writers

http://www.inkspot.com/~ohi/inkspot/assoc.html

The Inkspot's list of writer-related associations.

The Authors Registry

http://www.webcom.com/registry/

A nonprofit organization that provides an extensive contact directory of authors, a royalty collection and distribution service, and a licensing service—sort of an "ASCAP for writers." Complete information about the registry can be found at the Web site.

See **Horror Writers Association** under **Science Fiction, Fantasy, and Horror**.

International Women's Writing Guild

http://www.iwwg.com/

Nonprofit organization that serves as a network for women writers.

National Writers Union

http://www.nwu.org/nwu/

A trade union for freelance writers, the NWU publishes industry news of interest to freelance writers, how-to articles, market information, member news, and networking opportunities.

Publishing Industry Organization

http://www.well.com/user/asi/orgpub.htm

Names, addresses, phone numbers, URLs, and e-mail addresses compiled by the American Society of Indexers.

See **Science Fiction and Fantasy Writers of America, Inc.** under **Science Fiction, Fantasy, and Horror**.

See **Society of Professional Journalists** under **Journalism**.

The Writers Guild of America

http://www.wga.org/wga.cgi

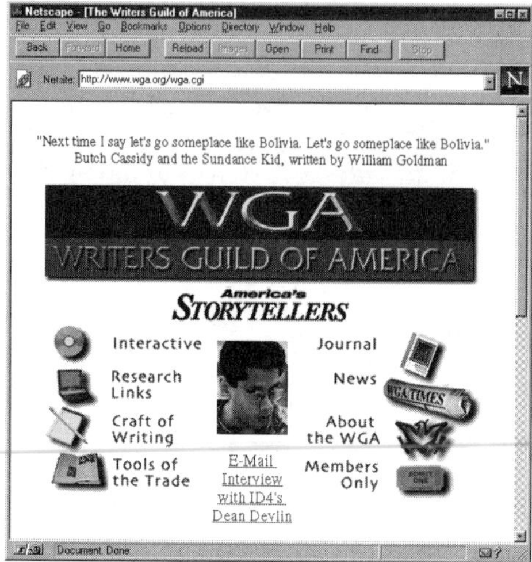

The Writers Guild of America contains useful articles about the writer's craft with special attention to screenwriters. It also contains excellent reference links, including tables of "experts" on topics in medicine, science, technology, and more.

Mailing Lists and Newsgroups

ACW E-mail Discussion List

Discussion of a wide variety of issues concerning computers and writing, including teaching strategies, where to find Internet resources, and other pedagogical tools.

Send an e-mail message to **listproc@unicorn.acs.ttu.edu**. Leave the subject blank. In the message area type: **subscribe acw-l *yourfirstname yourlastname***

Science Fiction, Fantasy, and Horror

Be sure to check the horror sites for topics related to science fiction and fantasy. They tend to blend together.

Science Fiction Web Sites

Doug's SF Reviews

http://www.astro.washington.edu/ingram/books.html

Short reviews and sci-fi links.

Fantasy BookList

http://www.mcs.net/~finn/home.html

Fantasy authors and some reviews of their books.

Feminist Science Fiction

http://www.uic.edu/~lauramd/sf/femsf.html

A directory of feminist sci-fi and fantasy on the Net.

Internet Top 100 SF/Fantasy List

http://www.clark.net/pub/iz/Books/Top100/top100.HTML

A list of top 100 sci-fi and fantasy books selected by Internet vote.

MIT Science Fiction Society Homepage

http://www.mit.edu:8001/activities/mitsfs/homepage.html

Touted as the largest online collection of science fiction texts.

Science Fiction Authors

http://www.oneworld.net/SF/authors/index.html

List of Web pages about sci-fi authors.

Science Fiction and Fantasy Writers of America, Inc.

http://www.sfwa.org/sfwa

Encourages public interest in science fiction literature and provides organization format for writers, editors, and artists within the genre.

Science Fiction Omnicon

http://www.iinet.com.au/~fanjet/sfomain.html

Sci-fi characters and the places they inhabit.

Speculative Fiction Clearing House

http://polarbear.eng.lycos.com/sf-clearing-house

Sci-fi and fantasy resources from the Net.

Spiffs World of Science Fiction and Fantasy

http://http.tamu.edu:8000/~sdd2252/Docs/SciFi/ SciFi.html

Sci-fi writers and books. Web pages devoted to sci-fi and fantasy.

Horror Web Sites

The Cabinet of Dr. Casey

http://www.cat.pdx.edu/~caseyh/horror/index.html

Another big, popular horror site index.

DarkEcho's Web

http://w3.gwis.com/~prlg/

Authors, reviews, resources, and art pertaining to the dark side of fiction.

The Dark Side of the Net

http://www.cascade.net/dark.html

The mother of horror site index pages.

The Fright Site

http://www.fright.com/

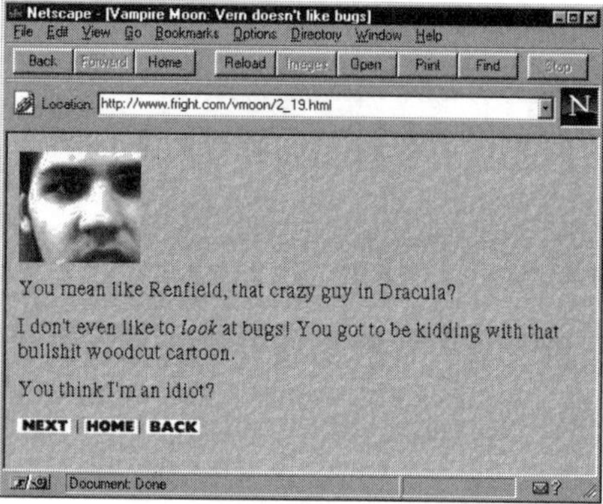

Hypertext fiction and excellent reviews of classic and contemporary horror films.

Horror Writers Association

http://www.horror.org/HWA/

An association that brings together writers and others professionally interested in horror and dark fantasy. Affiliated with Dark Echo's Web. Includes market and membership information.

Mailing Lists and Newsgroups

alt.horror

Dark Fiction/Horror Writers Newsletter

Useful weekly newsletter containing markets, reviews, contests, and resources for horror writers.

Write to **darkecho@aol.com** for subscription information.

rec.arts.sf

sci.classics

Mysteries and Detective Fiction

There are many Internet resources for mystery writers. Whodunits are especially big on the Web.

Web Sites

221 Baker Street

http://www.cs.cmu.edu/afs/andrew.cmu.edu/usr18/mset/www/holmes.html

You can never get enough of Sherlock Holmes.

Bullets and Beer: The Spenser Page

http://mirkwood.ucc.uconn.edu/spenser/spenser.html

Robert B. Parker's detective fiction.

ClueLass ~ A Mystery Newsletter

http://www.slip.net/~cluelass/

Self-described as "everything for mystery writers and fans."

Genre Fiction: Mystery and Suspense

http://www.vmedia.com/shannon/mystery.html

Detective and crime fiction.

The Mysterious Homepage

http://www.db.dk/dbaa/jbs/homepage.htm

Mystery resource links.

MysteryNet

http://www.mysterynet.com/

Premiere source for online mystery fans. Cases to solve, the history of mystery, and plenty of links.

The Mystery Zone

http://www.mindspring.com/~walter/mystzone.html

Touted as the first magazine of mystery, suspense, and crime fiction on the Net.

Sherlockian Holmepage

http://watserv1.uwaterloo.ca/~credmond/sh.html

Everything about the famous Sherlock Holmes.

Tangled-Web

http://www.thenet.co.uk/~hickafric/tangled-web.html

British mystery site with links.

Mailing Lists and Newsgroups

alt.fan.holmes

bit.listserv.dorothyl

rec.arts.mystery

Journalism

The Web is a treasure trove of research and commentary resources. See Chapter 21 for lists of news sites as well as online magazines and newspapers.

Web Sites

American Journalism Review

http://www.ajr.org/

The latest monthly issue, letters to the editor, grants and fellowships, and the study of journalism.

Ask questions of experts

E-mail the following organizations with questions requiring an expert's opinion:

Profnet (Ask the professors), **profnet@vyne.com**.

Hoosier Source (Professors in Indiana), **hoosiersource@uns.purdue.edu**.

CyberWire Dispatch

http://cyberwerks.com:70/1/cyberwire

Self-described as a "take no prisoners news service that concentrates on issues related to cyberspace."

Freedom Forum

http://www.nando.net/prof/freedom/1994/freedom.html

A private organization. The site contains speeches, reports, and articles about the changing roles of journalism, new media, and free speech concerns.

A Journalist's Guide to Finding Data on the Internet

http://nilesonline.com/data/

Links to sites devoted to agriculture, business, crime, health, the military, politics, weather.

Journalism List Redux

http://www.cais.com/makulow/vlj.html

Includes links to news sources (daily, topical, and global), and collections and archives covering many subjects. Excellent meta-page for reporters covering cyberspace and the Internet.

Links to Potential Story Data

http://nilesonline.com/data/

Reference links for finding information on a variety of topics. Part of the site is A Journalist's Guide to Finding Data on the Internet.

Media Watch Home Page

http://theory.lcs.mit.edu/~mernst/media/

Data on media watch and anticensorship groups.

National Press Club

http://npc.press.org

Links, headlines, and resources of interest to news reporters.

The Online Journalist

http://www.online-journalist.com/

News, commentary, and resources for the online journalism community.

Scoop Cybersleuth's Internet Guide

http://www.evansville.net/courier/scoop/

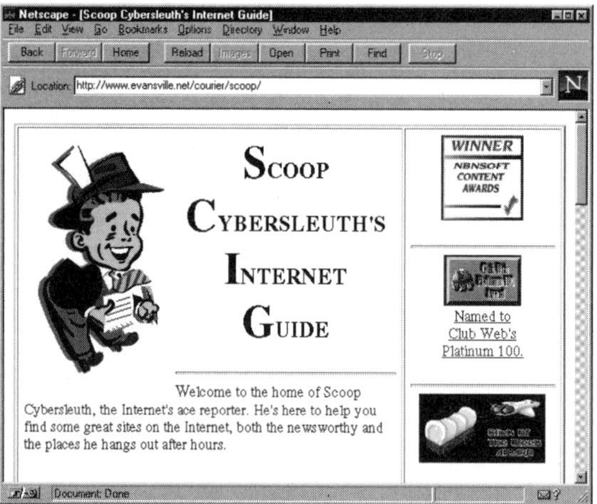

Research sites for government, business, technology, law and crime information, sports, online newspapers and magazines, medical, and entertainment sites. Also lists sites that relate to recent news events.

Society of Professional Journalists

http://npc.press.org

Membership directory, Freedom of Information act information, member publications, and benefits. Includes e-mail list, FTP archive, and links to journalism and news sites.

WebCrawler's Writing and Journalism Reviews

http://gnn.com/wic/wics/hum.write.html

A select list of writing and journalism sites reviewed by WebCrawler.

Mailing Lists and Newsgroups

alt.journalism

The primary newsgroup for journalists. Keeps you up-to-date on trends in journalism, research resources, and other topics of interest to journalists.

alt.journalism.newspapers

alt.news-media

alt.politics.media

Technical Writing

Refer to the "Standards and Practices" section of this chapter for more sites of interest to technical writers.

Web Sites

The Editor's Pen

http://www.nauticom.net/www/dwlacey/

A compendium of advice and links for technical writers, editors, and indexers.

Society for Technical Communication

http://stc.org/

The largest professional organization serving technical communicators. Provides regional and chapter information, resources, publications, educational opportunities, membership requirements, and more.

Writer's Block

http://www.niva.com

Quarterly online newsletter about technical writing and the business of documentation. It contains material of interest to communications specialists, including writers, editors, graphic designers, and desktop publishing operators.

Mailing Lists and Newsgroups

alt.books.technical

Newsgroup with details on the craft and business of technical writing.

Technical Writers Mailing List

The list (based at Oklahoma State University) deals with topics of interest to technical writers. To subscribe, send mail to: **listserv@vm1.ucc.okstate.edu**.

In the body of the message, type **subscribe techwr-l *yourfirstname yourlastname***.

The human administrator can be reached at: **techwr-l-request@vm1.ucc.okstate.edu**.

Romance

The romance genre is a growing area on the Internet. Be sure to check for new sites and newsletters.

Web Sites

From the Heart

http://www.teleport.com/~cedarbay/romance.html

Publishers, general resources, groups, mailing lists, and more for romance writers.

Joanne Reid's Romance Links

http://www.mbnet.mb.ca/~jbreid/

Useful information worth checking out.

Romancing The Web

http://www.romanceweb.com/

Information, sources, and publicity for and about romance writers and readers.

Mailing Lists and Newsgroups

Romantic Notions Newsletter

Publicizes newly-published writing. Contact **mmarr@cyberhighway.net**.

Romance Writers Mailing List

To subscribe, send mail to **listserv@sjuvm.stjohns.edu**. In the message body type: **subscribe rw-l *yourfirstname yourlastname***.

Children's Writing

Web sites exist for adults who write for children as well as children who are writers.

Web Sites

Books for Children and More

http://www.users.interport.net/~hdu/

Original articles, children's literature/writing links, images, publishing, and reference information.

Children's Literature Page

http://www.ucalgary.ca/~dkbrown/index.html

Comprehensive resources related to books for children, organized by category. Includes resources for parents, teachers, storytellers, writers, and illustrators.

Children's Publishers on the Internet

http://www.ucalgary.ca/~dkbrown/publish.html

An excellent list of publishers for children's books as well as industry news and guidelines.

The Children's Writing Resource Centre

http://www.mindspring.com/~cbi/

Contains excerpts from Children's Book Insider (CBI), books and tools for children's writers are available through the CBI, market tips, etc. CBI also has its own discussion area and file library on CompuServe (GO WRITER).

The Inkspot

http://www.inkspot.com/~ohi/inkspot/home.html

Resources for young writers, Children's Author Directory, Children's Illustrator Directory, workshops, conferences, tips, reviews, and much more.

Mailing Lists and Newsgroups

Children's Writers And Illustrators List

To subscribe, send e-mail to: **majordomo@lists.mindspring.com**.

In the body of the message type: **subscribe childrens-writing**.

Children's Writers' Mailing List

Writing aimed at the children's and young adult market—fiction, nonfiction, poetry, textbook chapters, vocabulary-controlled stories, picture books, and novels. To subscribe, send e-mail to: **listserv@psuvm.psu.edu**. In the body of message type: **subscribe yawrite**.

rec.arts.books.childrens

Poetry

Poets are finding an enormous, inexpensive distribution network on the Web.

Web Sites

The Academy of American Poets

http://www.tmn.com/Artswire/poets/page.html

Founded in 1934 to support American poets at all stages of their careers, the Web site features academy information (contests, press releases, membership information, etc.) and a variety of poetry links.

Poet Warrior Press: Writer's Resource Center

http://www.azstarnet.com/~poewar/writer/writer.html

Articles and resources of interest to poets and writers in general. Includes consumer magazine lists, book publishers, classic works, authors, writing festivals, market information, and more.

Ultimate Poetry Links Page

http://www.kiosk.net/poetry/links.html

Poets, books, haiku, workshops, etc. Provided by the National Library of Poetry.

Yahoo's Poetry Links

http://www.yahoo.com/Arts/Humanities/Literature/Genres/Poetry/

Yahoo's extensive list of links pertaining to all types of poetry and poets.

Mailing Lists and Newsgroups

rec.arts.poems

Original poetry often accompanied by critique and discussion.

Screenwriting

The Web sites dedicated to screenwriting are growing at a phenomenal rate. Registries and genre magazines are of special interest.

Web Sites

A.M. productions

http://www.amfilm.com

A.M. productions site with reference pages for screenwriters.

Film Diary

http://www.instruments.org

Follow the day-to-day filming of a current production.

Film and Video Related Newsgroups and FAQ

http://www.echonyc.com/~mvidal/news.html#faq

Miscellaneous newsgroups for film buffs of all kinds.

The Inkwell

http://theinkwell.com/

Screenwriter biographies, industry news, and related links.

Reference Library

http://www.re/playwriting/

Excellent reference library for screenwriters.

Screenwriters Online

http://screenwriter.com/insider/news.html

Download scripts, interviews, WGA demographics, and statistics. Opportunities to interact with the pros. Includes The Screenwriters Insider Report e-zine.

Screenwriters and Playwrights Page

http://www.teleport.com/~cdeemer/scrwriter.html

An excellent screenwriting and playwriting resource site.

Screenwriters Utopia

http://www.wic.net/cpwehner/utopia3.html

Resources, advertising, and advice for beginning and experienced screenwriters.

Mailing Lists and Newsgroups

misc.writing.screenplays

rec.arts.theatre

Screenwriting Mailing Lists

Over 800 subscribers and many daily posts. Send mail to: **listserv@tamvm1.tam.edu**. In the body of the message type: **subscribe scrnwri**.

The Writer's Guide to the Internet
Chapter
21

Research Sites Online

The following compendium of sites can get you started in your online research projects. Remember that new, better sites are coming online everyday.

News

Several news resources exist on the Web, growing in quality and quantity on a daily basis. Many of these sites are fully searchable and some maintain archives of past stories.

NPR

http://www.npr.org

Provides access to the many stories covered on "All Things Considered," "Morning Edition," "Fresh Air," and other NPR news programs. The NPR FAQ posted monthly in the newsgroup **alt.radio.networks.npr** contains e-mail and snail mail addresses for most of the broadcast programs and their producers.

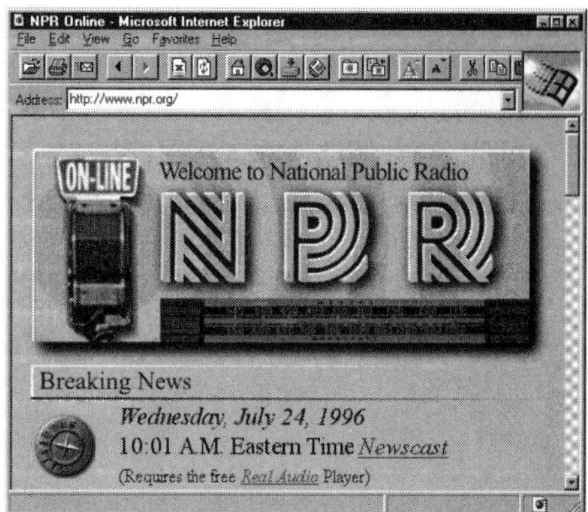

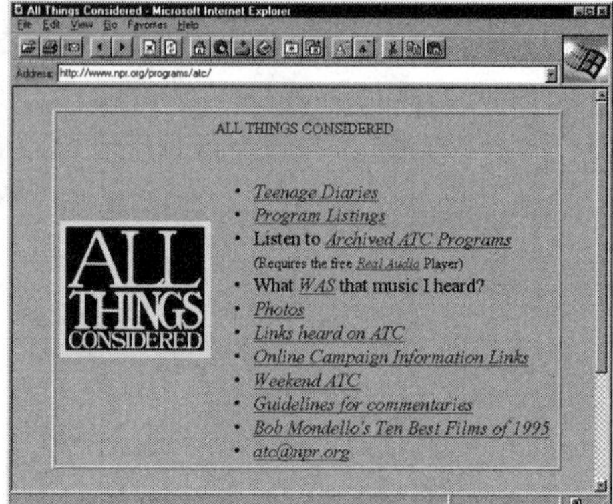

Notably, NPR also provides streaming audio files of current stories. Streaming audio technology lets you hear an audio file as it is being transmitted, instead of having to wait for the download to finish. This is especially helpful with longer audio recordings, such as those generated by NPR.

To facilitate the use of streaming audio, the NPR site presents links to the RealAudio home page (**http://www.realaudio.com/**) where you can download a RealAudio player program. (If you don't have the program, you won't be able to hear the broadcast.) As with other sound files, you'll also need to have a sound card installed in your computer.

Associated Press

http://www.trib.com/NEWS/APwire.html

Briefs and updates.

CBS News: UTTMlink

http://uttm.com/

UTTMlink stands for "up-to-the-minute" link.

CNet

http://www.CNet.com/

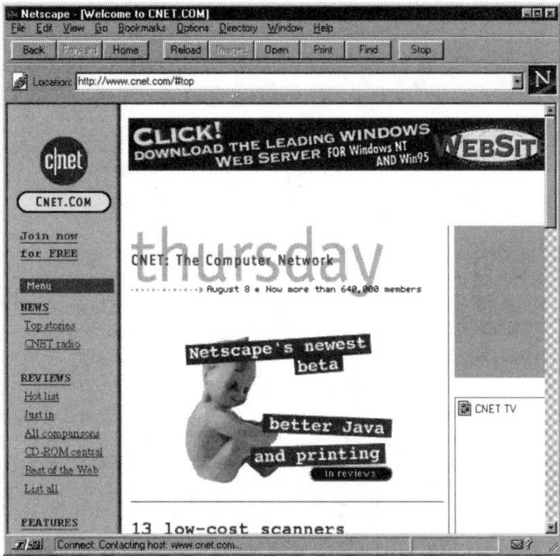

Related to CNET Television, this excellent site offers daily news, product reviews, columns, and feature stories about Internet topics and the software industry.

CNN Interactive

http://www.cnn.com/

News from the CNN network.

Computer News Daily

http://nytsyn.com/live/Latest/

A site produced by the New York Times Syndicate, it includes timely news, features, and columns about the technology and the world of computers.

Crayon

http://crayon.net

A site that lets you customize your own newspaper. Read only the news you care about. Free service.

The Electronic Newstand

http://www.enews.com/

The oldest repository of magazines on the Web. Usually one or two articles are available for download.

Federal Web Locator

http://www.law.vill.edu/Fed-Agency/fedwebloc.html

Links to all federal agencies. Search engine helps you find what you want.

Lead Story

http://www.bnet.att.com/leadstory/

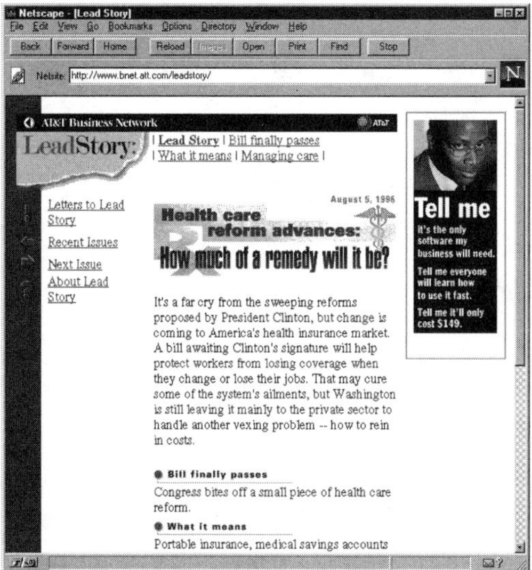

A tight, well-organized site brought to you by the AT&T Business Network. It culls the Web for in-depth coverage of one major news story each day, Monday through Friday. A good morning-coffee read.

Media Online Yellow Pages

http://www.nlnnet.com/yellowp.html

A directory of media outlets and connections.

NewsPage Home Page

http://www.newspage.com/

A fee-based news retrieval service.

Newsletter Library

http://pub.savvy.com

A searchable list of free newsletters organized by subject.

Newspaper Indexes

Because so many newspapers and magazines are getting wired, sites that index and catalogue these publications are becoming a necessity.

Web Sites

Arastar Internet News Page

http://www.arastar.net/news

A comprehensive compendium of online newspapers and magazines. An excellent resource.

Chaplin's News

http://www.geocities.com/Heartland/2308/

A very good resource for newspapers, magazines, and other news reference sites online.

Ecola's 24-hr Newstand

http://www.ecola.com/news/

A huge index of media sites indexed by location. U.S. newspapers also indexed by type: daily, weekly, alternative/art, business.

Editor & Publisher

http://www.mediainfo.com

Media-related columns and articles. An enormous database of newspaper home pages catalogued by country and, in the U.S.A., by state. Searchable database. Some downloads are fee-based.

The Electronic Newstand

http://www.enews.com/

News links divided into categories of newspapers, magazines, TV-radio, money, the economy, computers, sports, etc.

The European Journalism Page

http://www.demon.co.uk/eurojournalism/

Links to publications in Europe.

Newslink

http://www.newslink.org/menu.html

An exceptional resource for news links, surveys, stories, and top ten lists.

See **Scoop Cybersleuth's Internet Guide** under **Journalism**.

WebWise—Library

http://webwise.walcoff.com/library/index.html

Media and publications with an online presence.

Newspaper and News Publications

Boston Globe **http://www.boston.com/globe/glohome.htm**

The Christian Science Monitor **http://www.csmonitor.com**

Daily Record and Sunday Mail From the U.K. **http://www.record-mail.co.uk/rm/**

The Daily Yomiuri (Japan) **http://www.yomiuri.co.jp/**

The Electronic Telegraph (U.K.) **http://www.telegraph.co.uk**

Evening Times Online (Scotland) **http://web2.cims.co.uk/eveningtimes/**

The Gate (*San Francisco Chronicle* and the *San Francisco Examiner*) **http://www.sfgate.com**

The Guardian WebSite (U.K.) **http://www.guardian.co.uk/**

The Haight Ashbury Free Press (San Francisco) **http://www.webcom.com/haight**

The Hindu (India) **http://www.webpage.com/hindu/current/weekly.html**

Hong Kong Standard Newspapers **http://www.hkstandard.com**

The Irish Times **http://www.irish-times.com**

The Jerusalem Post **http://www.jpost.com/**

Jewish Post of New York Online **http://www.jewishpost.com/**

Mercury Center Home Page **http://www.sjmercury.com**

The Nando Times **http://www2.nando.net/nt/**

The New York Times on the Web **http://www.nytimes.com**
http://www.nytimesfax.com (digest version)

The Observer Life Magazine (England) **http://www.observer.co.uk/**

The St. Petersburg Press (Russia) **http://www.spb.su/times/**

USA Today **http://www.usatoday.com/usafront.htm**

The Wall Street Journal Interactive Edition **http://update.wsj.com/**

The Washington Times National Weekly **http://www.washtimes-weekly.com**

Webzines and Magazines

The Atlantic Monthly	**http://www.TheAtlantic.com/**
The American Prospect	**http://epn.org/prospect.html**
Barron's	**http://www.enews.com/magazines/barrons/**
Business Week	**http://www.businessweek.com**
CM's TechWeb	**http://techweb.cmp.com/current/**
Conde Nast Traveler Online	**http://www.cntraveler.com/**
Epicurious	**http://www.epicurious.com/epicurious/home2.html**
George	**http://www.georgemag.com/**
Internet World	**http://www.iworld.com/**
Jinn Pacific News Service	**http://www.pacificnews.org/jinn/**
Life	**http://pathfinder.com/Life**
Maclean's (Canada)	**gopher://gopher.enews.com/ i 1/collected/macleans/**
Mother Jones	**http://www.mojones.com**
The National Enquirer	**http://www.nationalenquirer.com/**
New Republic	**http://www.enews.com/magazines/tnr/**
ONE	**http://www.clark.net/pub/conquest/one/home.html**
The Paris Review	**http://www.voyagerco.com/PR/**
PC World Online	**http://www.pcworld.com/**
People	**http://pathfinder.com/people/**
Premiere	**http://www.premieremag.com**
Private Eye	**http://www.intervid.co.uk/eye/**
Redbook	**http://homearts.com/rb/toc/**
Slate	**http://www.slate.com/**
Smithsonian	**http://www.si.edu/resource/**

Der Spiegel	**http://www.spiegel.de/nda/spiegel/index.html**
Sports Illustrated	**http://www.pathfinder.com/si/welcome.html**
Time	**http://www.pathfinder.com/time/**
Time Warner Pathfinder	**http://www.pathfinder.com**
US News and World Report Online	**http://www.usnews.com**
The UTNE LENS	**http://www.utne.com/lens/**
Vibe	**http://www.vibe.com**
Washington Free Press	**http://www.speakeasy.org/**
Wired Magazine	**http://www.hotwired.com/wired/**
WorldNews Today	**http://www.fwi.com/wnt/wnt.html**
YO! (Youth Outlook)	**http://www.pacificnews.org/yo**
ZD Net	**http://www.zdnet.com**

Reference Books and Indexes

Britannica Online

http://www.eb.com/

Electric Library

http://www.elibrary.com

An excellent research resource. Very reasonable prices and a free trial period.

Grolier's Interactive

http://gi.grolier.com/

Reference Shelf

http://www.nova.edu/Inter-Links/reference.html

A jumping off point for references to geographic data, phone numbers, words, weights and measures, and more.

Reference Sources on the Internet

http://www.well.com/user/asi/refbooks.htm

An excellent list of business, computer, humanities, and science reference documents (acronyms, dictionaries, etc.). Also fact books, libraries, and general reference resources. Compiled by the American Society of Indexers, so you *know* it's accurate!

Roget's Thesaurus

gopher://gopher.odie.niaia.nih.gov:70/77/.thesaurus/index

Virtual Reference Desk, University of California, Irvine

gopher://peg.cwis.uci.edu:7000/11/gopher.welcome/peg

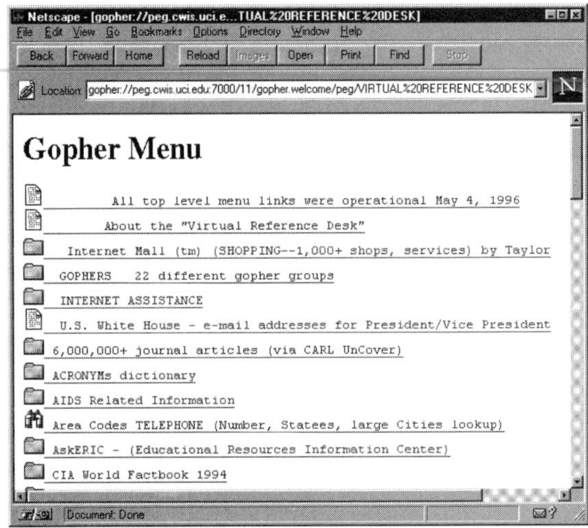

A comprehensive Gopher site with frequently-sought information sources and tools. The menu selections range from specific tools (such as dictionaries) to lists of resources (under topic headings such as Medicine and Federal Government).

Webster's Hypertext Dictionary

http://c.gp.cs.cmu.edu:5103/prog/webster/

WWW Virtual Library

http://www.w3.org/pub/DataSources/bySubject/Maintainers.html

Other Writer-Related Internet Resources

The writer's world includes more than writing and reading. It usually involves travel, reading about other writers, querying publishers, and most important, procrastinating. In this chapter you'll find a variety of Web sites, newsgroups, and mailing lists that cater to each of these critical areas.

Travel

Writers must frequently travel to research stories and promote publications. Fortunately, travel information is an exploding topic on the Internet, especially the Web. Literally thousands of Web sites describe destinations, offer travel advice, promote tours, sell tickets, even track weather. Online travel purchases are growing rapidly. Some surveys estimate that up to ten million pleasure travelers use the Web.

Sites such as Expedia, which represents Microsoft's entrance into the online leisure travel booking arena, are rapidly coming of age. The Mungo Park travel e-zine, **http://www.mungopark.com/**, enables travelers to make airline, car, and hotel bookings online.

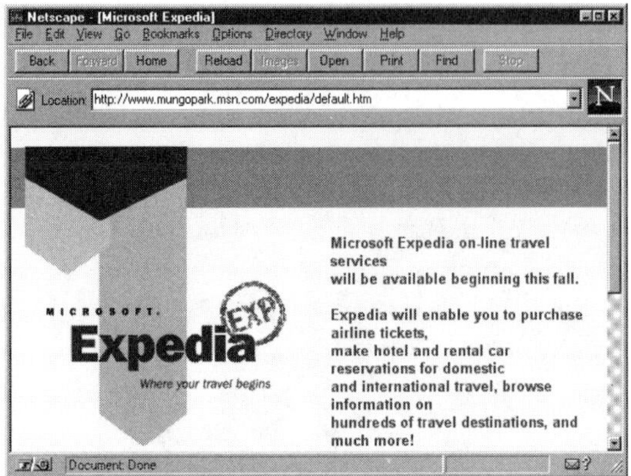

Expedia employs Secure Sockets Layer (SSL) encryption and Private Communication Technology (PCT) authentication to ensure secure credit card transactions. Other sites that sell tickets over the Internet will employ similar forms of security protection.

A good example of a multipurpose company Web presentation that helps you plan trips and purchase tickets is the American Airlines site, **http://www.americanair.com/aa_home.htm**.

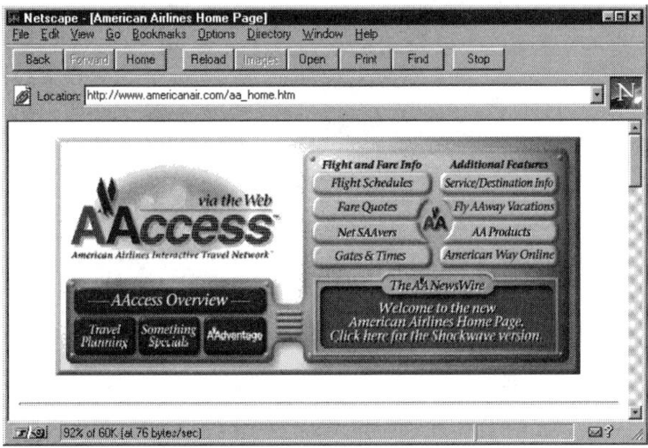

It includes a travel reservation program, Internet saver fares, a silent auction, and frequent flyer information. It also includes flight schedules, fare quotes, up-to-the-minute scheduling and gate information, route maps, product catalogues, a mailing list for discount fares, and much more.

If you have questions that can't be answered by a Web site or travel agent, check the travel-related newsgroups. Travel advice abounds on Usenet.

Web Sites

Airlines on the Web

http://www.itn.net/airlines/

Passenger carriers, 800 numbers, aviation organizations, frequent-flyer programs, and much more.

GNN Traveler's Center

http://gnn.com/meta/travel/index.html

Global Network Navigator (GNN) keeps track of travel resources, up-to-the minute deals, and other travel-related information. To receive GNN Traveler's Center updates via e-mail, send mail to **majordomo@gnn.com**. In the body of the message, write: **subscribe trav-talk**.

Internet Travel Network

http://www.itn.net/cgi/get?itn/index

A public reservation system that provides free Internet access to air, car, and hotel information and reservations.

Northwest Airlines

http://www.nwa.com

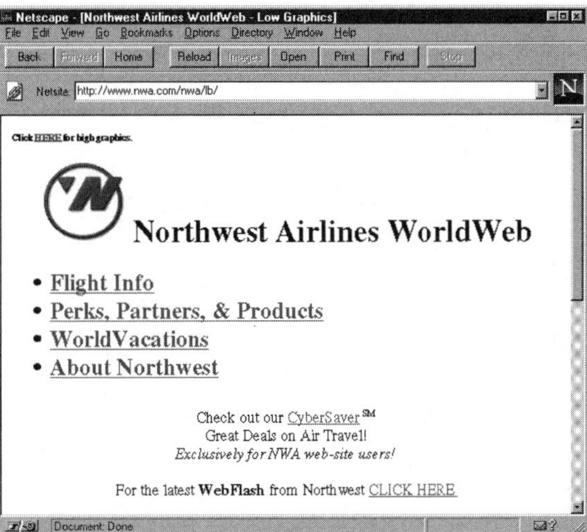

In addition to standard flight information and destination topics, Northwest Airlines lists discounted fares, some of which are exclusive to Web visitors.

Parent Soup: Traveling with Kids

http://www.parentsoup.com/

Traveling parents will find this site interesting, entertaining, and best of all, useful.

Travel Web

http://www.travelweb.com/thisco/global/travel.html

Lodging, travel-related news and information, and travel links.

Travelocity

http://www.travelocity.com

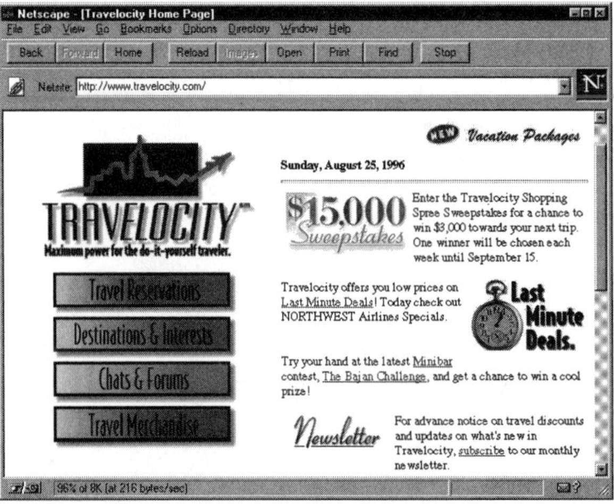

This site includes tons of destination information, including restaurants, hotels, and museums, as well as a link to the simplified version of Sabre (the computerized flight reservation system used by travel agents).

Travelwiz

http://www.travelwiz.com/

Avis-sponsored directory of information about bus and railroad travel, airlines reservations, hotels, tourism offices, travel hints, rental cars, and other travel resources. This is a comprehensive site.

USAir

http://www.usair.com

Discounted airfares furnished via e-mail. Sign up for their mailing list.

Miscellaneous Travel-Related Resources

Fedex

http://www.fedex.com

Track your Federal Express packages online.

ILISA Foreign Language Site

http://travlang.com/languages/

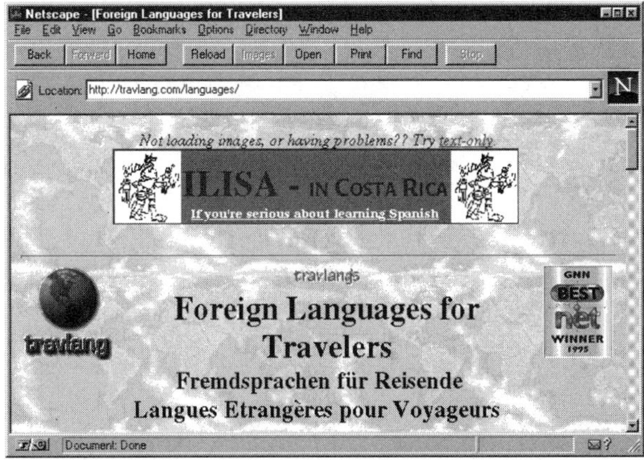

Learn the language of your travel destination online.

MapQuest

http://www.mapquest.com/

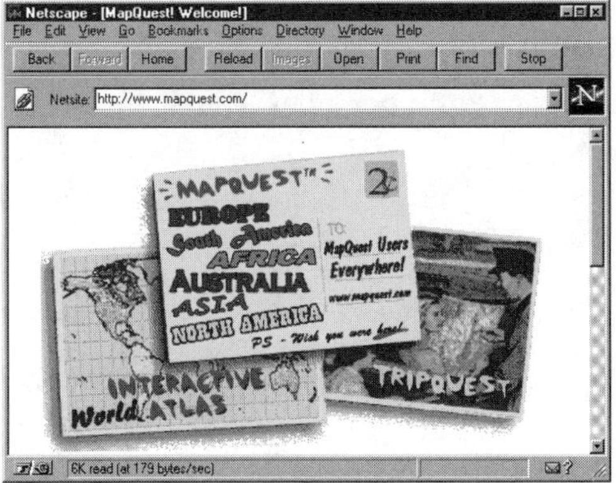

Free interactive street atlas of the continental United States. Provides directions for driving between cities in the continental United States, Canada, and Mexico.

Usenet

rec.travel.air

misc.transport.air-industry (Moderated)

alt.airline.schedules

sci.aeronautics.airliners

UPS

http://www.ups.com

United Parcel Service shipping.

Authors, Publishers, and Bookstores on the Web

There are many famous and not-so-famous authors with Web sites. Some of them are maintained by the individual authors; most are maintained by adoring fans. Author Web sites usually include related links and occasionally FAQs about collected works.

Rather than list the hundreds of individual newsgroups, mailing lists, and Web sites dedicated to published authors, I've listed three index pages of author sites. I've also included an incomplete list of author Web sites. If your favorite author isn't included in this list, don't despair. Many authors have newsgroups and mailing lists that are not listed here. Simply go to any search site (see Chapter 17) and search on the author's name.

Authornet

http://www.imgnet.com/auth/

Authornet is a venue for information about current literature and contact with authors.

BookWire Author Indexes

http://www.bookwire.com/index/Author-indexes.html

An index of author index pages.

Authors on the Web

Edward Abbey	**http://www.abalon.se/beach/aw/abbey.html**
Warren Adler	**http://www.authornet.com/auth/adler/WADLER.html**
Maya Angelou	**http://web.msu.edu/lecture/angelou.html**

Isaac Asimov	**http://www.clark.net/pub/edseiler/WWW/ asimov_home_page.html**
Margaret Atwood	**http://www.io.org/~toadaly**
Jane Austen	**http://uts.cc.utexas.edu/~churchh/janeinfo.html**
Clive Barker	**http://www.webcom.com/tby/cbarker.html**
Aphra Behn	**http://ourworld.compuserve.com/homepages/r_nestvold/**
Madison Smartt Bell	**http://www.cais.net/aesir/fiction/msbell**
Mario Biondi	**http://joshua.micronet.it/italian/mariobiondi/letture.ing.html**
William Blake	**http://www.aa.net/~urizen/blake.html**
Jorge Luis Borges	**http://www.microserve.com/~thequail/libyrinth/borges.html**
Truman Capote	**http://www.serve.com/Critter/Authors/capote.htm**
Lewis Carroll	**http://www.students.uiuc.edu/~jbirenba/carroll.html**
Raymond Carver	**http://world.std.com/~ptc/**
A. G. Cascone	**http://www.bookwire.com/authors/cascone.htm**
Willa Cather	**http://www.fas.harvard.edu/~newstrom/cather.html**
Raymond Chandler	**http://www.byronpreiss.com/brooklyn/marlowe/books.htm**
Margaret Chittenden	**http://www.techline.com/~megc/**
Arthur C. Clark	**http://www.lsi.usp.br/~rbianchi/clarke/**
Samuel Taylor Coleridge	**http://www.lib.virginia.edu/etext/stc/Coleridge/stc.html**
Douglas Coupland	**http://www.cybercity.hko.net/toronto/s_chung/coupland**
Michael Crichton	**http://http.tamu.edu:8000/~cmc0112/crichton.html**
Linda Davies	**http://www.ex.ac.uk/~RDavies/arian/linda.html**
Daniel Defoe	**http://www.li.net/~scharf/defoe.html**
Samuel R. Delany	**http://www.mbc.umt.edu/~ogd/neveryona/**
Antoine de Saint-Exupéry	**http://www.sas.upenn.edu/~smfriedm/exupery**
Charles Dickens	**http://hum.ucsc.edu/dickens/index.html** **http://lang.nagoya-u.ac.jp/~matsuoka/Dickens.html**

Emily Dickinson	http://www.cc.columbia.edu:80/acis/bartleby/dickinson
Sir Arthur Conan Doyle	http://www.cs.cmu.edu/afs/andrew.cmu.edu/usr18/mset/www/holmes.html
Dorothy Dunnett	http://lynn.efr.hw.ac.uk/EDC/endinburghers/dorothy-dunnett.html
T. S. Eliot	http://www.usl.edu/Departments/English/authors/eliot/
Erasmus	http://www.ciger.be/erasmus/index.html
William Faulkner	http://www.mcsr.olemiss.edu/~egjbp/faulkner/faulkner.html
F. Scott Fitzgerald	http://acs.tamu.edu/~jtc5085/index.htm
Diana Gabaldon	http://www.cco.caltech.edu/~gatti/gabaldon/gabaldon.html
Elizabeth Gaskell	http://lang.nagoya-u.ac.jp/~matsuoka/Gaskell.html
Allen Ginsberg	http://www.charm.net:80/~brooklyn/LitKicks.html
Nikki Giovanni	http://athena.english.vt.edu/Giovanni/Nikki_Giovanni.html
Eileen Goudge	http://www.hamptonsweb/goudge
J. Clark Hansbarger	http://www.cais.net/aesir/fiction/JCH
Nathaniel Hawthorne	http://www.tiac.net/users/eldred/nh/hawthorne.html
Seamus Heaney	http://sunsite.unc.edu/dykki/poetry/heaney/heaney-cov.html
Ernest Hemingway	http://www.ee.mcgill.ca/~nverever/hem/cover.html
Langston Hughes	http://ie.uwindsor.ca/jazz/hughes.html
Samuel Johnson	http://www.english.upenn.edu/~jlynch/Johnson/
Dylan Jones	http://imagenet.com/auth/djones/djones.html
J. V. Jones	http://www.jvj.com/
Robert Jordan	http://www.cs.unc.edu/~garrett/jordan/jordan.html
James Joyce	http://www.mcs.net:80/~jorn/html/jj.html
Franz Kafka	http://www.serve.com/Critter/Authors/kafka.htm
John Keats	http://www.cc.columbia.edu/acis/bartleby/keats/index.html

Jack Kerouac	http://www.charm.net:80/~brooklyn/LitKicks.html
Stephen King	http://phrtay10.ucsd.edu/~ed/sk/
Milan Kundera	http://www.du.edu:80/~staylor/kundera.html
Wyndham Lewis	http://130.54.80.49/lewis/lewis.html
H. P. Lovecraft	http://nti.uji.es/CPE
Maud Hart Lovelace	http://virtumall.com/homepages/navaho/Betsy-Tacy
Ben Marcus	http://www.cais.net/aesir/fiction/marcus
Michael Martone	http://www.cais.net/aesir/fiction/martone
Cormac McCarthy	http://pages.prodigy.com/TN/dctw04a/cormac1.html
Carson McCullers	http://www.cathouse.org/Literature/CarsonMcCullers/
Herman Melville	http://www.melville.org/
N. Scott Momaday	http://users.mwci.net/~lapoz/N.Scott.Momaday.html
Lucy Maud Montgomery	http://www.gov.pe.ca:80/info/lucy/index.html
John Mortimer	http://wxgods.cit.cornell.edu/mortimer.html
John Muir	http://www.sierraclub.org/history/muir
Vladimir Nabokov	http://www.libraries.psu.edu/isaweb/nabokov/nsintro.htm
Dorothy Parker	http://128.174.53.170/Literature/DorothyParker/parker.html
Edgar Allan Poe	http://www.cs.umu.se/~dpcnn/eapoe/ea_poe.html
Thomas Pynchon	http://www.pomona.edu/pynchon/uncollected/barthelme.html
Anne Rice	http://www.maths.tcd.ie/pub/vampire/intro.html
Tom Robbins	http://www.rain.org/~da5e/tom_robbins.html
Dante Gabriel Rossetti	http://jefferson.village.virginia.edu/rossetti/rossetti.html
Salman Rushdie	http://www.nyu.edu/pages/wsn/subir/rushdie.html
William Shakespeare	http://www.shakespeare.com/ http://the-tech.mit.edu/Shakespeare/works.html

Percy Shelley	**http://www.cc.columbia.edu:/~svl2/shelley/**
Ilan Stavans	**http://www.cais.net/aesir/fiction/istavans**
Bruce Sterling	**http://riceinfo.rice.edu:80/projects/RDA/VirtualCity/Sterling/index.html**
J.R.R. Tolkien	**http://www.lights.com/tolkien/rootpage.html** **http://www.csclub.waterloo.ca/u/relipper/tolkien/rootpage.html**
Mark Twain	**http://hydor.colorado.edu/twain/** **http://web.syr.edu/~fjzwick/twainwww.html**
Walt Whitman	**http://www.cc.columbia.edu:80/acis/bartleby/whitman/**
William Wordsworth	**http://www.cc.columbia.edu:80/acis/bartleby/wordsworth/**

Author, Author!

http://www.li.net/~scharf/author.html

Writing resources and author Web sites.

Publishers

After a somewhat slow start, publishers and booksellers are developing a strong online presence. To view a hierarchical list of publishers by category, visit Yahoo, **http://www.yahoo.com/Business_and_Economy/Companies/Publishing/**. Another comprehensive list of publishers organized by genre can be found at **http://www.inkspot.com/~ohi/www/publishers.html**. The following is a partial list:

Addison-Wesley	**http://aw.com**
Alpha Books	**http://www.mcp.com:80/alpha/**
Bantam Doubleday Dell	**http://www.bdd.com/**
BRP Publications	**http://brpinc.com/**
Doubleday	**http://www.bdd.com/read**
Cambridge University Press UK	**http://www.cup.cam.ac.uk/**
Circlet Press	**http://www.apocalypse.org/circlet/home.html**
Cloverleaf Gold Publications	**http://www.cloverleafgolf.com**
Del Rey Books	**gopher://gopher.panix.com**

Franklin, Beedle & Associates	**http://www.fbeedle.com/**
Library of Congress Publications	**http://marvel.loc.gov**
Hayden Books	**http://www.mcp.com:80/hayden/**
Houghton Mifflin Company	**http://www.hmco.com/**
McGraw-Hill	**gopher://mcgraw.infor.com:5000/**
NESFA Press	**ftp://grand.central.org/afs/transarc.com/public/jmann/html/nesfa.html**
O'Reilly Publishing	**http://www.ora.com**
Oxford University Press	**http://www.oup.co.uk/**
Penguin U. S.	**http://www.penguin.com/usa/**
Prentice Hall	**http://www.prenhall.com/**
Random House	**http://www.randomhouse.com/**
Scholastic	**http://scholastic.com**
Steel Dragon Press	**http://www.player.org/pub/flash/steeldcat.html**
Time Warner	**http://www.time.com/**

Services to Publishers

Book industry professionals have special interests and issues to address. Sites such as BookWire (below) are becoming indispensable resources to publishers and booksellers alike. To find the latest services, visit Yahoo's Publishers Listings.

Bookport Services **http://www.bookport.com/welcome/9545**

BookStack's Publisher Place **http://www.books.com/place1.htm**

BookWeb **http://www.bookweb.org**

Bookseller and publisher information. Part of the American Booksellers Association, book news, author tours, media guides, bookstore directories, top U.S. markets.

BookWire **http://www.bookwire.com**

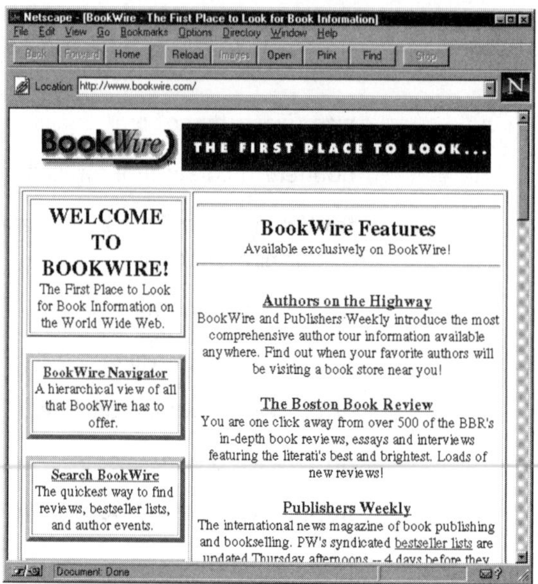

Includes *Publishers Weekly*, calendars of book events, a categorized index of booksellers, publishers, and libraries, and hundreds of other book-related resources on the Internet. Home to BookWire Insider, a news and information service for book industry professionals.

Bookstores

This is a sampling of bookstores on the Web.

Amazon Books	**http://www.amazon.com**
Book Look	**http://www.macroserve.com/booklook/home.htm**
Book Stacks Unlimited, Inc.	**http://www.books.com/scripts/news.exe**
BookZONE (specialty books)	**http://bookzone.com/bookzone**
BookWire Online Bookseller List	**http://www.bookwire.com/index/booksellers.html**
BookWeb	**http://www.bookweb.org**
Future Fantasy	**http://www.commerce.digital.com/palo-alto/FutureFantasy/home.html**
Internet Book Shop	**http://www.bookshop.co.uk/**
University Press Books	**http://www.fractals.com/upb/html/upb_intro.html**
The Virtual Book Shop	**http://www.virtual.bookshop.com**

Diversions and Distractions

Sometimes you reach a point in your writing when you simply have to get away from the project. Take a breather. For the happily wired, the realm of diversions expands from the real world into the virtual playground of the Internet. Here are a few time-wasters:

- Read or write e-mail. It's the number one diversion for anybody online.
- Play Duke Nukem, (Figure 22.3) at **http://www.3Drealms.com**. This is a nasty fight game in a politically incorrect blood-and-guts universe. The action is wild and the graphics are memerizing. A shareware version of Duke Nukem can be installed from the CD accompanying this book. Duke Nukem is surreal, violent and when you're in a rotten mood, quite satisfying. Not for young children or sensitive natures. You've been warned.

- Play Solitaire. For the gentler set, the simple game of online solitaire (available in most Windows setups) is just the kind of banal, low-key activity that gives the brain a rest. Plus if you win, you get a little Easter egg of visuals that makes you smile.
- Chat with another writer. If you're using an online service with chat options, you might want to jump into a forum or meeting room to visit with other writers. Start by telling the truth: you're exhausted and you have writer's block. They'll love talking with you about it.

- Visit the Elizabethan Curse Generator (Figure 22.4). Create an insult worthy of your worst publishing nightmare, e.g. thou wanton fat-kidneyed dogfish. **http://www.tower.org/disease/insult.html**.

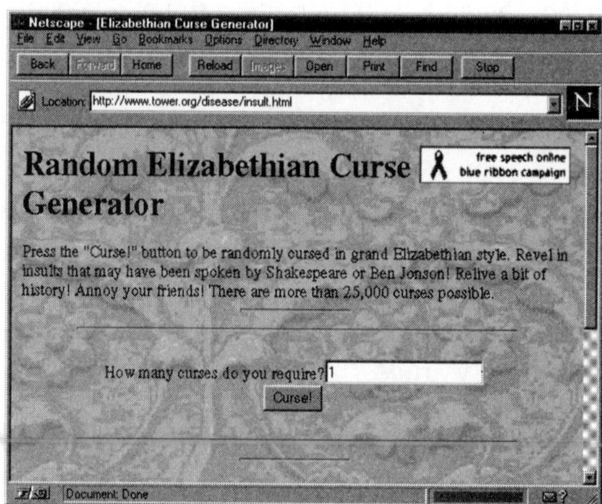

- Recite bad dialogue. At Taglines Galore! you'll never run out of obnoxious phrases. Find gems such as, "A beer would never make fun of your new outfit." There's 296,271 more where that came from. Oh, boy. **http://www.brandonu.ca/~ennsnr/Tags/Welcome.html**.
- Visit SpinnWebe. The SpinnWebe site explains, "we're a draw for the unusual, the non-conformist, and the slightly odd. And we hope that includes you." **http://spinn.thoughtport.com/spinnwebe/**.
- Tour the NASA home page, **http://www.nasa.gov/**. This is a fascinating site with more than you'll ever want to know about space travel, astronomy, and lots of cool images.

- Visit The Onion, **http://www.theonion.com/**. A satirical newspaper with stories like "U.S. 'Sends Message' to Iraq With Massive Display of Beefcake," "Blind People are Faking It," and "Would-Be Superhero Can Only Fly When Naked." News you've only dreamt about.

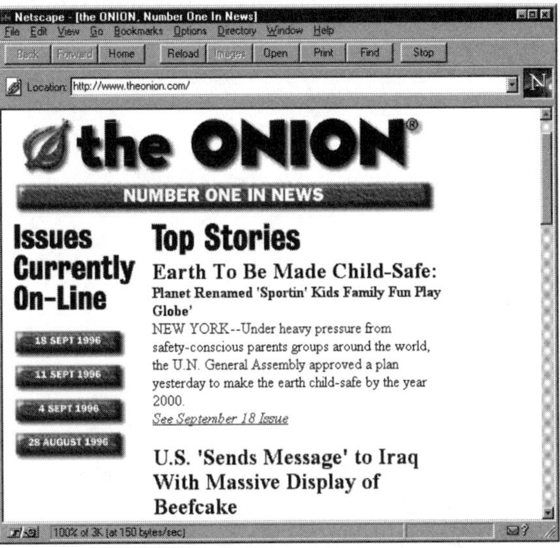

- Play with The Word Wizard. Enjoy interesting word games, contests, stories, quotes, excerpts from famous diaries, and much more. **http://www.wordwizard.com/**.

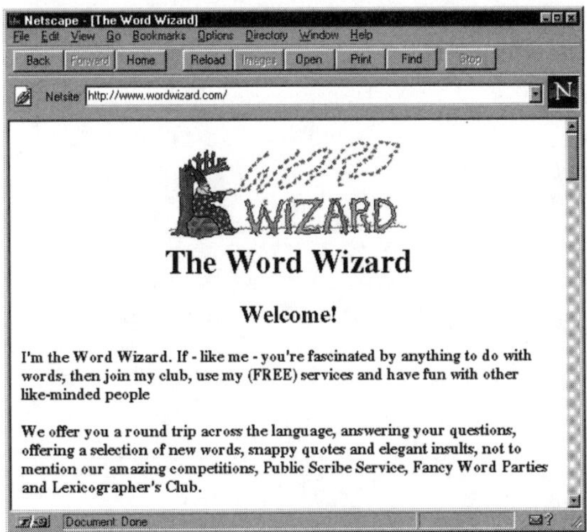

- Explore other odd, interesting and unusual references that could appeal to writers at The Writers Source. **http://www.cloud9.net/~kvivian/oddrefs.html**.

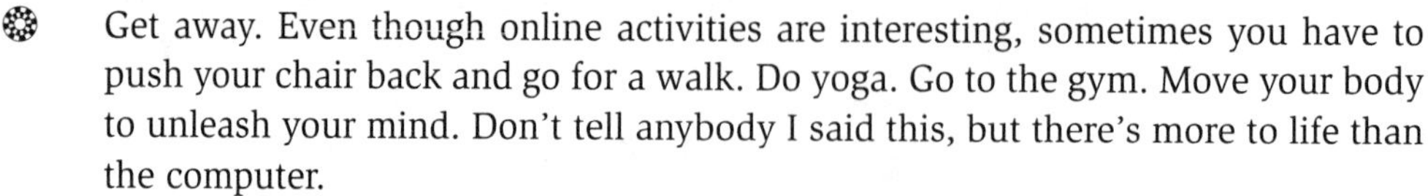

- Get away. Even though online activities are interesting, sometimes you have to push your chair back and go for a walk. Do yoga. Go to the gym. Move your body to unleash your mind. Don't tell anybody I said this, but there's more to life than the computer.

Frequently Asked Questions

Question	Page Reference
What is a FAQ?	33
What is the Internet?	1
What is the Web?	10–11
What are URLs?	12
What is Usenet?	2–4
What is E-mail?	4–5
What is Gopher?	5–6
What is FTP?	7–8
What is Telnet?	8–9
What do I need to get started online?	17–19

What should I expect from my Internet Service Provider (ISP)?	19–20
I'm overwhelmed with all these Web sites and newsgroups. What should I do first?	20–23
What is an Online Writing Lab (OWL)?	24–26
How do online classes work?	26–27
What are the advantages of an online class?	28–29
How do I use Usenet newsgroups?	31
What are the rules of conduct for Usenet communication?	33–35
What are some good newsgroups for writers?	35
What is a mailing list?	36
How do I subscribe to a mailing list?	37
I need a mailing list about a specific topic. How can I locate it?	38–39
Can you list some good mailing lists for writers?	39–40
Do my favorite authors have Web sites? Where are they?	220–224
Do you have a list of Web sites and newsgroups organized by genre?	192–204
Why should I publish online?	45
What are the drawbacks to publishing online?	44–45
What forms can my online publishing take?	46
How do I build a Web page?	48–50
What are HTML tags?	50–51
How do I use the tags?	52–54
What are links and how do I use them?	55–60
This isn't enough. What are some other resources for furthering my studies of HTML?	67–68
How do I start developing the content and organization of my Web site?	86–87
What is hypertext fiction?	107–108
How do I publish an e-zine?	97–100
How do I publish material in newsgroups and mailing lists?	101–103
What's so great about publishing a FAQ?	103–104

What do I need to consider when I write for the Web?	113–119
Why is it harder to read a monitor?	116
How can I compensate for the difficulties presented by online reading?	119–121
What is a search directory?	149–150
What is a search index?	155
What is a metasearch site?	163
How can I keep my Usenet messages private and inaccessible to search engines?	132–133
What are Boolean operators?	129–132
What is the best way to conduct an effective, efficient search?	139–142
How can I use e-mail interviews to further my research projects?	167–168
How do I structure and conduct an e-mail interview?	168–172
How can I promote my Web sites once I create them?	123–126
Is there any money to be made in Internet writing?	175–177
Where can I learn about online copyright protection?	182–185
What are some good timewasters?	227–230
How can I manage my travel plans via the Net?	215–220
What are some good news resources online?	205–211

Glossary of Acronyms, Terms, and Emoticons

Glossary of Acronyms

ARPA	Advanced Research Projects Administration
ASCII	American Standard Code for Information Interchange
ASJA	American Society of Journalists and Authors
CERN	Centre European pour la Recherche Nucleaire
CGI	Common Gateway Interface
DoD	Department of Defense
DTD	Data Type Definition
EFF	Electronic Frontier Foundation
GIF	Graphics Information File
HTML	Hypertext Markup Language

HTTP Hypertext Transfer Protocol

IRC Internet Relay Chat

JPEG, JPG Joint Photographic Expert Group

MIME Multipurpose Internet Mail Extension

NCSA National Center for Supercomputing Applications

SGML Standardized General Markup Language

TIFF Tagged Image File Format

URL Uniform Resource Locator

Glossary of Terms

absolute address Describes a complete pathname (often in a link) in reference to URLs. Example: **http://www.foo.com/directory/doc.html**.

address On the Web, the electronic address used as an e-mail destination. Example: **joe@foo.edu**.

anchor The HTML **<A>...</A>** tag that delineates a link to an outside resource. Also references a destination for an incoming link. See *hypertext*.

ASCII (American Standard Code for Information Interchange) seven-bit character code representing 128 characters.

attribute In HTML, a property that modifies a start tag. Some attributes are mandatory; others are optional. Examples: **<IMG SRC="image.gif">** includes the mandatory attribute SRC, indicating that the following address is a URL; **<A NAME="text">** includes the optional attribute **NAME**, indicating that the following text serves as a link destination.

bandwidth On the Web, refers to electronic carrying capacity. The greater the bandwidth, the faster the data transfer.

body In HTML, the structure containing the bulk of the HTML document. Separate from the HEAD.

CERN (Centre Européan pour la Recherche Nucléaire) The European Center for Particle Physics in Geneva, Switzerland; the birthplace of the World Wide Web.

CGI (Common Gateway Interface) The specification on how browsers communicate with HTTP servers. Used with forms and other server queries.

character entity In HTML, a string of text representing a special character or number. Always begins with & and ends with a semicolon.
Examples: < is the character entity for the less-than symbol < ; @ is the @ symbol.

client An end-user program that retrieves data from a server. On the Web, the browser is the client.

definition list An HTML list structure **<DL>** that includes terms and definitions. Also known as a glossary list.

directory list An HTML list structure, defined in HTML versions 1.0 and 2.0, but not in 3.0. It creates a list of short paragraphs, which are supposed to be formatted in columns.

domain A nonnumeric name used to identify computers on the Internet.
Examples: **www.foo.com**; **skycat.com**; **www.bsd.uchicago.edu**.

element Commonly describes the basic unit of HTML. Each tag is an element.

flame To send or receive a hostile message. Usage: "I got flamed." Also refers to the hostile message itself: "I got a flame."

form HTML documents that solicit information from the end-user. Data is sent to the server where responses can be generated based on user input.

GIF (Graphics Information File) A commonly-used graphic format on the Web.

helper programs Utility programs that help browsers render specific kinds of data such as video or audio.

home page A type of Web page that serves as a starting point for Web travels. Also the hierarchical head of a Web presentation. Home pages often include lists of hyperlinks.

hotlist In a browser, constitutes a quick-reference list of favorite Web sites. Click and go.

HTTP (Hypertext Transfer Protocol) The Internet communication protocol used to transfer Web-formatted data between servers and clients.

hypertext The text or image on a Web page that, when clicked, links you to another Web resource or document. Also describes the system of presenting text and graphic information linked to other resources on the Web.

HTML (Hypertext Markup Language) The source code of every Web-formatted document. A subset of Standard Generalized Markup Language (SGML), which is a language for describing structured documents.

imagemap A clickable (active) graphic image. Typically, various regions of a graphic are designated as links to other parts of a Web site.

inline image An image that is automatically downloaded as part of the Web document text (unless the automatic download feature is disabled in the browser).

Internet A global network of networks that facilitates data exchange in a variety of formats.

JPEG, JPG (Joint Photographic Expert Group) A commonly-used graphic format on the Web. Used primarily with photographs.

layout Describes elements that make up a Web-formatted document in terms of both structure and appearance (indentation values, font, and point size). *See* structure.

link Hypertext that associates one HTML document to another. (The visible text or graphic is known as a "hotspot.") Also used in reference to anchoring tags.

list element An item in an HTML list, designated by **<LI>**.

logical character format (soft format) The markup tags that suggest character styles. Visible formatting varies among browser software.
Examples: Emphasis **<EM>**, Strong emphasis **<STRONG>**.

Lynx A character-based Web browser.

menu list An HTML list structure **<ML>**, defined in HTML versions 1.0 and 2.0, but not in 3.0. It creates a list of short paragraphs.

MIME (Multipurpose Internet Mail Extension) A scheme that allows multimedia (text, sound, images, video) to be included in e-mail.

Mosaic Software used to view World Wide Web documents. Some browsers are graphical (Mosaic) and others are text-based (Lynx).

nesting The practice of embedding elements inside other elements. In HTML, lists are frequently nested in other lists. Tags are often nested within other tags.
Example: **<P>This is <EM>important</EM>.</P>**

ordered list An HTML list structure **<OL>**, usually numbered.

Perl (Practical Extraction and Reporting Language) The best language for writing CGI scripts.

physical character format (hard format) The markup tags that dictate character styles.
Examples: Bold **<B>**, Italic **<I>**

platform References the combined hardware and software you're using. HTML is written to be platform-independent.

relative address Describes a pathname (often in a link) relative to the current document address. Examples: directory/doc.html is one directory in from the current directory; doc.html is in the current directory; .../doc.html is one directory up from the current directory.

server Refers to the networked computer that runs server software or the software itself. Servers respond to client programs.

service provider An organization or business providing Internet access.

SGML (Standardized General Markup Language) The ISO standard describing markup languages. Facilitates platform-independent document transfer. HTML is a subset of SGML.

structure The elements that make up a Web-formatted document. These elements include paragraphs, six levels of headings, three types of lists, citations, addresses, four kinds of links, and much more. Structure dictates organizational hierarchy, not layout appearance. (Level 1 headings are higher up the ladder than level 2 and 3 headings, and so on). *See* layout.

tag In HTML, the typed text that describes HTML elements. Tags are bracketed by less-than and greater-than symbols. Empty tags contain no extra information, such as **
, **<HR>. Container tags include supplied information, such as **<IMG SRC="foo.html">**.

thumbnail A reduced version or portion of a larger graphic image.

TIFF (Tagged Image File Format) A graphics format you may encounter on the Web.

transparent image A GIF image whose background matches the background color of a Web document. This makes the image appear to "float" on the page.

Uniform Resource Locator (URL) The addressing scheme used to identify documents and resources on the Web.
Example: http://www.fedex.com.

UNIX The most common operating system running Internet servers.

unordered list An HTML list structure **<UL>**, usually denoted with bullets or inline graphics.

Commonly Used Emoticons

Many people enjoy inserting smileys (emoticons) into their e-mail to indicate irony or pleasure, or simply to jazz up a message. The following list includes commonly understood smileys. For a more comprehensive list, visit EFF's Guide to the Internet, **http://www.eff.org/papers/eegttii/**.

> *A word to the wise:* beware of overloading e-mail with too many smileys. It can obscure your message and make your writing appear immature.

:-) or :) or :>

Happy, having fun, or making a joke.

:-(or :(or :<

Unhappy, sad, or angry.

;-) or ;) or ,-)

Winking. Tongue-in-cheek comment.

:-/ or :\

Wondering. Confused or concerned. Not sure.

:-o or :o

Uh, oh! Oh, no! Oh, dear! Yelling.

|-)

Tee-hee.

|-D or :D

Ho, ho, ho. Belly laugh.

:-|

Hmm. Not sure.

[] or {}

Hugs.

:*

Kisses.

8-)

User wears glasses.

(-:

User is left-handed.

The Writer's Guide to the Internet
Appendix
C

Commercial Online Services

It isn't the purpose of this book to go into detail about the contents of commercial online services. MSN, AOL, CompuServe, Prodigy, etc., all have relatively similar types of information organized into unique on-screen interfaces. Generally speaking, AOL and MSN are easier to manage because their graphic interfaces are so well structured. CompuServe tends to have more professional forums. Prodigy is known for excellent chats. All of this material has to be written by someone. Many of the moderators, teachers, and online advisors for these services are freelance. Most services offer free online time, or software in trade, or both. Some pay for your efforts, depending on the topic you choose, the value of your name (are you famous?), the number of students attracted to your class (if you are teaching) and the timeliness of the material.

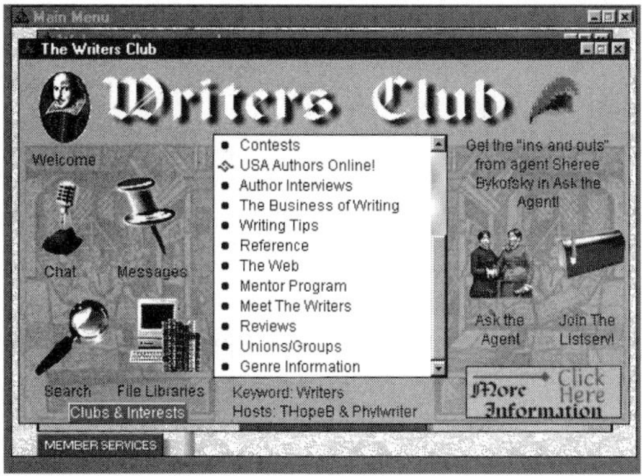

Figure C.1 AOL Writers Club

All services offer introductory periods, usually ten hours or so, to explore their corner of the electronic universe. Spend time digging around the writer forum areas in these commercial provider communities (for example, CompuServe GO LITFORUM, AOL Writers Club (Figure C.1), MSN Writer Forum (Figure C.2), Prodigy Writing Workshop). Before deciding which service you want to embrace, check them all. Take advantage of the freebies and get to know your resources. See where your publishing ideas will fit in, and do some exploration. Other forum or club leaders will be happy to share their insights with you.

America Online	800–827–6364
CompuServe	800–848–8199
Prodigy	800-PRODIGY
Microsoft Network	800–386–5550

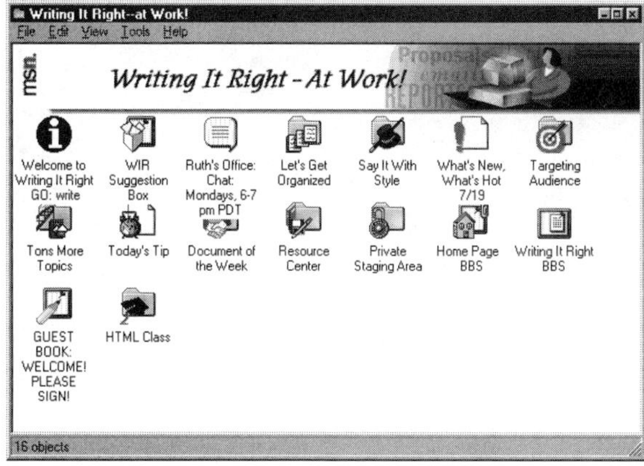

Figure C.2 MSN Writing Forum

If you fancy becoming a forum leader or instructor for one of these services, be assertive and pitch your ideas to them. If they give you a shot at a forum—presto!—instant audience. You have an electronic column, complete with deadlines and a demanding readership. Anyone who's written for a weekly or monthly column knows the value of producing topical information on deadline. It develops a backlog of materials that you can eventually gather together for another type of publication, perhaps a book or Web site.

> *Hint:* If you're looking to use your published pieces as a way of marketing yourself, don't subscribe with a clever nickname. Use your real name. Do you want people to remember "writergal" or Dawn Groves?

The Writer's Guide to the Internet
Appendix
D

Audio and Video Files

Audio and video technology is commonly used to enhance Web sites. The following paragraphs briefly discuss the pros and cons of simple audio and video. To learn more about them (along with other forms of multimedia enhancement), visit the Webreference.com Developer's Corner at **http://webreference.com/dev/**.

Audio Files

Sound files add musical clips, welcome messages, warning beeps, even background noises to your Web page. Sound files can be generated at home with a proper microphone, sound card, and digitizing software. Public domain sounds are also archived at various locations around the Internet and on CD-ROM.

Like images, sounds must be formatted appropriately to be interpreted by the browser. Unlike images, sounds are less common enhancements because many Web travelers don't want to wait for the time it takes to download the sound file, or they don't have a sound card installed on their platforms. A one-minute sound-bite of a speech, for example, could take up to ten minutes to download.

Sound file formats
Macintosh AIFF (scream.aiff), Windows WAV (scream.wav), platform-independent AU (scream.au). Platform-specific formats produce a better quality sound than AU, but they're obviously limited in terms of who can play them.

Player
A program external to the Web browser. A player lets you "view' specific kinds of files. For example, some audio and video files can't be enjoyed unless a specific player has been installed on your system. Most players are widely available as freeware or shareware; some come as standards with your operating system.

With proper software, you can also take advantage of streaming audio technology. Streaming audio lets you listen to sound clips *as* they are downloading — much better than waiting for an audio file to download completely before listening to it. Radio sites such as National Public Radio (Morning Edition in its entirety) at **http://www.npr.com** and ABC News Reports at **http://www.realaudio.com/contentp/abc.html** use streaming audio to broadcast news, music, and a variety of other radio programs. One of the most popular streaming audio "players" can be downloaded from the RealAudio Web site at **http://www.RealAudio.com**. Other streaming audio systems include Streamworks at **http://www.xingtech.com/**, Winplay at **http://www.iis.fhg.de/departs/amm/layer3/winplay3**, and VocalTec at **http://www.vocaltec.com/**.

A few notes regarding audio:

- Sounds are an important part of the multimedia enhancements being added to the Web, but unless your written work depends on sound files, (such as a multimedia production some other movie/animation-oriented site) don't feel that you must include them. Images and text are a lot less trouble.
- Sound files tend to be quite large. When you provide sound links on your Web page, be sure to list the file size and the format. To keep the size down, try recording your sound bites in mono instead of stereo. If at all possible, especially if your sound file is large, use streaming audio technology.

Video Files

Video adds "digitally encoded" motion video to your Web pages. The most common video formats on the Web are MPEG (movie.mpg), and Apple's "QuickTime" format (movie.mov). As with other external files, you must have a proper viewer application to play movie clips.

Streaming video technology (viewing the video as it is being downloaded instead of waiting for it to download in its entirety) isn't as accessible as streaming audio. Video files are much bigger than audio files, making the video slow and choppy as it is downloaded over a standard modem connection. At the time of this writing, the best way to view video files transmitted over a modem is to download them first.

A few points regarding video:

- Video files can be generated at home with a properly-configured computer. But your best bet is to locate video archives on the Net or purchase some royalty-free clips. As with all media files, if you borrow someone else's work, make sure you have permission to do so.
- Not everyone can play videos, which means that many people won't be able to enjoy your video files. The Web page should make sense without them.
- Like sound files, video files tend to be quite large. Be sure to list the file size and the format next to the video link.

To learn more about video—and other multimedia enhancements—take The Web Multimedia Tour at **http://ftp.digital.com/Webmm/fbegin.html**. This tour offers lots of information about video as well as a host of links to downloadable video and audio players.

Index